Hello Life!

A Year Without a Scale

Volume 2 (July 2013–January 2014)

Shira Lile

Contents

Acknowledgements 5
Introduction 6
Six Months Earlier – January 2013 7
July 2013 9
August 2013 30
September 2013 80
October 2013 129
November 2013 188
December 2013 240
January 2014 299
About the Author 342
Author's Thanks 343

To my brother Edaan, who saw the vision for this book long before I ever did, and to the many fighters around the world who said my blog saved their life.

Acknowledgements

I LEANED on many people in my life during my recovery from my eating disorder, many of whom I still lean on now.

A special thank you to my family who were, and continue to be, my rock.

Thank you to E, who undoubtedly, along with my blog, saved my life.

Thank you to the hundreds of people who followed my blog, and who uplifted me, encouraged me and inspired me, even without ever meeting me.

Last but most definitely not least, thank you to my husband Brock and son R.J, who remind me daily that I am loved exactly as I am.

Introduction

"HELLO LIFE!"

THOSE were the only words that I could say the moment I gave up my scale for an entire year.

What would I be without my scale? What would I use as my identity? I felt completely lost but never more alive – both at the same time.

I knew I would need accountability. That is when my blog, 'Hello Life: A Year Without a Scale', was born. After completing my one-year blog, six years of recovery (including an entire pregnancy without a scale), and dozens of people saying the blog saved their life, I decided it was time to turn my blog into a two-volume book. It's my deepest hope that this book finds the eyes of someone who, while they may be deep in the darkest trenches of an eating disorder, know that they are not alone.

May this book serve not only as a reminder that people are never alone in their pain, but as a reminder that hope does exist.

Six Months Earlier – January 2013

About My Blog

LET me take some time to introduce myself and tell you a little about the purpose behind my blog.

At the time of starting the blog I was twenty-two years old and in recovery from an eating disorder. I was studying journalism at CSUN and hoped to be an awesome reporter one day.

I had a few reasons why I was doing the blog. The first reason was to help myself. I realized that if I was going to go on the journey of one entire year without a scale, I was going to need some kind of outlet to express every emotion I was feeling.

What would those emotions be? I wasn't totally sure – actually, I wasn't sure at all. All I knew was that whatever it was I was feeling and going through, I was going to post it all in the blog to document my journey.

The second reason I wrote my blog was to help others who were struggling like me. If you are someone who is battling an eating disorder, my blog, and now this book, are for you. If you are someone who has ever been at odds with the person staring back at you in the mirror, this book and my blog are for you. If you are someone who has ever felt insignificant or undeserving of anything short of the best, then this book and my blog are for you.

I wrote my blog for those brave and courageous souls in the world, with or without an eating disorder, who have ever challenged themselves to do something and made the painstaking decision to stick with it and fight as hard as they can to make sure they succeed. As I said at the outset of my journey: *This blog, my fellow fighters, this is for us.*

July 2013

Day 182: And Now I Know the True Meaning of Love

YESTERDAY had been one of the most beautiful days I had ever experienced in my life.

I knew that reaching my six-month milestone of being scale-free and of living in recovery would mean a lot to me and to those close to me, but I had no idea that there would be such a huge outpouring of love behind it.

Monday, July 22

First, I got to celebrate with my mom, her husband, my sister and my grandma on Saturday night at a steakhouse, where they customized our menus to write: 'Hello Life Shira ... 6 Months!'

Then during the day on Sunday, I received so many beautiful comments and emails from my blog followers, subscribers, friends and family.

My dad, who is currently in Israel, even left me a comment on yesterday's blog post, just showing me that even though part of my family is halfway across the world right now, they are still with me in spirit for this huge milestone. Even without his comment, I would have known that and felt that, but it was nice to put words to it.

At night, my best friend and her boyfriend got me the most beautiful cake, with inspiring sayings all around it. We went out for dinner afterwards and celebrated not only my accomplishment, but the friendship that we all have.

I have my aunt and cousins, who I will be celebrating with later this week ... and a few more friends too.

Now, I am going to put the fancy dinner, comments, emails and chocolate cake aside, because yesterday was really not about all those things.

Yesterday was about love.

It was about a love that I never could have been open to receiving when I was living in my eating disorder. When I was living trapped inside Ed, only judging myself based on a number on a scale, I didn't let anyone in my life to love me, because I didn't even know how to love myself.

I didn't know what love was. I thought love was me trying to be a perfect girlfriend for my now ex-boyfriend. I thought love was me trying to fit into his perfect mold of who he thought I should be. I thought love was a certain number on a scale. I thought love was someone loving me even though I was obsessed with my weight.

After these past six months, and especially after yesterday, I know now that is not love – it never was. Love starts with me. It starts with learning to love me for me, and from that stems the beauty of other people's love into my life.

Along this journey to recovery and this journey to finding self-acceptance, I have found that the more I learn to accept and love myself, the more love I let in from family, friends and even strangers, and that is what happened yesterday.

My biggest fear when I started recovery, other than gaining weight of course, was that those people who are close to me in my life wouldn't like the new me. I wasn't sure whether I would even like the new me, so how could I know whether they would like it?

I didn't know who I would be without my weight and calorie counts, and without my skinny body, and I was scared of what I would find at my core without all of it.

But I am not scared anymore. I am falling in love with the person at my core – with her strength, with her compassion for others, and with her love to simply enjoy life. And I am not scared that those who love me won't accept the new me anymore, because very obviously they do love me – the recovered me – and it's not because I am a different person, it's because I can finally let them in, one person at a time.

This whole time I thought love was centered around making others happy, or making a man happy, or making my family happy. Now I see the true meaning of love.

Love is unconditional, it's support, it's family, it's friends, and most importantly it's me. I love myself enough to let myself receive the love from others in my life who want to love me back just how I love them, and it's a beautiful thing. That right there, that is love.

I am so grateful that I am surrounded by so much love in my life, and I am beyond appreciative to everyone who has opened their hearts to me along my journey to recovery.

Embracing love and living in an eating disorder are two things that can never exist together.

I choose love, and to that I say: Hello Life!

******

Day 183: Focusing on New Facts

After much time and careful consideration, I had made the final choice on this day to let go of someone from my recovery team, my nutritionist, Karen.

When I had first begun seeing her a few months previously, she had been an essential part of my recovery. She knew what my body needed, and she had listened to my feelings and needs about food and my body. However, over the previous few weeks, those needs were no longer being respected or heard.

The first time was after she told me I had gained one pound, even though I had told her the week before that I didn't want to know whether I had lost or gained weight.

The second time was when she said it was okay for her that I tried to lose weight, even though I was in recovery for an eating disorder.

The third time was last week, when she told me that I 'thought' my way into my body feeling sore after I had eaten too much.

Tuesday, July 23

There was a time in my recovery when I didn't know what I needed; I only knew that I needed to rely on the guidance of my recovery team and I had to put my physical and even emotional needs in their hands. But I can now say that I have reached a place where I know what I need, physically, and most definitely emotionally.

On an emotional level, I know that I can't have someone on my team who questions my truth. Whether that truth is that my body is feeling sore, or if that truth is me wanting to stay clear of hearing about me gaining or losing weight, it cannot and should not be questioned.

I already battle with Ed on a daily and sometimes even hourly basis about what my body looks like, and for someone to try to tell me that the feelings I am feeling within my body, such as the soreness, are not true, is not acceptable for me or for my recovery.

I didn't just walk away from Karen, I explained to her in an email why I will no longer be seeing her.

I know that, for me, my eating disorder flourished when I felt undermined or not valued, because then I would turn to it for praise and false hope that losing weight would make me feel valued again.

If I am going to learn to live in freedom from Ed, I need to begin to shut down the channels in which he swims and lives, and one of those is communicating to others when they have made me feel that my words are not valued.

By standing up for myself to Karen and speaking only my truth about what I perceived had happened (because her perception could be much different), it made Ed non-existent. I stood up for myself and I felt good about it, and no kind of restricting can give me that kind of satisfaction.

However, this now means I will no longer be stepping on a scale at all. I am not going to be seeking out another nutritionist, at least for now, because I don't feel I need one at this point. I know my meal plan and I follow it well.

Why should I torture myself and stand on a scale every single week, just for someone else to look at that number and make me wonder what it is? I know I am at a healthy weight. Although I don't know the number, I know it's healthy for me, and that is all I need to know.

On one hand, I feel relieved to not be stepping on a scale anymore or to hear whether I have lost or gained weight. On the other hand, I am terrified. At least with Karen, if I had a bad week and she told me I gained a pound, I knew about it. The facts were clear and they were known.

I could have gained weight this week; actually, I 100% gained weight this week because I actually ate amazing food and desserts with family and friends.

By letting go of Karen, I am stepping back into the unknown. I used to be much more scared of the unknown. I didn't know how to live with it. I had to know how many calories I ate every day, how much I weighed, and how much food I ate.

During my recovery I had to give up knowing my weight, but I held on to knowing whether I gained or lost weight, and I held on to seeing how much food I ate by keeping a food journal. Those are no longer going to be part of my recovery. It's terrifying, but it's so freeing at the same time.

Screw those facts about food, weight and calories. Screw those facts about losing a pound or gaining a pound every week. I so hope that I can forget the facts and let go of the rigidity around those facts, and embrace living in this period of the unknown.

I don't know how much weighed I gained this week – a true fact – but I do know that I experienced the most love I have ever experienced in my entire life this week, and that is also a true fact. Maybe it's time I focused on those kinds of facts instead of focusing on facts about food and weight.

I guess I am not really stepping into a whole new world of the unknown again, but rather I am just deciding to step into a world of new facts. I can still have my truths and my facts that are known, and therefore safe to me, but they will just be different facts.

Gaining or losing weight is no longer a fact in my life. Knowing that I have the most incredible family, friends and support team fighting with me every step of the way during this journey is now a fact that will replace my old facts.

Screw the old facts about food and weight. The best fact of all is that I get to say to myself every single day that I live in recovery from this eating disorder, Hello Life!

******

Day 184: If You Want to Judge, Go Ahead, I Am Staying True to Myself Anyway

Today, my blog had been used as a tool to pass judgement on my character and on who I was as a person. I didn't name the person who was responsible for doing that, since they had told me that calling some people out publicly on my blog wasn't the right thing to do, so I all I said was that it was someone very close to me and deeply involved in my life.

According to this person, my blog had been angry yesterday because I had said "screw food and calories," therefore it was "vulgar."

According to this person, the stronger I was becoming from this eating disorder, the more angry I was becoming. Although they were not around me often, they had concluded this from reading my blog posts and from seeing me every few weeks. They said other people had told them this too, although I had no idea who those other people were.

At this time I was the happiest I had been in my whole life and I could now finally express myself if I felt that someone had wronged me. This wasn't being an angry person, this was me standing up for myself.

According to this person, because I had felt hurt last weekend by my sister, I was supposedly not a happy person. Can't happy people have bad days, where they are hurt or where they just feel like crying? I am pretty sure they can.

Here is the worst part, and the part that pained my heart and soul. Not only did this person question the words of my blog, that were supposed to be used for my truth only, they attacked my character.

They had said, "You think your eating disorder is all about you, you, you. You don't care about your family and friends who have watched you suffer for years."

That couldn't have been further from the truth.

Wednesday, July 24

Since the very beginning of my recovery, I have written about how deeply my eating disorder interfered with my relationships with my loved ones, and how beautiful it is to me to see these relationships blossoming again.

I have written about setting a good example for my younger brothers, and eating with them, even if it makes Ed fight with me like crazy afterwards.

Two days ago, I wrote about how I have been so blessed to be surrounded by so much love in my life, and how I am so grateful that I am in a place in my recovery where I finally feel I deserve to receive that love.

To say that I think this eating disorder is all about me, when I have opened my heart to so many people, and when I go so out of my way to embrace other people in my life, such as going to family dinners and lunches that at times make me uncomfortable, is beyond hurtful.

And as for saying that my blog comes off as angry, well, I am sure it does sometimes. I was angry with my nutritionist for not respecting my needs, and I have a right to be, and no one should believe that they have the right to tell me otherwise. People get angry. Good for me for sticking up for myself and not resorting to my eating disorder to soothe those feelings.

As for saying this blog was vulgarly written yesterday – it's my blog. First of all, I don't think saying the word 'screw' is vulgar. Secondly, this is my blog and it's my truth, and it really doesn't matter to me how others perceive my truth. These are my words, my feelings and my experiences only. All I can do is share them with whoever wants to read them.

"If your eating disorder is all about you, then I guess I have no reason to read your blog," they said to me today. Well, guess what, this blog is about me. It's about my journey and my path to discovering true self-acceptance and true happiness, and if someone doesn't want to read about that, then please don't.

My eating disorder is not all about me, but it's about my journey to finding true happiness and freedom. If that means having some angry posts, or some sad posts, or some frustrated posts, then so be it.

Never did I think this blog would become a weapon for someone to use against me in my recovery. Never did I think it would become something for people to judge me by, or to think they can use it to make assumptions about my character.

I express my feelings, my struggles, my pain and my joy on this blog, and it's not intended for someone else to judge those feelings or who I am as a person when I write them. But that did happen today, and it's a sad day because of it.

The saddest part is to hear someone so close to me tell me that this eating disorder is all about me, when I am one of the most selfless people I know, with family, with friends, and with recovery. Nothing has ever been all about me, and I never planned it to be. But if you want to judge, go ahead.

I am staying true to myself, to my writing, to my blog, and to my recovery anyway ... Hello Life!

******

Day 185: No Need to Defend, I Know Me

In the previous day's post, I had written about an argument I had with someone close to me. They had spoken, I had spoken, and hurt had been caused on both sides. I wasn't going to spend this day writing about it, but I was going to write about what I had learned.

I had spent a lot of time the previous day defending my opinion about myself, my feelings and my character. I had defended it on my blog, and I had defended it to my family and friends. But then I had read this quote while browsing on my phone, and I realized that that was probably my biggest loss yesterday:

> *"The difficult part in an argument is not to defend one's opinion but rather to know it"* ~André Maurois.

It wasn't a loss that I had stood up for myself, because I was glad I had done so, but it was a loss to argue and become emotionally drained trying to defend my feelings or who I was, when I already knew myself, my feelings and my opinions about who I was as a person.

Thursday, July 25

I think this is the first time in my life where I am actually secure with who I am. It's the first time that I don't feel I need to seek approval from others or from Ed.

I could have looked to Ed today to help me restrict and feel temporarily better, but I didn't need to do that. Ed couldn't touch me today. I feel that because I am so in touch with myself, my beliefs and my character, I don't even need Ed to try to 'make me better'.

I am happy with who I am. I am happy with my views of myself. I am happy with my own opinion of myself. I see now that this is truly what matters.

It's going to have to be okay with me that other people are not always going to be happy with who I am, what I am saying or what I am writing, even if it's hard to hear. I see now, I don't need to defend my words or myself to anyone. All I need to do is know myself and where I stand within me.

I am not just referring to my argument of yesterday. I am referring to the many times in my life where I have fought to seek approval – from Ed, from friends, from teachers, from bosses and from family. And if I didn't get that approval, I defended myself as to why I should get it, or I let Ed come in so I could get approval from him.

Both of those things no longer exist for me anymore. I don't need to defend myself. I don't need approval. My heart is open to others – their views and their truths.

But in the end I have to know my truth the most. I am content with who I am, and I know my opinion of myself, and that to me is really what matters.

When I am secure with who I am, I don't need Ed. I don't need a number anymore to tell me how good a person I am. I don't need calorie counts anymore to tell me how disciplined I am. And I don't need to fight others about it either. I only need my core beliefs about who I am, and those I have worked long and hard to establish.

There is no need for me to harbor any negative energy within myself anymore. I am not angry with anyone, and I am not upset anymore. I understand everyone has their own views, as they should. I know me – no need to defend it.

The best part is, I am finally getting to know who I am, without a number on some scale attached to it ... wow, who knew six months ago that would even be possible? Hello Life!

******

Day 186: There Are Other Things More Important than the Way My Body Looked Today

Today's post was to be short and to the point, because I was really physically tired.

Friday, July 26

I came home really late last night, and I knew I would have a big day ahead of me, helping to take care of my grandma, and also to take some time to catch up on some lost sleep. Therefore, I cancelled my morning gym session so I could sleep for an extra two hours, and I spent the rest of the day helping my grandma.

Simply stated, these things, such as being there for my family and giving myself an extra period of sleep instead of working out, are things that are far more important than Ed.

In between helping today, feeling tired and trying to get some rest, I didn't even make time for myself to stand in front of the mirror and look at my body for too long. I did it for a second, and that was it.

I was too tired to care about what I looked like today and, truthfully, there were just other things that were more important than the way my stomach looked in the mirror this morning. Resting was more important. Taking care of my grandma was more important.

I feel good that I was able to help someone who I love today. It's a different kind of good feeling than the one I used to get when I used to see that I was 'x' number on the scale, or that I had eaten 'x' number of calories.

It's a totally different kind of self-satisfaction. It's one I can get used to and it's one that I like. Hello Life!

******

Day 187: Too Busy Living

I had to be ready to leave my house in less than one hour when I suddenly remembered that I had forgotten to blog on this day.

Do you know what this meant? This meant that I was so busy living life without Ed inside my head all the time, that writing about him just wasn't as 'thought about' as usual.

It was actually a pretty amazing thing.

Saturday, July 27

I took care of myself today. I got my nails done, and I even got a new pair of jeans. And I didn't reward myself with these simple acts of self-care because I weighed a certain number today, I did it because I wanted to feel good about myself, a new concept, but one that I like.

These jeans that I bought were a size bigger than all my other jeans, but the fact that I have friends and people to wear them out with was more important to me than the size. I bought a new pair of jeans so I can feel good going out with people, the main focus being that I actually enjoy going out now.

A year ago, if I were to only fit in a bigger size jeans like I did today, there would be absolutely no way that I would still go out that night, especially to eat dinner, which is what I am going to do tonight. I would have stayed home, taken some kind of laxative, and felt miserable until the next morning. And during the night I would have weighed myself over and over again to remind myself of why I was home alone and not out having fun.

I wouldn't have been living then. I would be only existing in Ed's world, and a weak existence at that.

I am living now. I am not staying home tonight because these jeans are a size that Ed doesn't like. Instead, I am going out with friends, and I am wearing these jeans despite the number on the tag. I feel good in them, and I am going to have a good time.

I used to think that it was impossible to be able to live without Ed, but here I am, living, loving, and learning how to be without him a little more each day.

Hello to being busy living, and Hello Life!

******

Day 188: Back in the Unknown

It was 8p.m. and Ed had just started to creep back next to me, so I decided this would be a good time to write.

Sunday, July 28

I thought I was having a good day earlier. By good, I mean that I was sticking to my meal plan, had a late lunch, and therefore had the opportunity to kind of miss the snack before dinner (okay, good to Ed, not good to recovery).
Well, dinner came and it passed, then I had this sweet tooth attack. And I mean, major sweet tooth attack. It felt like the feelings of a binge. I haven't felt these feelings in a long time, and it was scary to re-feel them. It's the feeling where your mind and body are craving something so intensely that your hands are reaching for something and your mouth is eating it, but you are not even enjoying it. It's not even tasteful. It's just an act of impulse.
I let myself have the chocolate, cookie and few other things I was craving, then I went upstairs to tell my grandma that I felt I was having this sweet tooth attack. Right away, the urge to binge went away. Something about saying it out loud and making it a known fact, as opposed to a deep dark secretive feeling I had to keep to myself, made me feel a sense of control again.
So now I feel satisfied with my sweets. A little full, but nothing comparable to a binge or what a binge would feel like. However, Ed is here now.
As you all know, last week I decided to not see my nutritionist anymore for many reasons. Up until today I have enjoyed not getting on a scale and I have enjoyed not writing all my food

down in a food journal. But right now, with Ed right next to me, I am missing those things.

Maybe if I looked at the long extensive list of sweets that I ate today, it would stop me from doing it again. How will I know if I really messed up with my food these past two weeks if I don't stand on a scale and wait for my nutritionist to tell me whether I lost or gained weight? (no number of course).

With Ed, the one thing that always kept me sane when he tried to create chaos in my mind was facts. If he told me I ate too much food, I immediately weighed myself, so I could know if he was right or not, depending on what I weighed in that minute.

If Ed said I needed to lose weight, I could count calories, solid numbers, no guessing. Pure facts. Facts are what kept Ed alive for me. The number on the scale, the number of calories I ate, the size of my clothes, these facts used to make me feel like I had a sense of control over the repetitive thoughts about food that Ed would plant in my mind.

I don't have these facts right now and I am longing for them. But it's a lose-lose situation. If I have these facts, Ed continues to live on, and I continue to be his victim. If I don't have these facts, I sit here in blur and fog and I think about how much I have gained or how much I have eaten.

No one likes to sit in fog or in blur. I can't see in fog. I can't be me in fog. I am back in the unknown. That is really what this fog is. It's the unknown. I haven't been in the unknown for a while. Last time I was in the unknown was when I first gave up my scale.

I had forgotten just how much Ed loves to remind me that in a world of unknown, he is the only thing I know. But that is not true anymore. Ed is not the only thing I know, even in this space I am right now, filled with unknown fears and doubts.

I might not know what I used to know about my weight, but I do know that I am worth my recovery, even if it means trying to become friends with the unknown – getting to understand it, getting to accept it, and hopefully trusting it.

I would rather be in the unknown of recovery than in the known world of Ed – a world of entrapment, sadness and loneliness. Hello again unknown, and Hello Life!

******

Day 189: Exhausted

I was so exhausted, that I couldn't even write a lengthy post on this day.

Monday, July 29

I spent the day taking care of my grandma.

Long story short, I could have let this be a way to skip dinner, since she wasn't with me at home when it was dinner time, but I didn't, because if I don't feed my body, I can't be present and mentally and physically able to help my grandma.

So, I took care of myself. By doing so I was able to help take care of her. But I need to honor my body when it tells me I need to rest, so that is what I am going home to do right now.

Ed might be strong, but he is not strong enough to succeed in making me weak and unable to care for someone I love, and that is the reason I stuck to my recovery today, even though I easily could have gotten off track.

Good night, and Hello Life!

******

Day 190: My Body is Just a Shape ... I Am a Soul

Up until about five minutes ago, I had been too busy to really think about my body or the way that it looked on this day. But now that I had a minute, my first free minute all day, what did I decide to do with it? Yup, I decided to stare at myself in the mirror. And by stare, I mean that I analyzed every single inch of me.

I analyzed what my arm used to look like, how my legs used to look in these pants, and how they looked now. I questioned how they would look if I took off an inch here or there ... using my hands to pinch away the inches.

I stood at different angles and took various pictures. My photo cleanse had ended a few days previously, and I thought after this I needed to start a new one.

Tuesday, July 30

Why couldn't I just skip the mirror today?
But, even though I don't like what I see, it's not destroying me like it used to. I am actually more upset with the fact that I can't find the compassion within myself to not judge myself so harshly. I am so caring and compassionate when it comes to caring for other people in my life ... why can't I do it for myself?
But, I will say that even though I am not happy with how I look today, it doesn't make me unhappy with who I am as a person. Before I started recovery, I would have looked at myself in the mirror, seen me as too big and needing to lose weight, so I would have deemed myself as an unworthy person because of it. That is not the case today.
Maybe I don't have the body I want today, but I am still a good granddaughter, daughter, sister and friend. My imperfect image of my body can't take that from me.

Ed is trying, and will continue to try to tell me that those things about me are not true because I am not skinny anymore. How can I still think I am a worthy person and not be skinny? That is what Ed says.

I see now that my body and who I am as a person have nothing to do with each other ... it's something that has taken me a long time to discover.

My weight is a number. My body is a shape. That is all they are – numbers and shapes. They are not me. I am a heart, a soul, a person with dreams and passions, and a person who cares and loves others.

On days that I am hating my body, I will need to focus on loving the person I am on the inside. That is what I will need to do today, every time Ed is with me when I look in the mirror.

I am a good person Ed, even without the body you want me to have. So ... go away. Hello Life!

******

Day 191: What If ...

From the beginning of my day, I hadn't been having a good body day. I don't need to explain anymore at this point what that means. I was hating the way I looked today, simple as that.

Later I had been browsing for some inspirational quotes like I did a lot, and I came across a poem called 'If' by Rudyard Kipling. I must have already read it at least fifteen times by then, and each time I discovered that it made me think about another aspect of my life.

I posted the poem at the end of this day's blog so everyone could read it. But for me, the part of the poem that stood out to me the most, considering the place I was in with my body at that moment, was this part right here:

> *"If you can bear to hear the truth you've spoken*
>
> *Twisted by knaves to make a trap for fools,*
>
> *Or watch the things you gave your life to, broken,*
>
> *And stoop and build 'em up with worn-out tools."*

"If you can bear to hear the truth you've spoken, twisted by knaves to make a trap for fools," – this sentence was symbolic of Ed in my life right then. I had spoken my truth about him, what he had done to my body, to my mind and to my life, very publicly on my blog. I had exposed him. I had fought him. I had taken what were once my biggest fears about recovery, which was freedom from Ed, and turned them into my truths. Ed was the knave who twisted this truth to make it a trap for fools.

Wednesday, July 31

Some days, I become Ed's fool again. I don't let him make me restrict, but I become his fool. I let him tell me my body is not good enough, therefore I am not good enough. But like the poem says, even when the truth I have spoken is twisted, I can still bear to hear it. I can still look in that mirror and say to myself that I am not stopping recovery now, just because Ed is telling me to.

> *"Or watch the things you gave your life to, broken,*
>
> *And stoop and build 'em up with worn-out tools."*

This is where I am at today, and really in my recovery as a whole. I gave my life to Ed. Every second of it, every meal of it, every fun experience of it, every accomplishment in the past three years of it, I gave it all to Ed.

And now that life is broken. It's broken because I chose to break it. I chose to break free from Ed and start living in a world free of him. But now that my life with Ed has been broken, I have been building it back up without him – a new life for myself. As the poem says, "And stoop and build 'em up with worn-out tools."

No one is going to give me a new beautiful magic wand to build my life back up again. No one can give me a replacement body that will suddenly be good enough for Ed and me. No one can do recovery for me but me.

I am not a new soul. I am not a new person. Essentially, I am the worn-out tool that needs to find the strength within me to build my new life up. And not only do I have to build my new life up, but particularly in this moment I need to build my new self-esteem up about this new healthier body of mine.

I have been building with these worn-out tools since day one. None of my recovery has ever been polished or easy. But now I need to find the balance between building up myself and my new life without Ed, and learning where to sit back and accept it for what it is.

Maybe right now I need to stop building and start accepting. Building has become so second nature to me that I am scared I will never know how to simply accept. I won't be a worn-out tool forever. Ed wore me down, but the more free of him I become, the more rejuvenated I will be.

The title of the poem is called 'If'. What if I really will be successful in rebuilding my new life and new self-esteem without Ed? What if I am already doing that, but I am too busy building to take a step back and see it? What if the time has come for this worn-out tool to stop building and start accepting? Hello Life!

If ~ Rudyard Kipling

('Brother Square-Toes' – Rewards and Fairies)

If you can keep your head when all about you

Are losing theirs and blaming it on you,

If you can trust yourself when all men doubt you,

But make allowance for their doubting too;
If you can wait and not be tired by waiting,
Or being lied about, don't deal in lies,
Or being hated, don't give way to hating,
And yet don't look too good, nor talk too wise:
If you can dream – and not make dreams your master;
If you can think – and not make thoughts your aim;
If you can meet with Triumph and Disaster
And treat those two impostors just the same;
If you can bear to hear the truth you've spoken
Twisted by knaves to make a trap for fools,
Or watch the things you gave your life to, broken,
And stoop and build 'em up with worn-out tools:
If you can make one heap of all your winnings
And risk it on one turn of pitch-and-toss,
And lose, and start again at your beginnings
And never breathe a word about your loss;
If you can force your heart and nerve and sinew
To serve your turn long after they are gone,
And so hold on when there is nothing in you
Except the Will which says to them: 'Hold on!'
If you can talk with crowds and keep your virtue,
Or walk with Kings – nor lose the common touch,
If neither foes nor loving friends can hurt you,
If all men count with you, but none too much;

If you can fill the unforgiving minute
With sixty seconds' worth of distance run,
Yours is the Earth and everything that's in it,
And – which is more – you'll be a Man, my son!

August 2013

Day 192: Lessons Are Clothed in Gray

TODAY had been another busy day, and a gray one at that. Usually my days were very consistent. Either they were extremely busy and hectic or they were very relaxing and calm. Sometimes I ate exactly on my meal plan, sometimes I didn't at all. Either way, I was able to tell when my day was white, black or gray.

Thursday, August 1

Today was definitely a day lived in the gray, and it felt weird to me. I wish I could sit and think of a better or more articulate word for it, but weird or out of place are the two descriptions that come to mind.

I went running today on what I thought was a three-mile loop at a park. Okay, well, I had intended to go running the whole time, but I stopped and walked part of it – gray area number one.

Then, after I got back to my car, I looked at the app on my phone that tracks how far I walk or run, and it said only two miles, and I thought it was three mile – gray area number two.

For lunch, I wasn't really in the mood to eat, so I got a little bit of frozen yogurt and only ate half of it. Does that count as restricting or am I just listening to my body that it wasn't hungry? – gray area number three.

Life in general right now is gray. I don't have specific plans for my weekend yet, but I know I will make some – even that is gray for me.

So much gray today, yet here I am at the end of the night, sitting and writing about it so matter of factly. I am not saying I like living in the gray because I don't – I don't at all. It feels like a big blur to me, but I do like that I can recognize the gray now. Before recovery, my life was only black and white, and I couldn't imagine it any other way.

> *"Genius and virtue are to be more often found clothed in gray than in peacock bright" ~ Van Wyck Brooks*

I like this quote because I think, over time, it's going to prove itself to be true to me.

Maybe it's days like these, where I walked instead of ran the whole time, or where I had to figure out whether my lunch was really what I wanted or what Ed wanted, or on weekends when plans are not set in stone – maybe these are the times I will discover the most about my journey and most about myself.

When things are black and white, there really is no discovering left to do, all the answers are right there in front of you. Living in the gray areas means giving room and space to thinking about the answers that are not there. For example, even asking myself the simple question: "What do I want to eat for lunch?" instead of eating the same thing I always do when I am in my black-and-white state of mind.

The gray is kind of scary, don't you think? It gives us the undeniable time to think about why we are doing what we are doing, and if we are satisfied with it.

For me personally, I wasn't satisfied with some of the decisions that I made today, and the gray areas helped me see that. I should have eaten what I wanted and how much I wanted for that lunch, and I should have walked more and ran less if I felt tired on my run. More than that, I should not even have checked the distance tracker.

But the shoulds are not important in the gray areas of life, they are only important to the black and the white. Should, would, could – those words belong to the world of black and white.

Learning and experience – those words belongs to the grays. These learning experiences about how to live my life in recovery, whether it be about food or people, will indefinitely be clothed in gray.

So, today was dressed in gray, and that is okay. Gray skies are nothing but clouds moving anyway, so maybe tomorrow it will be a little bit more clear ... and if not, I will look for the lessons and beauty hidden in the gray anyway.

Hello Life!

******

Day 193: I Am Rich

After a long and exhausting night and day, I was feeling kind of drained. Up until a few minutes ago, I hadn't even known what I would write about, because I was just so tired that my heart was having a hard time speaking to me about what I truly wanted to write about on this day.

I knew I didn't want to write about food, because it hadn't been a part of my day – a true relief.

Friday, August 2

I have been sitting at home just by myself for a few hours now, and it gave me a chance to reflect back on these past few days.

You know what I thought about when I looked back on these days? Not about the food I ate; although it was bothering me yesterday and the day before, because it was foods I don't normally eat.

But I didn't think about that today. I didn't even think about the fact that I am tired right now. I thought about the amazing friends and family I have, and how much support and love they have been surrounding me with lately.

I am rich. I am rich with love and support. I got to talk to my brother and sister, who are in Texas right now, for an hour on the phone today. I am rich with beautiful siblings.

My best friend has kept me upbeat and laughing even when I haven't been in the greatest mood. I am rich with amazing friendship.

E asked me how I was doing today. I am rich with support.

Even spending some time with my grandma, who doesn't feel very well right now, and have her tell me I am doing a good job ... these people, these moments, and these things, are the wealth that I focused on today. I might feel physically lonely at home right now, but I know I am surrounded with an army of love.

Food just wasn't a part of my recovery today; hating my body wasn't part of my recovery today. Today, my recovery was safe and secure in those precious moments where I realized how rich I am.

No number on a scale or no amount of weight loss can ever compare to that kind of safe and secure feeling. There is not a skinny enough body in the world that can make me feel this kind of rich.

At one time, Ed was the one who filled me up. He was the one adding those coins to my piggy bank every time I lost more weight, and I thought that was wealth.

No, Ed. You made me poor. Recovery is making me see how rich I am without you. With the utmost gratitude, I end today's post by saying: Hello Life!

******

Day 194: Grabbing Life

Last night I had been having Friday night dinner with my family, where I met a fifteen-year-old boy named Orr. He was vising America from Israel, and it was his birthday.

So, I just assumed that he was like every other fifteen-year-old kid – having fun, smiling and joking around.

Saturday, August 3

We were singing happy birthday to Orr, when my uncle leaned over to me and said, "He might not be here next year... and we think we are the ones with the problems." I didn't get what he meant. "He has cancer, Shira," he explained.

I remember that exact moment so vividly in my head, because the minute he told me Orr had cancer, I picked up my head from looking down at my cell phone, and I just watched this boy blow out his birthday candles. I wonder what he wished for.

I remember looking over at him, and just seeing someone who was so in the moment. I had no idea he was battling cancer. He was laughing and smiling and he was being so present. It was as if his cancer wasn't even allowed to invade his space that night.

I am not saying that we should minimize our problems because, trust me, I know I still feel the same about the issues in my life and you all feel the burden of your daily problems too. They totally suck, but this helped put them in perspective.

I can't get over how happy Orr looked last night when he saw his birthday cake. It was like nothing else mattered to him in that moment. Is that what it takes to have to be able to truly be happy with the small, simple moments in life, like getting a birthday cake? The fear of losing our own life? I hope not ... but then, what does it take?

I have tried for months now to be happy living in the present moment, and many times I have been, but I never looked like Orr did yesterday. He was lit up. He was angelic. He was on a cloud no one could reach.

There is nothing like knowing that someone twenty feet in front of you might lose their life any day now to make you want to jump up and grab your life as fast as you can.

I am grabbing my life, that is for sure. Grabbing it back from Ed. Grabbing it back from negativity and pain. Grabbing it back from self-doubt. And I am pulling it back to me.

Now that I have grabbed it, I need to hold on tight, because Ed will fight hard for it back. I am ready to hold on.

Hello Life!

******

Day 195: Sunday Funday

I happily started this day's post by saying that today was 'Sunday Funday'. I had got a massage, spent some time with my grandma, and had gone to dinner and hung out with my best friend and her boyfriend.

Always on Sunday Funday, there is yummy food involved, but that food is something that creates bonding time with my friends.

Sunday, August 4

Before I started recovery, Sundays were what I called my 'Fat Sundays'. They were my binge days. Food was a manipulator of

Ed's on Fat Sundays. He used the food he let me eat on Sundays as his guilt trip for me to restrict the rest of the week.

Food on Sundays is no longer Ed's pawn. Now it's my pawn; my way to bond and have some fun with others.

Yes, I am already planning on what I will do in the gym tomorrow because I am a little uncomfortable with all the food from today, but I am okay with that. I have learned by now that I can't win every single part of Ed all the time. So if working out for an hour tomorrow is helping me be not as hard on myself today, then so be it.

Recovery is not meant to be perfect, and I am glad I finally don't expect myself to be perfect all the time either.

Hello to Sunday Funday, and Hello Life!

******

Day 196: The Greatest Necklace I Have Ever Gotten

On this morning, before I had gone to see E, I had woken up with Ed right beside me. My body was feeling a little bit sore from whatever I had eaten the day before, an indicator to me that I must have eaten too much. So, right away, Ed had snuggled up next to me under my covers before I could even turn my bedroom light on.

Monday, August 5

I was five minutes late for my appointment with E because I got so consumed in taking pictures of myself in my mirror that I lost track of time.

One picture after the other. One mean comment to myself after the other. Actually, it was Ed making the mean comments to me. I was just the one pushing the camera button. He was like the puppeteer and I was the puppet. He got me to turn on the camera, and I snapped the shots.

When I was taking those pictures, all I could think about was that I am way over the weight I want to be at. Of course, I don't know what I weigh, due to going a year without a scale, but when I was taking those pictures in the mirror, numbers were all I saw.

I could literally go through a camera roll in my head of how my body looked at each and every weight I ever was in my life, and I could tell you exactly what weight I am in each photo, depending on what my body looks like in each one.

So, can I know for sure that my judgement of what weight my body looked like today is correct? No. I could be wrong, I could be right —more gray to add to my life.

I am not about to step on a scale and ruin everything that I have worked so hard for in my recovery, and then end this blog. So, I guess I will just have to live with not knowing what I weigh.

I know the best way to get Ed to leave me alone on days like today is to keep busy, stay productive and stick to my meal plan. I am so proud to say that I did all those three things today, not because someone told me to, but because I wanted to for me.

I worked out, but only for forty-five minutes, which is another big deal, considering the fact I wanted to stay longer. I got an oil change, a car wash, I took a shower, and I tutored two of my kids back to back.

The little girl who I tutor is very special to me. She reminds me a lot of myself when I was young. She is so talkative and sensitive, and she likes to be the boss and know absolutely everything about everything. Definitely a mini version of myself.

Anyway, when I walked in to see her today, she brought a necklace to the table. It was a heart that was broken into two pieces, that said 'best friends'. She wanted to keep one half for herself, and she wanted me to have the other half. It was such a selfless, pure, innocent and kind act. It was the opposite of everything I was feeling earlier in the day with Ed.

Ed wanted me to focus all day on me and my body; he likes obstructing purity and replacing it with twisted deviance. He likes replacing kindness for myself with harsh judgements. He thrives from telling me how I am not enough.

This necklace said to me, 'I am enough'. To the girl I tutor, I am enough, not because of how I dress, how much I weigh, or what I didn't or did eat today, but just because I am me. It was as if she broke the cycle of cruelty that Ed was working so hard to continue to push round and round in my head.

I love that necklace. It's the best necklace I think I have ever gotten. I put it on right away. I am still wearing it now.

Every time I see it, I am going to remember, how to this one seven-year-old girl, on a typical Monday night, I was enough.

Hello Life!

******

Day 197: I Am that Butterfly

My plan for this day was to wake up early and go work out. Well, I had woken up, but then I had laid in bed and turned on my TV, and I really didn't feel like moving. I felt so perfect and comfortable doing exactly that.

This was the first day in such a long time that I had nowhere to be, and I just wanted to relish that moment. But Ed hated that. Oh, he really, really hated that. He kept trying to tell me that I needed to work out, since I hadn't worked out the previous week and hadn't eaten very healthily.

After an hour of me consistently turning him down, I was finally able to leave that conversation he and I were having in my head.

Tuesday, August 6

For those new readers (in the past day the blog has gotten a few new followers), Ed is the name I have given to my eating disorder. I treat Ed as a separate person who is in my life. If he is going to be part of my life, I decided I would personify him.
Weird? Maybe. But it works.
So, with me being able to quieten Ed, I was able to cuddle in my bed with no one other than me and myself. Just us. No Ed. And I loved it.
I even brought myself breakfast and coffee in bed, something I never do, as eating anywhere but at a table seems to be something I am uncomfortable with (not sure why), but I think it has to do with being mindful of the act of eating.
I spent the whole day with myself. I relaxed, I watched a movie, I made myself lunch, and I tanned outside while listening to music.
Ed came back to say hi to me when I was getting dressed, and a few more picture were taken. I am not proud of it, but it ended faster than it did yesterday, and I deleted them right away. I am proud of that. I am going to continue my day with me and myself, and leave Ed out of the picture.
I saw a photo today online, and it really symbolized my recovery. It shows a butterfly attached to a rock by a piece of string. The rock is at the bottom of some stairs and the butterfly is on the third step. I am that butterfly and Ed is the rock. Yup, it's me dragging Ed up the stairs, not him dragging me down.
Rocks are lifeless. They have no voice. They have no power. The more my recovery progresses, the more Ed is becoming a rock – lifeless and powerless.

If I had seen this picture at the beginning of my recovery, I would have seen it as that rock holding that butterfly down. Not now. Now that butterfly is moving that rock all by herself.

I am that butterfly. Here is to another day of the little butterfly within me who keeps proving to Ed time and time again that she is stronger than she looks.

Hello Life!

******

Day 198: I Wore a Bikini

Today I had finally done the one thing I had been trying to run away from all summer long. Yes, I had put on a bikini, and actually worn it outside to the pool, not just in front of my mirror.

How did I feel? Chubby. Not fat, but very chubby. All I had seen was my old body in my mind, but then I would look in the mirror and see my new body and just be overwhelmed by the major changes.

Wednesday, August 7

I have all these curves and body mass that I never had before, and I can't escape seeing it in a bikini. But the whole reason I even put on the bikini in the first place was because my three little brothers wanted me to go swimming with them.

They always ask me, and I always say no. First off, I hate water. Don't ask me why, but I do. Secondly, I hate being in a bikini, not because of what other people will think of me, but because of what I will think of myself.

Anyway, after standing in front of the mirror looking over every inch of me, with Ed right by my side, I remembered the whole reason I put on that bathing suit in the first place.

I didn't put it on for Ed to criticize me. I didn't put it on to punish myself, although to me it would have felt appropriate to do so once I saw the way I looked. I put it on to go and be a part of my brothers – to go swim with them, to go experience life with them.

They didn't care or even notice which love handle was poking out the most, or which leg was rubbing against the other. They cared that for the first time in two years I was about to jump into the pool with them.

One of my brothers had the video camera to record us, and the other two counted to three with me. One ... two ... three ... and then we did it. I did it. I jumped into the water, and my brothers cheered and clapped the whole time.

I watched that video twenty times afterwards, trying to see how my body looked. I even took a snapshot of the video so I could zoom in on my body. And then I finally gave up.

What I see today might be different to what I see tomorrow, and how my body looks today is not what is important. It may feel very important to Ed, therefore I feel like I need to give it immediate attention, but in the bigger picture of life, it's not that important.

What was important was that I jumped into that pool after two years of Ed not letting me.

Hello Life!

******

Day 199: Silently Screaming

It had all started when I came home and put on a pair of stretch leggings. Last time I had worn them they were falling off me. Today they were tight.

From falling off me only five months before ... to now being tight. I was already not having the most loving relationship with my body after seeing myself in a bikini yesterday, then these leggings just solidified everything I was already thinking and feeling.

Thursday, August 8

I feel like I have traveled through this whole day silently screaming in my head. I tried to get out of it, and I tried really hard too. I tried distracting myself by spending time with my brothers. I tried watching a movie. I tried focusing on the amazing things in life, such as my family and friends, but the screaming didn't stop.

Part of the time, I was screaming with anger at my body. Why does it look like this now? Why does recovery have to mean me having this body that I dislike so strongly? (I won't use hate, because hate is a strong word, and I don't think it's hatred, at least not right now).

Then sometimes I was screaming at myself. Why did I go out all those nights and eat all those bad fattening foods? Why did I give myself the excuse 'you are living your life', when I should have told myself 'you will just make yourself fat'?

Then the other part of me was screaming at Ed for making me scream at myself in the first place. And after all this silent screaming has been going on all day within my own head, now I don't even know what I am screaming anymore. It's just noise ... so much noise.

I tried to imagine taking myself to a mountain somewhere, screaming in real life, and really letting it all out that way, but something within me doesn't want to do that. Something about my screams being silent today is holding a lot of power over me. Even writing about it right now feels like I am exposing some big dark secret that I have been holding to myself.

But now that I have exposed it, maybe it will calm down. I don't want to be stuck hearing my own screams and Ed screams all night; I want to enjoy my night. I want to enjoy my weekend. I want to enjoy me.

I remember this feeling of silently screaming from when I was trapped inside Ed. It used to happen to me at night, when my heartbeat would speed up, then slow down, then speed up again, because I was so scared about what I was doing to my body by not eating and I didn't know how to save myself.

It would always be in the middle of the night, and I used to stare off into the darkness, crying and promising myself that the next morning I wouldn't weigh myself – but it never worked. I used to dread going to sleep because of it. I felt like I was my own worst enemy.

The good thing is, this time I know that those silent screams inside my head are nothing but Ed. At least now I know who I am fighting against. Before, I used to think I was fighting against myself. I used to think it was me who was my own worst enemy.

No, Ed is my enemy. I am the good one here, the one saving me from him. We are two different entities. I will continue on with my night as I planned, because that is what I need to do to stay in the real world, and not in Ed's world.

Do I still feel like I am silently screaming? Yes and no. The screams are there but they are not technically silent anymore, now that I have shared them with you all, and there is a lot of power in that.

Even though today has been hard for me, and it's been draining feeling trapped inside my head all day with Ed, I just realized as I titled this post that today is Day 199 of a year without a scale. That means tomorrow is Day 200. Almost two hundred days of being in recovery and of not weighing myself, yet I am still fighting Ed.

On one hand, it's disappointing that I am still here fighting him after all this time. But on the other hand, it's incredible, that I am still here, nearly two hundred days later, still fighting and giving it my all, instead of giving up.

Almost two hundred days of not giving up on myself ... I think it might possibly outweigh the silent screams I had to endure all day.
Hello Life!

******

Day 200: Two Hundred Days of Not Giving Up on Myself

This day I celebrated two hundred days without weighing myself and of recovery from my eating disorder.

Did I like my body? No. Did I accept it? No again. But I loved myself more than anything right at that time for spending the last two hundred days fighting for the life that I knew I deserved, free of Ed.

I loved myself more than I loved my eating disorder, and that may have meant something right then – I might have just needed to be uncomfortable with my body.

Friday, August 9

On Day 31 of my blog I wrote a post about celebrating my first one-month milestone in recovery and of being without a scale. In that post I wrote:

> *"I have begun to fight for my future, a future where I know that whatever I lost from this eating disorder or from my recent heartache, God will restore me double, and when he does I will not only be a fighter, I will be the world champion of the title that my eating disorder tried so hard to keep – the title of my life."*

Here we are, on Day 200, and I am proud to say that I am the champion of that title now. I am not only fighting now, but I am living too. I am living as the champion of my life.

Yes, on some days Ed tries to steal the title away from me, and sometimes I let him touch it for a second, or run his fingers over the outlines of it, but I never let him grab it back. That title is mine. I earned it. I fight to keep that title of the champion of my life every single day. It's a fight where each day is a new round, and each day my punches become stronger.

Sometimes Ed wins a few rounds, but he is never the one who gets to raise his hand in victory. Every night that I go to sleep knowing that I lived another day in recovery, I am the one who gets to raise my hand as the winner.

My side of the boxing ring never rests and, truthfully, never does Ed's either. But my corner is stronger than his. I am stronger than him. Ed stands alone. I stand with everyone who has been supporting me in my corner since Day 1.

Thank you to everyone who is still in my corner, cheering me on, two hundred days later. Without you, I don't have the power to win. I am the ultimate fighter, but you all are my gloves that I hit with, and that I protect myself with.

Today I celebrate two hundred days of me not giving up on myself, and to that I say with deep appreciation and gratitude: Hello Life!

******

Day 201: Insanity

In my blog, I had started telling everyone that I had started taking pictures of myself in the mirror again. After deleting over five hundred pictures about two months previously, I had put myself on a thirty-day photo cleanse.

Well, the photo cleanse had ended, and the picture obsession had begun again. It was no surprise to me that this picture taking had restarted at the same time that I had been having trouble accepting my body.

The week before, I only took a few pictures a day, then deleted them right away. I would take the picture, look at it, then delete it immediately. Now, I was taking the pictures and saving them until later, so I could look at them when I felt like it.

Every time I looked at them, I criticized every single part of me. Sometimes I told myself that maybe next time I would like what I saw. But then I thought, no, this would never happen.

Saturday, August 10

Albert Einstein's definition of insanity is doing the same thing over and over again and expecting different results. I keep doing the same thing over and over again with these pictures, expecting that I will like them, but I won't. I am living the definition of insanity with these pictures.

It's not like I am looking at photos that someone else has taken of me; I am purposefully taking these pictures to judge myself. I don't even want to take these pictures, I just do it as if I am on autopilot.

It reminds me of when I used to weigh myself every day. I didn't want to do it, but Ed had so much control over me that I would wake up and do it anyway. It was a set routine. Wake up, pee, weigh myself.

For the past two days, I have been in this autopilot routine with taking these pictures. My body is just taking these pictures without me even knowing what I am doing. Ed is being the controller and I am being the puppet. Get up, get dressed, take a picture.

So, two days of picture insanity later, and I am left with thirty-two new undeleted pictures currently sitting in my phone. I know I will be ready to delete them soon, when I am ready.

I think that it takes a strong person to know when they succeed, but it takes a wiser person to know when they fall or take steps backwards. These pictures are a step backwards for me, and I am not afraid to see it or admit to it.

It won't be the end of my recovery that I have started taking pictures again. It will, however, be a reminder of how hard it is to pick your feet up again after you have planted them two steps behind where they used to be.

But it's okay. I am not scared to take steps back, because they will motivate me to take three steps forwards tomorrow.

Hello Life!

******

Day 202: When Someone Else's Ed Takes Their Life

Today I had been to see an old friend of mine from high school, who was also my neighbor. He was in the hospital, living off life support, after taking too many prescription pills a few days previously.

As I was standing in the room, his mom took his hand in hers, and said, "He loved everyone, but himself ... all he wanted to do was escape the pain."

He hadn't wanted to overdose. He hadn't wanted this to happen. All he wanted was an escape. But when she said that he loved everyone but himself, it really struck my heart, because that was the struggle that I had been fighting every day for the past seven months – learning how to love and accept myself just the way I was.

Ed was my escape from me not loving myself; pills were his. We were no different. For me, I had my eating disorder. For him, he had his pills. It made me think about how everyone in life had their own Ed in their own kind of way.

Sunday, August 11

My Ed is my eating disorder. Maybe someone else's version of Ed is drugs, maybe for some of us it's athletics. Whatever it is, I so deeply understand what it's like to love everyone but yourself, and to let those other Eds be your comfort for that. Whether your Ed is food, drugs, alcohol, or anything else, they all serve the same purpose – to escape from yourself.

I understand wanting to escape from a world where life just seems too overwhelming. For me it was overwhelming with food or numbers, for others it might be other things.

Is this the ultimate destination for those who will never find the path to true self-acceptance and love? The death of your own soul? The death of your body?

I don't care anymore today about what I cared about yesterday. My shell of a body that I let my own Ed tell me to take pictures of in the mirror ... that just doesn't matter as much when you see a family trying to put the pieces together of how their son ended up on life support.

They were devastated, confused, speechless. But I understand how he got there. I understand because, had I not started recovery, it could have been me. I understand how easy it is to start to think that those escapes that make us feel so temporarily good can so quickly become the worlds that we want to immerse ourselves in.

I remember the high I would get from not eating. It could last me days. It took me a long time to start to realize how it was affecting my life. I didn't want to harm myself, I just wanted to escape. And that is all my friend wanted to do – he wanted to escape.

A life is gone. A life is gone because another person's Ed won.

In honor and out of respect for the life that was essentially already lost today, there will be no "Hello Life!" at the end of today's post. Instead, there will be a moment of silence.

If you are reading this post right now, I ask you to please take a moment of silence with me, as I not only pray for my friend and his family, but for all those souls who are fighting to stay alive in a world where they feel they need to escape because they are not good enough the way they are.

******

Day 203: Taking Back the Reins

Today had been very simple: I took back some of the control that Ed was having over me during the previous few days with all this insane picture taking I was doing.

E had summed it up perfectly: "It's okay to be in that Ed chaos for a little, but now it's time for you to take back the reins."

She was right.

Monday, August 12

It was time to take back control and show Ed who is in charge of my life. It's not him, it's me.

So, what did I do? E sat with me, and I deleted over forty new pictures that I had taken in the past few days and saved on my phone.

One by one ... delete, delete, delete.

I felt like I had lost something precious to me afterwards. It felt like the same feeling I had when I gave up my scale. Those pictures had become my scale lately, and now they are gone. Those pictures had been my way of identifying myself lately. I had grown attached to them. I knew every single one of them. They had become a reminder to me about why I should let Ed be the dominant one in our relationship, because of how 'bad' my body looks now.

Just how the numbers on the scale would make me feel as if I was constantly trapped in my mind running laps, unable to stop the craziness, that is how these pictures made me feel.

Now that they are deleted, I am scared of what I will do next. I don't want to take anymore pictures. But it's not like a scale, where I can take it out of my house. I have my camera on my phone next to me at all times. Temptation is always there.

My fear is not what will happen if I don't take anymore pictures. My fear is: What if I do? What if I take more pictures, after I have told myself I don't want to anymore? That would be like standing on the scale after I promised I wouldn't do it for a year. It would lead to disappointment in myself, and that is far worse than the feelings I have of shame for even taking the pictures in the first place, or the feelings of self-loathing I have for my body when I look at those pictures.

The extremist in me wants to say, "No more pictures forever," or "No more pictures for a year," just like I did with my scale. But giving up my scale for a whole year didn't just happen in one day. I attempted to give it up many times before I made that year commitment.

At first it started with not weighing myself for one day. That one day turned into three days, and those three days turned into a year. So for a moment here, I am going to be a realist, instead of an extremist, and try to find some balance.

I know that tomorrow will be a hard day for me, as I will be attending the funeral of my friend who passed away today from overdosing yesterday. On top of that, I will be seeing a lot of old friends who haven't seen me since my eating disorder started. The last thing I need is to let my Ed take over me on a day where I am so strongly reminded of how someone else's Ed took their life away from them.

So for now I will say that for one day, tomorrow, I won't take pictures of myself. That is it – one day only. This is so opposite of what my black-and-white personality wants to do, but I am going to flow with it.

A one-day commitment of no pictures. I can do that. It's a step towards taking back the reins from Ed, and to that I say: Hello Life!

******

Day 204: A Beautiful Way to Be Remembered

Today I had attended the funeral of my old friend, who was twenty-four, and who had overdosed on pain medication a few days before. There were hundreds of people there. Hundreds of people who wanted to show their love and respect for him.

As his friends and family spoke about him, they all kept one main theme within their speeches: He loved everyone around him, and he gave so much love to those around him, yet he kept no love for himself.

I kept wondering why someone who had so many people in his life who loved him and cared about him, felt the need to take these pain pills all the time and escape. And then I realized, I could ask myself the same question.

Why had I felt the need (and sometimes still felt the need) to turn to an eating disorder, even though people in my life cared and loved me so much?

The answer was simple: He didn't love himself, and I didn't love myself. I realized that if we don't love ourselves, there is no way we can even be open to receiving the love of others in our lives.

Tuesday, August 13

It has only been during the past seven months since I started recovery that I am able to create deep and meaningful relationships with people in my life. Before, I couldn't even be open to seeing how much I wanted those relationships because I was so busy being wrapped up in my eating disorder, trying to make me into a 'skinnier', therefore 'better and perfect' version of myself.

Unfortunately for my friend, he never got to take the journey to self-acceptance like I am doing now, therefore I don't know whether he ever knew how loved he really was. I don't know whether he saw it, and that makes me so sad for him.

During the funeral, my friend's mom spoke to her now passed-away son: "Everyone knew that you were a talented artist and musician, but they didn't know that your best talent was loving your mother."

Even though he used his body as a canvas for tattoos, even though he got a nose job, even though he didn't love the way he looked, none of those things were what he was remembered for. He was remembered by his mom for loving her.

How fortunate would we all be if, when we leave this earth, we are not remembered for our bodies, our weights or our hair style, but for how beautifully we loved one another.

Hello Life!

******

Day 205: Three Steps Forwards

A few days previously, I had written a post about how I was taking so many pictures of myself in the mirror, and how I knew it was a step backwards for me in my recovery.

However, in that same post, I also wrote that that one step backwards would motivate me to take three steps forwards.

Today, I took those three steps forwards.

Wednesday, August 14

Today I took one of my younger brothers to a water park and then to dinner and dessert. Yes, me and a water park – with a bikini.

I didn't take a picture of myself yesterday or today. I knew that if I took that photo this morning, I wouldn't be able to enjoy my day with my brother, and he deserved me to be with him today, not Ed.

Sure, there were times during the day when I was checking myself out in mirrors in the bathroom, but never more than a quick glance. It wasn't easy, but I did it. This was a huge step for me today. That is why I say it was more like three steps.

I put on a bathing suit, in a time where I am so uncomfortable with my body, and I forced myself to fight every single urge Ed presented me with, from when I tried the bathing suit on in the morning, to lunch in the afternoon, and to dinner and dessert at night, and I won.

I didn't just beat Ed for me today, but I did it for my brother. That selflessness right there is recovery.

Hello Life!

**

Day 206: A Little Boy Being Excited to Show Me How He Writes His Name on His Paper —That's Happiness

"Wow, I can't believe I ate all that food yesterday." "How could I eat all that dessert last night?" "Of course, I wake up feeling sore." "Okay, extra hard working out for me today."

Those were the thoughts that I had when I first woke up on this morning. Had I not needed to leave the house by a certain time to take my little brothers to school, I might have stood in front of the mirror and body checked over and over, but I wanted to be on time, so I didn't do that.

Thursday, August 15

As I was walking my youngest brother into his kindergarten classroom, he asked me to stay with him five extra minutes.

"Do you want to show me where you sit,?" I asked him. He nodded, smiled, rushed over to his desk and showed me his pencil box that had his name written on it. He was so excited to share this new part of his life with me. I sat next to him as he wrote his name on his paper, all by himself – another big deal that he wanted to show me.

I don't know what it was about those few minutes of sitting there with him in his classroom, but something inside me just didn't want to leave, but I knew I had to. So I kissed him and left.

From the minute I left his classroom, I felt like I was this light feather who had no more burdens on her. I don't mean light as in weight, I mean light as in carefree and happy. It was as if I had little wings attached on my shoulders that decided to pop out and flutter for me.

Since I left his classroom, I never thought about all the food I ate last night again, working out too hard, or how I looked. Something about sharing that moment with my youngest brother was so powerful and touching that it made Ed disappear from my world.

These moments, like sitting next to my brother on his third day of kindergarten and him being so happy to show me his new seat and pencil box, are the moments that make life worth smiling for. Each tiny moment of happiness that I experience is slowly becoming my armor to protect myself and defend myself from Ed.

I hope everyone reading this blog today was blessed enough to experience a tiny moment of happiness too. If you did, what was it? Feel free to share your moment or moments of happiness on this post, as I know it would bring me and others so much joy to get a glimpse of the kind of happiness that other people feel.

I used to think I could only get that happy, light as a feather feeling by seeing a really 'good' number on the scale or by buying new clothes that were a size zero. I used to think I could only achieve happiness through Ed, through losing just one more pound.

No, that wasn't happiness. This little boy being excited to show me how he writes his name on his paper – that is happiness. No eating disorder in the world can stop me from enjoying that experience with him.

Hello Life!

******

Day 207: The Man Who Has Shoes but No Feet to Put in Them

I started off this day's post by saying thank you so much to everyone who shared their moments of happiness on the previous day's post. It truly brought me so much joy to see the kinds of things that made them all smile and it gave me a glimpse into their world.

Friday, August 16

So today I am in San Diego with my grandma. When we were sitting in the car, she reminded me of a saying my grandpa used to say a lot: "What about the man who has shoes but no feet to put in them."

He used to say that to remind us, and himself, to not complain about the small things in life and that there are others who always have it worse than you do. The man who has shoes but no feet to put in them, he can complain. He actually has a reason.

While that is very true, I take this saying as something more metaphorical. How many of us have feet to wear our shoes, yet we act like we have lost our limbs?

Sometimes I get mad that I have been dealt this eating disorder. On days like this past week, where I have been consumed by pictures and mirrors, that frustration heightens. But when I let that frustration take over me, I am acting like a man who has shoes but no feet to wear them – totally helpless.

I am not helpless. I am strong. God wouldn't give me shoes that I can't wear. He wouldn't give me battles I can't win. And he wouldn't give me feet that can't carry me through hard times.

I have feet and I have the shoes to wear on them, and I am damned if I will let Ed make me think otherwise.

Hello to being reminded that I am fortunate enough to not be the man with shoes but no feet to put in them, and Hello Life!

******

Day 208: Thankful for a Quiet Day

Plain and simple, today had been a quiet and therefore beautiful day for me. I got to relax by the beach, spend time with my grandma, watch TV, sleep and eat without overthinking it too much.

For some people, this may seem like just a typical relaxing Saturday, and you may wonder why it was a gift to me to have such a day.

Saturday, August 17

Since I know what it's like to have days where I am so consumed by Ed, a quiet day like today is a gift to me. It's not often that I get a quiet day, as even on the days that I am not as strongly affected by Ed, I keep myself extremely busy and productive.

I am so appreciative that I was able to let myself relax today, and I am so appreciative that Ed wasn't bothering me all day about it. I love that I am able to appreciate the beauty in the things that I once would have taken for granted not so long ago, such as a relaxing day.

I hope everyone reading this post was able to find some kind of gift in their day today, and if you would like to share it, I would love to read about it too, so please share what your gift was today.

Hello to finding the gifts in even the most ordinary days, and Hello Life!

******

Day 209: Walking into a Future Without Ed

I had to apologize for this post being so late, as I was driving home from San Diego and hadn't had time to write.

Today had been another great day. I could actually say that for the first time in a while I had truly eaten what I wanted and enjoyed it without feeling guilty.

Sunday, August 18

When I was driving home from San Diego today, I received a phone call from Donna, the mom of one of my childhood friends. My sister and I were best friends with Donna's daughter growing up, and we spent a lot of time in her house. She was like a part of our family.

I hadn't heard from her in a few years now, and for some reason she decided to call me just to see how I was doing. I was caught off guard, but at the same time I was so pleasantly surprised. It was a good feeling, a familiar feeling.

When she asked me how I was doing and what I was up to, I told her "I am finishing my last semester in school, about to graduate, and I am just enjoying my last week of summer with my family and friends."

I didn't notice until afterwards, that none of what I said to her had to do with my recovery, my eating disorder, food, losing weight or working out.

Had she asked me that question a year ago, I would have told her, "I am busy working out a lot and being healthy," because that is all that was important to me. And by healthy, I mean not eating. I didn't know any other way to describe my battle with Ed at the time, other than saying I was being 'healthy' (total opposite of what I was).

But that didn't happen this time. I told her how happy I am about school, about my family and friends, and about graduating college –none of which have to do with Ed. How exciting is that, right?

I used to write on this blog about how one day I knew that my life would be able to move on without Ed. I didn't know how, but I knew it would. The fact that I told someone on the phone today about how I envision my life in the next few months being all about school and relationships and gaining independence, that is me already moving on without Ed. I am already mentally preparing myself to be ready to walk into my future with him behind me.

The best part of this whole experience with talking to Donna, except for what I just wrote about above, was that I saw how great it felt for someone to reach out and just ask how someone else is doing. It was genuine, kind-hearted, and selfless. She made me smile and feel thought-about.

How long has it been since I have made someone else feel thought-about?

Tomorrow I am going to call someone who I haven't called in a while, in hopes that I can give them the same feeling that Donna gave me. Ed or no Ed, feeling cared about can lift anyone's spirits up, and we all need that from time to time.

Hello to starting my Monday tomorrow by hopefully enriching the life of someone else, hello to envisioning my future without Ed, and Hello Life!

******

Day 210: A Crazy Monday

This day's post was very short so I had to apologize in advance.

Monday, August 19

Today was a crazy day. I am stressed out. I am tired.
I know that it's crucial that I need to make time for myself this week. But right now, even after a long, unplanned, not-in-my-control kind of day, I am sitting watching a movie with one of my brothers.
If I can't control much of anything else right now – with life or body – the least I can do is seize this moment with him and wrap myself in his love.
Until tomorrow, which will hopefully be a calmer day ... Hello Life!

******

Day 211: Having Faith in What Will Be

"Surrender to what is. Let go of what was.
Have faith in what will be." ~ Sonia Ricotti

"Have faith in what will be." This has really gotten me through my day today.

At the end of the day, I didn't feel like sitting there and writing about the stresses or anxieties that I had been feeling lately, because I had realized that was just life.

Life was stressful sometimes, it could be anxiety-filled sometimes, it could be unplanned sometimes, and it could be a bit out of control sometimes.

But what mattered to me in that moment wasn't really what was happening in the now, although being present in something was something I tried to dedicate myself to often.

Right then, it worked for me to have faith in what would be.

Tuesday, August 20

In the next few days I will be starting school again. I have already started my position as senior reporter for the school newspaper.

I will writing. I will be productive. I will be emerged into a world where my success is measured by the content I write and the way I use my mind, not measured by my body or my food intake.

Being productive and being a reporter is not an Ed-controlled world. Ed has never been able to take away my passion for writing, or my strong desire to succeed in school, and after so much unpredictability this summer, I am really looking forward to seeing myself shine.

I shine when I write. I shine when I am productive. I shine when I have some stability and routine. All those things are what will be in my future, and just knowing that has made today a really good day.

I could have focused on Ed today. I could have thought about the ice cream I ate last night, or the fact that I didn't work out today, but why? Why focus on those draining things, when life is about to throw me so many opportunities to shine?

I have faith in what will be. I envision me shining. Ed is not stopping me.

Hello Life!

******

Day 212: Skipping the Scale at the Doctor's

I had had today all planned out. Turned out I didn't even need to, because fate took care of it for me anyway.

Since the previous week, I had known that I was going to the doctor today. I knew that they always weighed me when I went there. It used to be my favorite part. But this time, it had to be different.

I hadn't been to a doctor since my recovery had started, except for my initial exam by an eating disorder specialist, and that day had been the first time I had done a back weigh.

Wednesday, August 21

I have done many back weighs before with my old nutritionist. A back weigh is where you stand on the scale but don't see the number. But I was safe with her because I knew she would never blurt out the number.

I read a blog post about another girl in recovery for an eating disorder who went to her doctor, and the nurse accidentally said her weight out loud. I was so scared this would happen to me.

When I was walking in, I started thinking to myself, "I wonder what would happen if I did see the number today? Maybe I am ready to handle it." But because this entire blog is dedicated to one year without a scale, I didn't even give myself the option of going there.

Why give up now after I have come so far? And more importantly, in retrospect, I know that I couldn't have handled seeing that number today.

I walked into the office, and I saw the scale. It wasn't an electronic one, it was an old-school one, where they stand and move the little block until the scale tips. So even if I did a back weigh, I would have been able to feel where they stopped the little block and how far along they moved it.

I knew in that moment, I couldn't get on there. I knew I wasn't ready. I was trying to go over my lines that I practiced with E in my head on what to say to the nurse, but before I could even find them, the nurse said to me, "Do you know your approximate weight? Because if you do, we can just skip the scale."

I was in shock. "Um ... yeah, I know it," I told her.

I told her the closest number that I think I am. Who knows if it's even accurate or not, because the last time I saw a number on a scale was over seven months ago. But, whatever, it was good enough for her.

There are moments in life where things are meant to happen and when things are not meant to happen. Today, I wasn't meant to stand on that scale.

I remember sitting in the room waiting for the doctor, saying, "Thank you," silently to whoever was watching over me today from above, because someone definitely was. Never, in all the years that I have come for a yearly check-up, has the nurse given me the option to skip the scale. They didn't even know I am in recovery for an eating disorder.

I talked yesterday about having faith in what will be ... and today was a perfect example of that.

I can't end this post without giving myself the slightest bit of credit for fighting that temptation to not stand on that scale today. It's not the first time in my recovery that I have seen a scale in front of me and have had to walk away from it, but it's never easy. There is always Ed sitting in the back of my mind pushing me just to hop right on. But I didn't do that today. I listened to myself, instead of to him, and it's something that is getting easier to do each day.

The universe never seems to stop amazing me. What we put into it, we truly do get back. And today, after the many favors I have done for people in my life, the universe gave me back a favor and let me skip the scale at the doctor's.

As far as a good day goes ... I don't think I can ask for anything more. Hello Life!

******

Day 213: Tables Are Starting to Turn

For whatever reason, I felt like I was back at the very beginning of recovery on this day.

I had gone out for lunch with my grandma. I had been out to eat hundreds of times by that then, and to many different and new places, and I usually didn't have that hard a time with new and 'not safe' foods. But today, I had had a hard time.

I didn't like that the fish I ordered had oil on it, and I didn't like that it was a bigger lunch than I would normally have. It was something out of my routine. I still ate it and enjoyed it, but it was more of a reminder to me about where I once started in recovery.

Thursday, August 22

There was a point where having even just an apple for lunch was hard for me to do. There was a point where I couldn't even have gone out to lunch at all.

Experiencing the hard time I had today kind of grounded me and brought me back to those early days in my recovery of seven months ago. It makes me appreciate the many lunches I have been able to go to without Ed stepping in.

Today was a struggle, but it's when we struggle that we find our greatest strengths. I found my strength today when I ate that lunch anyway, and when I was able to sit with the discomfort of that and ride out those feelings, instead of just give in to Ed and restrict.

Instead of being mad at Ed for trying to pull me back to him today, I am actually a little grateful. Thank you Ed for reminding me of where I once started, and how far I have come. And thank you for showing me how strong I have become. You sat with me today at that table and watched me eat the lunch you so badly didn't want me to eat.

How did it feel to lose your control over me today? How did it feel to tell me not to eat, yet I didn't listen? How did it feel to see me trample on your demands with my own needs and wants? How does it feel for me to not listen to you? How does it feel for me to not care about what you wanted, and only do what I wanted?

Maybe now you have a glimpse into the way you made me feel for all those years that you were the one in control.

Well Ed, if you want to come into my head and tell me not to eat, then I have no other choice but to invite you to sit at my table with me. I am not afraid of you anymore.

And every time you yell at me to not eat, I am going to pretend like your voice is silent, just the way you did to me every time I told you to stop making me lose more weight.

The tables are starting to turn, dearest Ed. Hope you can get used to it.

Hello Life!

******

Day 214: I Love You, That's What

I was sitting with my brothers, thinking what to write about on this day. I was thinking I could write about the fact that I had eaten cake today, and how bad I felt about it, but that wasn't helpful to me in any way.

Friday, August 23

So as I was sitting here about five minutes ago, I said out loud to my little brothers, "Guys, I have nothing to write today." (They don't need to know I am uncomfortable about eating cake.)

"I love you, that's what," my four-year old brother said to me.

I think that sums everything up. My recovery, my dedication and my perseverance ... "I love you, that's what," sums it up pretty well.

What better way to end my Friday than with that, right?

Hello Life!

******

Day 215: Not Going to Fall

I sat writing this day's post in bed with a heating pad on my neck and Advil by my bedside. I had woken up ready to go work out, but I had slept wrong and I couldn't move my neck at all. I went to the gym anyway, only for my trainer to send me right back home, since I pretty much couldn't move at all.

I guess I had some kind of hope that she would let me work out anyway, because after eating a lot of food and sweets the day before, I really felt the need to burn some of it off.

Well, she didn't let me work out, and I was thankful for it, because I would have hurt myself even more. But, naturally, Ed and I were not happy about that.

Saturday, August 24

I was already in pain from my neck, and on top of feeling that discomfort, now I had to live with the feeling of not being able to burn off any calories from yesterday. It's annoying and it's frustrating, but at least I listened to my trainer, and I came home and rested all day. And I still ate today too, which is a victory for me and a loss for Ed.

In the midst of me driving myself to the gym, thinking I could actually work out today, I received a Facebook message from the dad of one of my old friends. This friend and I were friends in high school, and over recent years he had been battling some Eds of his own, although his wasn't food, his was drugs.

As I said in a post last week, everyone has their own Ed in life, whether it be food, alcohol, drugs, or anything else people might use as an outlet to deal with life. Anyway, he came home from rehab about two months ago.

I had spoken with him on the phone, but never saw him in person, as I didn't want to get too close to someone who I wasn't sure was strong enough to stay away from their addiction, and I didn't want him to introduce me to any new coping mechanisms like drugs. Ed is already enough for me to handle.

Over the past few days his parents kept asking me where he is, and for the phone numbers of the people he is with. I had no idea why they were contacting me, since we hadn't spoken in a few weeks.

Today I found out he had told his parents that for the past few weeks he had been hanging out with me and my friends. He knew his parents trusted me. He used me as his cover up, so he could go do whatever he is currently doing. I am not sure what it is, but considering he is not communicating with his family, I assume it's not good.

At first, I was so upset. How could someone use me to cover up for them doing harmful things to themselves, like possibly using drugs? Especially me. This guy and I were close friends. He was even the third subscriber to this blog. And then I realized, I can't even be mad at him. I can't be mad at him because this is not him doing this, it's his own Ed.

I remember when I used to use people to cover up for me and my dear Ed. I would use my brothers, and tell my boyfriend at the time that I ate dinner with my brothers already, so I couldn't eat with him. I would tell my sister I couldn't eat with her since I had to make dinner for my boyfriend. The list goes on and on.

I doubt my friend is reading this post today, because when you are back in that dark world of addiction, you don't pay much attention to the present world outside. But if you for some reason are ... I hope you know that no matter how many times you have fallen, you can still get back up. Right now, in this moment, you can stop, take back control and get back up.

I have to remind myself of this message today too. Ed is yelling at me that I should not eat because I didn't work out today. But I am eating anyway. Why? Because I know what it's like to fall victim to Ed, and how hard it is to find the strength to stand back up again.

I woke up this morning standing up to Ed, and I will go to sleep standing up to Ed. I am not going to fall today.

And to my friend who is struggling today, I hope you can find it within yourself to stand up too.

Hello Life!

******

Day 216: Being 'Me-Sponsible'

Today I had been 'me-sponsible'. I had been responsible for me, my health, my happiness and well-being. What had I done?

- I had eaten on my meal plan, although I didn't remember feeling hungry or having the urge to eat.
- I worked on two stories I was writing for my university newspaper due that week.

- I prepared everything for my first day of school the next day.
- I rested and didn't exercise, since I had injured my neck the day before.
- I took a nap because I was tired.

Sunday, August 25

I love the concept of 'me-sponsible'. I am the kind of person who is always responsible – I am on time to work, I complete my homework assignments a week before they are due, and I keep track of all my daily tasks in my phone.

But how often do we give ourselves the time we need to be 'me-sponsible'? I for sure don't do it enough, but over the past seven months of recovery, it's something I have learned to make time for in my life.

At one point, self-care was something that was a luxury to me. Getting my nails done, taking a nap or eating a meal, were luxurious prizes I would award myself with when I restricted. Now, self-care is a priority, not a luxury.

What kinds of things do you enjoy doing when you are 'me-sponsible'? As always, feel free to share, as it brings insight and ideas to myself and other readers.

Call it self-care or call it being 'me-sponsible', I hope everyone reading this finds some time this week to be kind to themselves, because we deserve it.

Hello to self-care now being a priority, hello to being 'me-sponsible', and Hello Life!

******

Day 217: First Day of School in Recovery

Ed had woken up with me today at 7:30a.m. when I realized that my neck was still injured, so I couldn't work out, yet again. The idea of not exercising for four days in a row was getting mentally harder for me to deal with every day and, of course, Ed wasn't helping me.

On top of that, today was my first day back at school. It was actually my last semester of college, as I would be graduating next December.

It brought me a lot of different emotions. Part of me was so excited and ready to end that chapter of my life, and move on to bigger things. Part of me was excited to start a semester as senior reporter for my university newspaper. But part of me was also scared and nervous.

Monday, August 26

When I started recovery in March, school was slowly ending, and I was still kind of figuring the whole recovery thing out. The eating part of recovery was still new to me at that time.

For a lot of people who don't have eating disorders, they think that the first step in recovery is eating, but it's not. The first step is even realizing that you have an eating disorder in the first place, and that is where I was around the time school ended before summer.

Today was the first day I had to go through a full day of school while totally living in recovery, meal plan and all. So here I was this morning, sitting with two options:

A) I could let Ed be in control of my very first day of my last semester of college and my first day of officially being senior reporter; or

B) I could find it within myself to stay true to what is important today – my future, my writing, my school and my recovery. Not eating or restricting just can't make the list.

So, I chose option B.

It was hard. Very hard. The words 'very hard' actually don't even give it justice. I literally felt like a robot on autopilot all day, just eating at the times I knew I had to, and eating what I knew was on my plan. It was automatic, with no feelings attached. When Ed gets to me and I disconnect from my hunger cues, it's easy to let him win.

I was already thinking of how great it was that I was so busy today with a full school schedule and work schedule, and how convenient it would be to be 'too busy' to eat. That was my excuse last year in school.

It's not a valid excuse for me anymore. I know if I want to be the best reporter I can be this semester, produce good quality work and make good grades, I need to eat to stay clear-minded.

As far as my first day of school in recovery goes ... I did it, but it wasn't easy at all. But that is okay, because in the end I won't remember the struggle of today as much as I will remember that I was in control today, not Ed, and that I won over him.

I can see this semester being a great one for me, now that Ed is not who I use to define myself by. I won't go into any more tests, presentations or interviews only thinking about what I weighed that day. I will be present.

I might struggle with Ed's thoughts versus my own thoughts, but this is my time to show myself what I am capable of without Ed or without a number on a scale bringing me down.

I worked too hard to get to this place in recovery to let Ed ruin this last semester for me. I am doing this. I am going to finish my last semester in college living in recovery.

Wow. Hello Life!

******

Day 218: Writing Calorie Counts on the Back of My Syllabus in Class

There I was, at 5:45p.m., sitting in my class on diversity and the media, writing down all the calories I had eaten that day on the back of my syllabus. I didn't even know how I had got there – I really thought I had been having a pretty okay day with Ed.

Tuesday, August 27

In the morning, even though I wanted to go work out really hard, I knew I couldn't because my neck was still hurting, so I walked instead. It still hurt to walk, and maybe it wasn't the best choice, but it was still only walking. And for me that was a total win, that I was able to do that and not go running instead. I wasn't satisfied with only walking, but it was enough exercise so that I was able to eat lunch and eat my snack.

I was talking back and forth with Ed a lot today, as you can see, but I felt like I was the one getting in the last word. So, how I got to writing my calorie count on the back of my syllabus in class I don't know.

I realized what I had done only after I had done it. I hated doing it though. It felt so automatic, so expected, and so part of my routine. Writing calories on pieces of paper in class used to be part of my old school routine, and it's not something I wanted to bring into this new routine when I am in recovery.

At first I thought about crossing the calorie count out, but now that I look at it right next to me, I want to leave it there. I want to leave it there as my reminder of what Ed can do to me when I let him take over my mind. He can distract me from class, and the end result is that calorie count on the back of that paper.

But really, what are those numbers anyway on the back of my syllabus? They are numbers. Just numbers. More and more numbers. Big numbers ... which I don't like, but in the end, just numbers.

Those numbers are what Ed thrives off. They are so factual and to the point. They are so unforgiving. Ed is unforgiving, but me, I am forgiving. I forgive myself for writing those calorie counts on the back of my syllabus, because I am doing the best that I can do.

Being okay with doing the best you can do is not a concept that is accepted for those of us who live with eating disorders, or any kind of addiction. The best doesn't exist in the dark world of eating disorders, until you give your life to it. There is always a lower weight to reach or a smaller size to fit into.

In recovery, doing my best does indeed exist and, to be honest, sometimes I don't even know what doing my best is. Yesterday it was eating even though I didn't exercise, today it was walking instead of running, and maybe tomorrow it will be something else.

For today, I was the best me that I could be, and to that I end tonight by saying: Hello Life!

******

Day 219: Once in a While, Blow Your Own Mind

I had completely and totally blown my own mind on this day. I had gone above and beyond any and all expectations I had of myself and I truly felt proud.

It had started at 12:30a.m. the previous night, after I found out that the story I had spent hours on, interviewing people about why faculty members at California state universities were not getting pay raises, totally got thrown out the window, since at 10p.m. the union had decided to give them all pay raises.

My title of 'CSU faculty have not received pay raises in over five years' totally got trashed, and instead I had to write a new piece about why they were now getting pay raises. The original story was supposed to be published the next day, which meant it had to be completed and perfect by 3p.m. today.

My editor said not to rush and that she would run the new version of the story the next Thursday. But, as you all know, this wasn't how I operated. I didn't like to wait for opportunities to come to me. This was an opportunity to publish my work, so I needed to tackle it.

By 12p.m. I had re-interviewed everyone I needed to.

By 1:30p.m. I had found time to eat lunch and nourish myself.

By 2:30p.m. my story was in my editor's hands ready to go to print for the next day's newspaper.

Talk about a lesson on going with the flow – last minute changes, and not turning to Ed for support.

Wednesday, August 28

I couldn't turn to Ed today when I was feeling overwhelmed; if I did, he would be all I focused on. I would have focused on my calories instead of my writing, or the way my clothes fitted instead of meeting my deadline. There was literally no space for him.

And on top of feeling so accomplished already, about one hour ago I got an email saying I have an interview tomorrow for a paid internship with NBC.

I applied for this internship only three days ago. It was a total whim and I didn't think they would even call me back, but something in me made me want to apply. There was something in me that made me believe in myself enough, that I had a chance to go for it.

I believed in my self-worth at that moment when I applied, because I believed I was good enough. I didn't think I was good enough because of what I weighed that day, or what I ate that day, and that is huge.

Even today, after seven months of recovery, I still am learning to mold myself into believing that my value doesn't rest on a number or size, but rather who I am, what I believe in and what I am capable of.

Ed didn't write that story for me today in six hours. He didn't get it published for me tomorrow. He didn't get me my interview. And a size zero didn't get me any of that either. I got me that.

Learning to believe in myself because of who I am, and not because of what I weigh, has been a long process for me, and it still is a process, but today I learned a really big lesson – the more I believe in myself, the less Ed exists.

I wrote a post about a week ago, saying how I felt my time to shine was going to come quickly. It has now officially come. The more I shine and the more I believe in me, the more dull Ed becomes.

And you know what? I am not even stressing about what will happen if I do or don't get that internship with NBC. Them just giving me that interview in the first place solidifies that I have the right to believe in myself. What greater gift could I ask for?

Hello Life!

******

Day 220: Three Dinners in Three Days

I had woken up this morning, done my video interview for NBC, gone to get my nails done, and then went to pick up a copy of my college newspaper so I could see my story published.

All good things, right? Actually, they were all great things.

Thursday, August 29

Up until about thirty minutes ago, I was happily enjoying myself in a slight world of la la land, where it was just me feeling proud of myself; Ed wasn't there. But, and I don't mean to take away from any of those beautiful times I spent without Ed today, but there is a but, then I got invited to dinner.

One of the families who I tutor for invited me to have Rosh Hashanah dinner with them next Wednesday night. It's a celebration of the Jewish new year. Of course I said yes because, firstly, it would be rude to decline, and, secondly, I really think it was such a kind and warm thing for them to do.

Then as I was driving home, it hit me. Wednesday night is dinner with my tutoring family. Thursday night is dinner with my dad's side of my family. Friday night is dinner with my mom's side of my family in San Diego. Three dinners back to back to back everyone. Three big, food filled, dinners.

If you can't already feel it by now, my anxiety level started to soar. I know it's a whole week away, but I already, or I should say Ed already has started planning what to eat on Saturday, Sunday, Monday and Tuesday, leading up to those dinners. He is saying they should be really light meals, and possibly extra cardio on those days.

Here is my question: Do 'normal' people (no one is really normal, but people without eating disorders) think about stuff like this? Do they get anxiety over having three straight dinners back to back?

I knew that the upcoming holidays would be a challenge for me, as any first in recovery is. And holidays can be especially difficult being that they are surrounded by so much food and so many people, the two things that Ed despises the most. I just didn't think it would start to affect me already.

The part of me that is not connected to Ed wants to enjoy these dinners. I want to enjoy getting to know the family I tutor, outside of the one hour I spend with their child. I want to enjoy my time with my brothers and my family on Thursday. I want to enjoy the beach and dinner with my grandma, mom and aunt on Friday night too.

But you see, with Ed in the picture, it will be a lot harder to get to those moments of joy. I know I can still have them, but I need to make that decision now. I need to decide that I will enjoy the upcoming holidays with my family and, yes, with the food too.

Decision made. I will enjoy it. The next step is how to fight Ed to get to that enjoyment.

Even though I have a lot of anxiety right now, part of my heart is so warmed by the fact that I was invited to dinner by someone I work for. They actually care about me and wanted to do something nice. That right there is me speaking, not Ed.

Anyway, I am opening up this post for any advice possible. What do you do on the holidays when you are surrounded by food? I don't think that people with eating disorders are the only ones who face this issue. If anyone, whether you have an eating disorder, are in recovery for an eating disorder, or don't even have an eating disorder, has any advice, I would love to hear it, because I truly do want to enjoy these dinners next week.

And I will enjoy them. It's just scary because it's the first time I am doing the holidays while being in recovery. But the fear over how to handle something new in recovery completely outweighs the fears that I used to have when I was living in Ed – fears like being scared to eat anything other than prunes for lunch, or being scared that the extra piece of gum I ate would throw off my weight the next morning.

Maybe this is not even a fear about these dinners. Maybe it's just something new. Doesn't everyone get a little anxious when they experience something new?

And I should point out to myself that three dinners in three days also means three times of spending time with people who love me. Hello Life!

******

Day 221: I Am the Driver

So, where was Ed at today? He was there like always, of course. I had felt him speaking to me a little louder than usual today for whatever reason.

For example, when I had gone to get frozen yogurt today, and I saw that it weighed 8.6 ounces, I let Ed tell me to throw half of it away when I got home.

You would think that I felt more comfortable once I had thrown half of it away, but I didn't. I felt the opposite. I felt ashamed and disappointed at myself that I even let Ed tell me to do that. I had obviously wanted that amount of yogurt for a reason, and I had let him tell me otherwise.

While that didn't feel good, to let Ed take power over me like that, I tried to remind myself that it was only one incident in my entire day when I let Ed back in. Just one.

Friday, August 30

There were times when Ed ran my entire life ... every day ... every hour ... every week. So, one incident today is not something I am going to beat myself up over.

However, there was also something great that happened today, that by far is better than pleasing any of Ed's demands, and it outweighs the disappointment I had in myself for giving in to him that one time today. After having my interview for a paid internship with NBC yesterday, I got notice that I have moved into the final hiring stage for KNBC, which is channel 4 news. Pretty much my dream come true.

I spent the first half of the day trying not to get too excited about it. Then I spent the second half of the day trying to shut Ed out completely. And then I realized – I don't think my goal for the moment is to shut anything out completely, even Ed. It's about balance.

I am actually pretty content with learning how to live my life, pursue my dreams and my school, even with Ed in the picture. It's not about demolishing him as a whole, because what takes years to create will probably take years to destroy.

It's about learning to navigate my life with me in the driver's seat. At one point, Ed was my driver. I was the passenger. We are still in the same car together, but now I am driving.

I have said that I am the driver in previous posts, and while I feel I have been driving the car for a while now, it's only now that I am starting to feel in control of the vehicle. The speed we go at, the lights we stop at it – most of the time now it's me, not Ed, especially this week. And I can sincerely tell you that I truly feel within my veins that I am driving myself somewhere great. Maybe by the time I arrive I will have dropped Ed off somewhere. And, if not, then he can sit back and watch me excel without his input.

Either way, I am the driver. Hello Life!

******

Day 222: A Hard Day in Recovery Doesn't Mean it's a Bad Day

To sum today up, recovery had been difficult. I was out with my little brothers all day, and they love to eat – everything. Candy, frozen yogurt, French fries, and a bunch more food I can't remember. I was really full all day and felt a little uncomfortable.

But with that being said, just because recovery was hard today, it doesn't mean I had a bad day.

Saturday, August 31

Not too long ago, I would have said a hard day in recovery meant a hard day overall, or a bad day. But that wasn't the case today. Yes, recovery wasn't easy today, and eating all that food was hard for me, but my day itself wasn't deemed bad by it. My day was actually great, if you take out the food part.

My brothers and I went to an arcade, and we went to lunch and pretended it was one of their birthdays to get a free ice-cream sundae (we always do this – don't judge me). We also went to see a movie and went shopping.

I think the highlight our day for all of us was when we were playing the game 'Deal or No Deal' in the arcade, and we chose the case that had one thousand tickets. To kids aged ten, seven and four it was like they won the lottery. Actually, even I felt like we won the lottery. They received a disco ball with all their tickets. Sure, the food was fun for them, and hard for me, but it doesn't come close to that moment of winning all those tickets that we shared together.

As I was dropping them off at home, one of my brothers said, "This was the best day of my whole life. Thank you Shira." That pretty much just made every bite of food and every moment of physical discomfort from being full totally worth it.

And I also think it's a pretty cool thing that even though recovery was hard today, my day was still good. A hard day in recovery doesn't have to mean I had a bad day, and that is really amazing for me.

And now that I think of it after writing this post, my recovery was pretty incredible today, even if it was hard. I was able to put all of Ed's thoughts aside, and still enjoy the precious moments in my day that mattered, like winning a thousand tickets at the arcade with my brothers, and to that I say: Hello Life!

September 2013

Day 223: The Power of Connection

I HAD watched a documentary today about a thirteen-year-old boy with Down's syndrome who was preparing for his Bar Mitzvah (basically a Jewish rite of passage for young men). During the film, it always showed him hugging people, holding people, and smiling at people.

He would sing a lot, as it later came out that his mom, who had died, taught him how to sing. But you could see that every time he sang he was somehow connected to her.

Everyone from his dad, his siblings, his friends, to his teachers, said that he was a special person, one who was connected with God and one that could connect with other people.

Even though he was facing so many hardships having Down's syndrome, he looked as if he was one of the happiest people I had ever seen, and I think it was because he knew how to connect to other people. And not only did he connect with them, but he loved them, he lifted their spirits, and he made them smile.

For example, there was another girl with Down's syndrome at his Bar Mitzvah party, and he had never met her prior to that day. She was the daughter of one of his dad's friends. After meeting her and only knowing her for ten minutes, he looked at her and said, "You are a really special person."

Her whole face went blank, like she had never heard someone say that. And here was this thirteen-year-old boy, who was able to enrich her life and make that connection with her that she would never forget.

Anyway, it made me think about connection, and how we as humans long for it and need it so badly.

Sunday, September 1

We long to connect to others, to connect to ourselves, to connect to a higher being, and we long to connect to love as a whole. And if you really look at it, isn't that why we turn to other sources of comfort in the first place? For some kind of connection.

That is why I turned to my eating disorder – to find a connection to something that I thought could bring me validation and happiness. Being connected to Ed was like being locked in a prison, but it was still a connection, nonetheless. It was a connection that reassured me, pound and pound again, and one that would never be broken if I didn't want it to be. Of course, little did I know that by staying so connected with Ed, I was disconnecting from the real love in my life, such as family and friends.

I can say now that I have found connections outside of Ed – actually way stronger than Ed – with family, friends and new people. Maybe all it takes is one of us opening our hearts to someone else and establishing that connection to keep them from searching for it elsewhere, like Ed.

I am not sure where I am going with this post, but I guess I just want to say how important it is, at least in my life, to embrace those connections with other people; to embrace connecting with love, with care, and with warmth.

I just came home from having dinner with my aunt, uncle and cousin, and it was a true reminder of how good it feels to be physically connected with others, even if it's just sharing a meal together.

I am hopeful that my days of finding connection through Ed are behind me, because the power of connecting with people who care about you, the power of connecting with yourself, and the power of connecting with the belief that something greater than you will always bring you out on top of any situation, is so much more powerful than any addiction could be. Hello Life!

******

Day 224: Playing it Safe

I had played recovery really safe today. What I mean by playing it safe, is that I pretty much stuck to 'safe' foods that I knew I was comfortable eating. I did an okay job of staying on my meal plan, considering it was a holiday, and I had only woken up at 12:30 in the afternoon.

Of course, the Ed in me was happy, because that meant we skipped our morning meal by sleeping, and we could just have breakfast at 1p.m., not leaving a lot of space for a proper lunch after that.

I didn't have a proper lunch. I had a snack for lunch. Was it my greatest choice in recovery? No, I could have chosen better. But it was the best choice I could have made for myself today, with my time schedule being off, and with not working out because I still wanted to rest my neck until the following day.

Monday, September 2

With all the major transitional changes going on in my life right now, such as starting school again, writing for the newspaper, and having three family dinners this week, playing it safe is going to be alright with me for today. It's not forever, it's just for now.

Ed got to me a little bit today. He got to me at lunch when I replaced the meal with a snack. He got to me at dinner when I really wanted to try to cook myself something new, but instead I stuck to a sandwich, because it was safe to me.

He is still getting to me right now as I think of all the events that are going to be surrounded by food for me this week. But, just like everyone else's life, my life is on a wavelength of ups and downs, goods and bads, and even okays in the middle. Sometimes, all of our Eds can get inside our heads a little too much.

My recovery is on a wavelength too. Today was okay in the recovery world. I will make sure tomorrow is better. And as long as I am still dedicated to always moving forward, I happily end tonight by saying: Hello Life!

******

Day 225: Recovery at its Finest

This night, right as I was heading home around 7:30p.m., my brother said he was coming over for dinner to eat with my sister, her boyfriend and me.

Earlier in the day I had cancelled my tutoring session that was supposed to be at 7:30p.m., because I knew that if I had gone I would have skipped dinner. I had taken care of myself, and in return I received the gift that this night brought me.

Tuesday, September 3

My brother Dean has been in Texas all summer and I haven't seen him in months, so right away, when I heard he was coming over, I decided to throw together a last-minute welcome home dinner for him.

My original plan for today was to eat super-safe foods, since I have my three holiday dinners in a row starting tomorrow night. But, like always, as I have learned time and time again in recovery, plans change.

When I was at the market buying the food, I saw a cake at the bakery. Ed told me not to get it, but I really wanted to. I wanted to write 'Welcome home Dean Bo' on it. What is a welcome home dinner without a welcome home cake, right? It's great in Ed's world, and very boring in my recovery world.

So, I got the cake. I also got a full dinner of chicken, rice, bread, sweet potato and wine. I was going to get them this food and get me a salad, but that is so Ed-like, and I didn't want that. I wanted to be like them. I wanted to fit in; to eat what they were eating.

Never ever would this night have happened had I still been locked in my eating disorder. There is no way. But because I chose recovery, it did happen.

The four of us spent the night eating, laughing, talking, and just loving one another. Food bonds people; it brings people together. I don't remember the last time my brother and sister and I all sat down and had a meal together, just us. I can still hear my brother and sister laughing downstairs right now as I write this, and my heart wants to go be with them.

Tonight was truly recovery at its finest, and to that I say with gratitude and appreciation: Hello Life!

******

Day 226: Family Dinner Number Two of the Week

I was late getting home on this night and was really tired, so my post was only brief.

Wednesday, September 4

Today was the second family dinner I had in a row.

After waking up sore this morning, I was worried about the food tonight at dinner. What could I eat? Would I be tempted to eat bad food? What would I do?

Well, here I am, very full, many dishes and desserts later, and I am not comfortable, but I am okay. I still spent a night with my family, soreness or not, Ed or not. And that is a win in itself. And my life and recovery will pick up tomorrow, fullness and all.

Tomorrow I am going to try to let myself really eat what I want. Maybe that way the temptation of overeating won't be as strong. Maybe not? And if not, I will still continue on to my next dinner tomorrow and to my next one the day after that. It's the holidays, and I would like to believe everyone eats a little indulgently during the holidays.

Either way, two family dinners in a row would never have happened before recovery. Here is to the third one tomorrow night.

Hello Life!

******

Day 227: "I Haven't Eaten Cake in Years"

This is who had been at the dinner table on this night – my third dinner out in row, remember: Me, a seven-year-old boy who I tutor, his nanny, his mom, his grandma, and his mom's friend. Here is what our dinner played out like.

Thursday, September 5

There was a huge, beautiful spread of food out on the table, with all kinds of bread, fish, salads and cheeses.

"Shira, eat the pastry I made. It's with meat. I can't eat it, I made it for you," said the boy's mom. She then proceeded to add one spoon of salad onto her plate and one tiny piece of fish too. That was it.

Her friend asked, "Can I have the bread that is stuffed with the meat please? I am going to eat only the inside and toss out the bread."

Then the boy's grandma added, "Oh, I am so full. I just get so full, even from salad." (She was thin as can be.)

Then there was me. The mom, her friend and the grandma all put different food on my plate. They couldn't stop asking me to eat more. Why? Because they didn't let themselves eat it, so they tried to mentally get full by physically feeding me.

I know this strategy because I used to be the queen of it. I was known by my brother and sister for always having a full fridge at all times, ready to cook them anything they wanted. By stuffing them, I could forget about feeding myself. Watching them eat sometimes literally filled me up.

So, back to my dinner:

Since it was the kid's birthday, I got him a birthday cake. After we sang happy birthday, his mom cut a few massive pieces of cake.

His grandma said, "I could eat a whole chocolate cake. I love chocolate." Yet when her turn came to eat cake, she picked at the middle, and quickly pushed it away from her.

His mom's friend said, "No thank you, I will just drink my tea. Can you give me the colonic tea you have?" Yes, she really did ask for a laxative tea at the dinner table.

Then I asked the mom whether she was having cake. "I haven't eaten cake in years. I enjoy my figure too much," she replied.

Years? Yes, she is skinny. But she hasn't had cake in years? That was so sad to me.

Here I was, literally sitting in the middle of three different women who all had Eds of their own – some less, some more, some not even knowing it, but I could feel it all around me. Their Eds wanted to come talk with my Ed. It was like a secret meeting only I could see.

Well, I did have cake, because I felt bad leaving the boy to eat his birthday cake all alone, and it was chocolate cake, so what else do I need to say?

I am still uncomfortable with the fact that this is the third night in a row that I had a big dinner, with cake. Three dinners and three cakes, all in three days – Ed's having a mini field day over here.

But I would so rather be the one sitting here saying, "I can't believe I ate cake three days in a row," and having got to celebrate the holiday with family and friends, than that mom at the dinner table during her son's birthday who hasn't had cake in years because she cares about her figure too much.

Hello Life!

******

Day 228: Fourth Family Dinner in a Row

Tonight had been my fourth and final big family holiday dinner in a row. A week ago I hadn't known how Ed and I would get through those dinners together. And yes, he had been there at every one.

I sat there on this night, still very full yet again, and anxious about all the weight I felt I had gained in the week. However, I sat there with a feeling of accomplishment.

Friday, September 6

I didn't know whether I could do these four dinners, but I had.

Last year I would have never celebrated the Jewish new year with four different dinners. Not ever. No way. But this year I had, even if it meant being outside my comfort zone, disobeying Ed and waking up with body soreness every day.

Tonight was particularly special because it was my family's first Jewish new year celebration at the new house my grandma just bought in San Diego. It was symbolic of change and of moving forward. A new house for my grandma, a new accomplishment in recovery for me, and a new year for us all to strive for whatever it is that truly brings us happiness.

Ed may be harsh on me right now and that is okay. He comes and goes, he is loud and then he is quiet. But my family, they are always here, and always loud (in a good way,) and that is why I know I will be okay.

Hello to the beauty of change and newness, and Hello Life!

******

Day 229: "I Actually Look Good in this Bikini"

Today had been the first time in years, even since the years I had been in my eating disorder, that I had actually looked in the mirror before going to the beach and thought to myself, "Wow, I actually look really good in this bikini."

Saturday, September 7

Yesterday, after I ate dinner, I was so full, and I was thinking about how much food I have eaten this week during the holidays. I thought all this gained weight showed on my body.

Then today I put on this bikini and liked how I looked. It's as if I was looking at myself through another set of eyes. I guess it just shows you how our minds can play such tricks on us. More so, it shows how Ed can play such mind tricks on me.

I don't know why Ed didn't play tricks on me today. I didn't try to block him out, and I didn't restrict; I have actually been eating anything I pretty much wanted today. But, for whatever reason, Ed cut me a break when I put on that bikini today.

He came back a little stronger throughout my day, but I know his mind games already. In this moment I could feel I look bad, and the next I could feel good. So, I am just going to enjoy the little break I got this morning. Sometimes all we need is a little slack, and for today that is more than enough for me to be grateful for.

Hello to not only putting on a bikini, but to also feeling good in it, even though I don't know what I weigh in it, and Hello Life!

******

Day 230: Life's 90/10 Rule

I had just been listening to Joel Osteen, as I did every Sunday, and he reminded me of a saying I had heard many times before:

"Life is 10 percent what happens to you, and 90 percent your attitude on how you respond to it."

I could go on for pages about this 90/10 rule and how many times in my life I had had to apply it to myself, but for today it just made me think about my journey to recovery.

Sunday, September 8

I didn't choose to battle with an eating disorder. I didn't choose to become a prisoner inside my own body and mind, trying to achieve this image of perfection that doesn't really exist. I didn't choose to be dealt Ed – no, that was life's 10 percent.

But I did choose to fight him. I did choose to let go of my entire life with Ed – our familiarities with one another, our constant reliance on one another, and of our image of what perfection was supposed to look like. This is my 90 percent right here and right now – my attitude towards this new life of recovery.

Sometimes I am bitter that other people don't have to struggle like me, and sometimes I can be envious of others who don't have to know what it's like to have your life tainted by an eating disorder and all the mental imprisonment that comes with it. But most of the time, 89 percent out of the 90 percent, I am grateful for this journey.

I am grateful because it's through this eating disorder that I found the strength within myself that I never knew I had. And it's also the reason I am on my Day 230 of life without a scale; life without a number to define me.

Joel is right, we can't choose the 10 percent of challenges life gives us, but we can choose what we want our 90 percent to look like.

Today I don't care about the 10 percent challenges I have been handed. I care that I can truly say, in terms of life being 90 percent how we respond to obstacles, that I am not only responding with determination, but also with grace and appreciation.

Let Ed give me his best 10 percent if he likes, because my 90 percent and I will always win, because I am worth every ounce of happiness that comes with recovery.

Hello Life!

******

Day 231: Sometimes You Are Just Hungry All Day

As if recovery wasn't hard enough as it was, without having a scale, without being able to restrict, having to follow a meal plan, and also with Ed in my head constantly, it didn't make it any easier on days like this, where I was literally hungry all day.

I mean seriously hungry. I was never full. I thought something was wrong with me, or that I was imagining my stomach rumbling, but I wasn't.

Monday, September 9

So, here I have my tummy making noises only one short hour after eating a full meal ... and, yup, there enters my dear Ed.

Ed hates it when I eat anything at all, but he especially hates extra snacks or extra food, especially today, when we are coming off a long week of heavy dinners and desserts.

Sometimes, Ed is like my ex-boyfriend – I feel like I need to just do what he wants so he can be quiet and leave me alone. But we all know what happens when we do that.

Just like my old relationship, things would be fine for a while. He would be nice for a while, but a few hours later something would be wrong again, and we would be back to square one. That is what happened today with Ed.

At first, I tried to drink water instead of eating more, and he was quiet. Then twenty minutes later when I was still hungry, Ed was mad at me yet again.

Like any relationship with two entities, I had to compromise. Not only did I eat my snack, but I also had an extra snack on top of that. The eating part wasn't the compromise that Ed liked – that part was for me. The part where I satisfied Ed was when I ate my last snack, which was an apple. Even though I was still hungry, I only ate half of it.

Do I wish I could have eaten the whole apple? Yes. I mean, it was an apple, not a piece of cake or a doughnut. But, in the moment, it was just too much. However, in the big picture, I still disobeyed Ed; I still ate when I was hungry, and I even ate more than he wanted me to.

Whereas seven months ago I would have starved all day for Ed, today I only gave up half an apple on Ed's behalf, and I am pretty happy with that progress at this moment.

And now that I ate a good dinner, I am feeling full for the first time today. But even though I am full, I still have space for dessert, like I always do, because sweets just make me happy – sorry Ed.

As for Ed, he got tired of fighting with me once I ate a full dinner, and I think he has gone for the night.

On that note, I am off to watch a TV show and enjoy my dessert with my grandma.

Hello Life!

******

Day 232: Testing ... One ... Two ... Three

Have you ever been at a concert or big event where someone is going to be speaking or singing, or something of that sort, then someone comes to the microphone on the stage and says, "Testing ... one ... two ...three"?

They say it about two or three times in a row, and once they see the microphone works, the main event takes place; either the singer debuts their new song, or the speaker gets a big introduction.

Well, right now, my life is in the 'testing ... one ... two ... three' zone.

Tuesday, September 10

As you all know, I started interviewing for a paid position at NBC about two weeks ago. I made it to the very last step so far, and last Wednesday I had a writing test.

This writing test was the last step of my interviewing process. Next time I hear from NBC, it will be to tell me that I either got the job or that I didn't.

Since last Wednesday, anxiety has been eating away at me. I haven't written about it because I was trying to focus on other things, but today it was a big part of my day. I have just been waiting and waiting, thinking and thinking.

Some moments I think to myself, how great it will feel to get that congratulating phone call. Other moments I am preparing myself for the worst. It's like the world is saying, "Testing ... one ... two ... three" to me right now. And very soon my main event will take place. This test is leading to something.

But what is it a test of? Is it a test about giving up control? Since I can't control whether I will get hired or not, that is a possibility. Is it a test about having faith? Is it a test about believing in myself? Is it a test about learning how to fail, if I don't get it? Is it a test about learning how to feel proud about success, if I do get it?

There is so much space here for questions to arise. All I know is that today the hiring manager said she will give me an answer by the end of the week. So, by the end of this week, my testing phase will be over, and my main event will have happened. But until then, I am in the unknown.

When you live in an eating disorder, you are never living in the unknown. Everything is known to you – your calories, your sodium intake, your fat grams, your weight, your clothing size, other people's calories, how much weight you need to lose, I can go on and on.

Living with an eating disorder is like living your life as a human calculator, just constantly keeping track of everything you can, but recovery is not like that.

While it's tempting to try to morph into my human calculator version of myself today, since it gives me some sort of factual comfort in a zone of absolute uncertainty right now, for the very first time it doesn't feel like a solution. I see now that trying to grasp onto things that are tangible, such as food and calories, won't fix my anxiety over this job.

When I say I am tempted to go back to being a human calculator, counting all my numbers, it's not because I am having a hard time with my body. I actually, very surprisingly, am okay with my body right now. I only am tempted because it's something that I know.

We all like to be around comforting things that are familiar to us in times of stress. But my mind is open to the bigger picture, which is that this is not about controlling my food or calories in an attempt to distract myself from waiting to hear back from this job.

It's about me learning some kind of lesson. Like I said, I don't know which test I am being asked to take right now, but one way or another, I will grow from it.

You can't grow from an eating disorder. You can't grow from being a human calculator of calories all the time, even if it's nice to have that familiarity. However, you can grow from life's tests that are thrown at you – that 10% of things that you are dealt with that you can't control.

When this testing phase is over this week, I will have grown, and in the meantime, I will just prepare myself for that.

Hello Life!

******

Day 233: In Honor of 9/11

I realized that people would have read this a million times already, but it was the twelfth anniversary of the tragic events of 9/11.

I had thought about 9/11 many times over the years as I had grown older; the lives that were lost, the families that were left behind, and the voices of so many that the world would never hear again. But today, I took a moment and reflected on it in another light.

Since this blog was about my recovery, I explained how it had affected me in the recovery sense.

Wednesday, September 11

I write a lot about how living in recovery from an eating disorder means giving up a lot of control over things that you once had power over, such as control over weight, calories, etc. Sometimes, well actually 99% of the time, giving up these controls seems like it's the hardest thing to do. Usually, at least for me, it takes all of my inner strength to do it.

Not to take away from the immense amount of inner strength and fight it takes to give up those eating-disordered controls, because it's extraordinarily hard to do, today when I thought about 9/11, it made me think about control in another way. What about those people on those planes and in those buildings who had no control over their lives? They had no control over when their last breath would be, over who the last person they saw would be, or over whether they would survive or not.

It made my battle with my seemingly massive controls over food and calories seem insignificant, and in the big picture of life and death, they are. It's easy to forget how the battles we all fight every day are not the only battles that are being fought in the world. Today, yes, I fought for my recovery, but at the same time there were families, children and loved ones fighting to hold on to memories of those lost to a tragedy no one could control or stop.

Every moment of every day we are all fighting battles. Mine is with Ed, yours is with someone or something else, but regardless, we are all just fighting for the same reason: To be at peace.

On days like today, where the lives of so many people are remembered, food really is not important, my tighter clothes are not important and my time at the gym is not important. What is important today, is to not only honor and remember those people and loved ones affected by 9/11, but to honor and cherish our own lives, that we are so incredibly lucky to be living.

Sending strength, prayers, healing and hope to all those affected by 9/11. And in honor of all those who lost their lives twelve years ago, I am not ending today with Hello Life. Instead, I will leave it up to you to decide what you want to say hello to, and feel free to share it on this post if you would like to.

Until tomorrow ... Hello (insert what touches your heart today).

******

Day 234: It Can't Hurt to Hope for the Best

You know those days where everything seems to not go your way? Well, that had been my day today. It didn't really have anything to do with recovery; in the recovery world, things were okay, my meal plan was on check, my time at the gym was good, and I didn't body check too much.

In one way, the fact that my eating disorder wasn't the reason my day wasn't that great was actually pretty amazing.

Thursday, September 12

There were days where my eating disorder was all I measured my entire day by, so the fact that it wasn't a huge factor in today being just one of those not-so-great days leaves me smiling.

I originally planned on writing about why today wasn't a good day, but now that I have just realized all those reasons have nothing to do with my eating disorder, today is not so bad anymore. It's actually better than I thought.

A day that wasn't so great because of other things that I cared about that didn't have to do with food or weight or calories ... maybe that is actually kind of refreshing.

I guess today really wasn't that bad then, thinking of it. I even had NEDA (National Eating Disorder Association) tweet about this blog, which is kind of an honor.

The only thing that still is weighing heavy on my heart (no pun intended with the word 'weigh'), is the fact that I still didn't hear from NBC about my job. The lady said she would let me know by the end of the week. Tomorrow is Friday, so that pretty much only leaves tomorrow to find out the answer, considering that Friday is the official end of the business week.

I feel like I am driving through a tunnel with both feet on the gas, and with my eyes closed, just hoping to make it to the other side. Whatever the outcome, I will keep pressing on that gas. But it can't hurt to hope for the best rest, can it?

Hello to tomorrow, hello to whatever outcome it may bring, and Hello Life!

******

Day 235: Goodbye to NBC

"Your writing test just wasn't up to par." That is what the lady had told me today when she called me at 5:15p.m. to tell me I hadn't got the position at NBC that I had been praying for.

I knew exactly what part of the test I had made mistakes on, because it was the one part I kept thinking I should have looked over. It had been the hardest part of the test, and it was also the last part, right around the three-hour mark. I specifically remember being so drained by that time that I had done the best I could and submitted it.

I didn't know which was worse: Admitting to the entire world on this blog that I hadn't got the job because my writing on that test wasn't good enough, admitting it to Ed, or admitting it to myself.

"… wasn't up to par." Also known as, "Not good enough."

To know that I hadn't got this position because my skills as a writer on that one single test were not good enough literally ate away at the core of my being. I knew I was better than that. At least up until today, I thought I was.

Friday, September 13

Here I am, in the midst of this journey to recovery from an eating disorder that has thrived off telling me I wasn't good enough just the way I am, to now be told I wasn't good enough for NBC either.

A few days ago I said that my life is in the testing zone right now, and that I felt I was being put through this emotional waiting game to hear about this job to learn some kind of lesson. I had a fellow blogger share her view that day on how not everything in life is always trying to teach us a lesson. I sit here today and I am starting to think that maybe in this case she was right.

What was the lesson here? Why did I need to go through this for the past two weeks, being hopeful that I might get the job of my dreams, only to hear I didn't because my writing wasn't good enough? What is the lesson in that?

I had all the signs from the universe telling me I got this job. My song that I have dedicated to my grandpa who has passed away, who I call my guardian angel, even came on the radio last week and this morning. And for what? To mess with my head?

It's just something I will never understand. I have already cried all tonight, and I know I am not done yet. But it's either crying and being sad, or restricting and letting Ed comfort me. To be honest, both options totally suck, but I know I have to go with the first one.

I feel like I have failed. Worse than that, I feel like I have failed myself for not doing better on that writing test.

Ed is begging for me to run to him right now so he can make this all better. My logic is begging for me to stay strong, and my heart is begging for me to just let it cry.

This is the first major disappointment I am facing in recovery. I will get past it. I won't resort to Ed, that is definite. But right now I need a moment to say goodbye to the vision I had of myself at that job. Then I need to delete the pictures I had of the NBC logo saved on my phone, ready to be posted to my Instagram and Facebook page when I envisioned myself getting the congratulatory call. And when I am done with that, I need to start the process of forgiving myself for feeling like I have failed.

We all know the saying from the famous movie Forrest Gump, *"Life is like a box of chocolates, you never know what you are gonna get." Well, today I got the one filled with the coconut or weird strawberry filling that no one likes. Maybe tomorrow I will get a yummy one.*

But until then, I say through my tears, with the utmost hope that tomorrow will be a better day: Hello Life!

******

Day 236: Time to Forgive Myself

Before I began today's post, I gave the most heartfelt thanks for everyone's support the day before – to all who sent personal emails, to those who commented, and to my family and friends, who I personally spoke to. I thanked everyone for their love and support. It had kept my spirits positive even when I felt crushed.

As for today, it was Yom Kippur, a Jewish holiday where adults are supposed to fast to atone for their sins during the year. It's also a day for reflection, a day to think about how you can improve yourself as a person, and a day to ask for forgiveness from others who you have wronged.

Saturday, September 14

Although I don't consider myself a highly religious person, being raised Jewish, fasting on Yom Kippur was something I had always done. It wasn't always for the right reasons once Ed came along, but nonetheless, I did fast.

This is the first year since I was eight years old that I am not fasting, and it was one of the hardest choices I have had to make. Going back and forth between fasting for the right religious reasons or fasting for Ed was confusing and, ultimately, it led to me feeling guilty.

I know I should have wanted to fast for the right reasons, but I knew deep down it wasn't. It made me feel really guilty. Even fasting when I was eight years old wasn't about repenting for my sins, it was about the fascination that I would save myself some calories.

And with guilt came the feeling of weakness. Am I really not strong enough yet to just fast for one day and then bounce right back to my meal plan? Yes, 80 percent of me says I am, but 20 percent of me is unsure. Even .000001 percent of uncertainty that could possibly lead me back to my eating disorder is enough to make me stay away from fasting, but it bothered me that I am not at that place yet.

So while I haven't fasted today (eating was actually much easier than I anticipated), I did think about the forgiveness aspect of Yom Kippur. Over these several months in recovery, I have learned how to forgive those who hurt me; those who I felt pushed me towards my eating disorder. Of course, if I have wronged anyone, as everyone in my life reads this blog, I ask for your forgiveness too.

Now I need to move on to the hard stuff of today. There are two people who I need to forgive in order to move on. I need to forgive Ed, and I need to forgive myself. I wrote a post on Day 51 of this journey that included a letter forgiving Ed, so the only thing left to do now is to forgive myself.

I wrote in yesterday's post how I feel like I have failed myself for not doing better on my writing test for NBC. It's been almost twenty-four hours since I heard that I didn't get the job, and I still feel the same way. But I don't think that it's by chance that Yom Kippur, the day of forgiveness, falls on today, the day right after I began to view myself as a total failure.

If I want to move on with my life and with my recovery, I need to do this. So here it goes. (Yes, I am about to write a letter to myself ... nothing is shocking or weird anymore on this blog. So let's just roll with it.)

My dear self,

It's never easy to forgive. It's never easy to forget. But to forgive you is by far the hardest thing of all.

While everyone else in the world can be tearing themselves apart, you can find a way to lift them up, but when you tear yourself apart, you are ruthless. You are your own meanest judge, after Ed of course.

You were excited that day of the test and you were nervous; you just wanted to get it done, and furthermore, you really did the best you could.

So the lady on the phone said you were not up to par; maybe she was right. But maybe not. Maybe her par is just different to your par.

I forgive you for not looking over that test that day. I forgive you for staying so hopeful and getting your hopes up for the past two weeks, even though your intuition told you not to. And lastly, I forgive you for calling yourself a failure yesterday.

You may be 'under par' or not good enough for NBC, but one thing you are not is a failure.

With forgiveness and love,
Me.

Here is to not only forgiving myself for not doing better on that writing test, but more importantly, here is to forgiving myself for calling myself a failure.

Hello Life!

******

Day 237: It's Time for Our Version of Events

I had a song on repeat on this day, over and over, and once I explain some of the lyrics to you, you will understand why. There were two lines in this song that stood out to me.

The first one was:

"If the truth has been forbidden then we're breaking all the rules."

This line could have been the opening sentence to the story of my recovery, and the recovery of so many others who I had spoken to, especially over the previous few days, since I had opened up my 'contact me' form.

The second line was:

> *"It's about time we got some airplay of our version of events."*

Once we take back the truths that our addictions created for us and made us shy away from, we get to create new ones; we get to create our own 'airplay of events', like the song says.

Sunday, September 15

Throughout all of our journeys there is one thing that is consistent for all of us who are not only seeking recovery, but who are seeking to learn how to love who we really are, and that is that we have all experienced living a life where our truth was once forbidden.

For me, personally, the entire time I was living in my eating disorder, the truth about almost anything other than my weight was forbidden. The truth about how isolated I was becoming the thinner I got was a truth that was forbidden to think about. The truth about the metal prison bars that felt like they were literally pressed up against my body at all times, keeping me trapped inside myself with nowhere to turn, was a truth that was forbidden to express to others. The truth about my deteriorating health, when my heartbeat would slow down at night, and when my hair would fall out in the shower, was one that was forbidden to say, even to my own doctor.

The truth of the matter was that I was stuck in a one-way relationship with my eating disorder, where either he would win or I would win. There was no space for both of us to live in.

I followed that rule about my truths being forbidden for years, and now, just like the song said, it's time to break the rules. All those rules that our eating disorders told us, from avoiding our own truths about our lives, to who we could or could not see, to what we were allowed to think about at night, are now being broken when we choose to live in recovery.

I don't think you have to have an eating disorder to know how hard it is to be brave enough to stare at your own truths. But the rewarding part in doing that is that once we look at the truths that our own Eds have been keeping us from, we can then create new ones.

To my warriors who are fighting for their recovery today, we deserve to create our own truths, our own version of our lives, our own version of what we are deserving of. We deserve to take those things back from our eating disorders.

If you had to choose one new truth to take back from something negative that once held power over you, what would it be? What is your new truth that you want to make for yourself today? If you don't want to write it here, I encourage you to say it out loud, say it to yourself in the mirror, or say it to whoever you are taking your truth back from.

We have the capability to vanish these shadows that our eating disorders/addictions follow us around in all day, so why not fill them in on who is in power now?

Here is my new truth today: Ed, I am two hundred and thirty-seven days into not weighing myself, and I love myself more today than I ever have, and you are not stopping me.

Ah, that felt good. I have years of twisted truths to take back from Ed, but for today, this one is good enough.

Hello Life!

******

Day 238: Alter Ego

Ed had woken up with me today, telling me his usual speech about my body. Most times I could brush it off, but this morning he just didn't stop going on and on about it.

From the minute I had woken up, I was instantly going through all the food I had eaten the entire weekend. I didn't even have time to get out of bed to put my workout clothes on before I was already planning on how to not let it happen again the next weekend. Ugh ... dumb, annoying, lying Ed.

Monday, September 16

Ironically enough, today's homework assignment for one of the girls I tutor was that she had to write a story where the main character was herself, but she had to change her name and give herself one superpower.

Her class is reading the story of Mulan, a young girl who disguises herself as a man to go fight in the army. She transforms herself into looking like a young man and she trains herself to learn how to fight like the guys in the army do. So I understood why she got this assignment.

Anyway, she is eight years old, and she looks up to me, and I love her for doing so. So, what did she want her new name to be in her story? Yup, she wanted it to be Shira. I tried to say no, because I felt embarrassed for some reason, but she insisted, so we went with it.

Being an eight-year-old girl, the superpower she chose for Shira was that she would be able to wake up every day in the mall. At first I wasn't sure if that was considered a superpower, but if flying is a superpower, then why can't automatically waking up in a mall every day be one too?

So she wrote her story about a girl named Shira, who woke up every day in her favorite store in the mall, and that is where she lived. She owned the mall and everything inside of it. She was the boss. I loved this Shira. She is the Shira that would be the boss of Ed too.

It made me think about myself for a moment as having this alter ego that this eight-year-old literally just created for me. Sure, she didn't fly or become invisible, but she did something even better – she chose to live every day in her favorite place where she ruled everything.

How awesome would it be if we all had an alter ego of ourselves, that whenever our addictions were talking to us, we could just switch modes into being our alter ego? Maybe not forever or maybe not all the time, because I would like to think that one day the real Shira will be able to defeat Ed on her own (as many days she has).

But on days like today, where Ed was so loud, the idea of an alter ego fascinated me. I have been sitting here trying to figure out what my name for my alter ego would be, and I have come up with nothing. But I know that she would wear huge eight-inch heels and she would crush Ed with them every single day.

If you had an alter ego, what would you name him/her? What would your superpower be? For tonight, I am going to just sit here and imagine my alter ego, whatever her name will eventually be, crushing Ed with her big high heels, over and over and over again.

Hello to the high heels, superpowers and super strengths that our alter egos will kill our Eds with, and Hello Life!

******

Day 239: When Your Pants Don't Zip Up in the Dressing Room

So there I was, standing in the middle of the Forever 21 dressing room during my break from school, almost about to cry. The pants I wanted to try on didn't even go up halfway up my leg. The size that six months ago would have been too big on me, now couldn't even get over my calves.

Okay, maybe they ran small I tried to tell myself. So I got one size up. They went up my leg, but they didn't zip or button. I literally tried everything I could to make them zip up – suck in, pull the material together, lay back – but nothing worked. I decided to just take them off and leave. But once I had taken them off, I found myself just staring at my body in the mirror.

Dressing rooms have the absolute worst lighting possible. For whatever reason, it's the kind of fluorescent light that shows every inch of your skin. Imagine that light plus Ed together, it was like a mini gang-up attack on me.

It didn't make me want to restrict, because I was still grateful for the place I had worked to get to in recovery, but it did make me just flat-out mad.

Tuesday, September 17

Is this what part of my recovery is? Being the girl in the dressing room whose pants don't zip up? I guess one of my biggest fears about becoming that girl came to life today. There was no denying it, that girl was me, but I left that dressing room because I had to go interview someone for a story I am writing for the school paper.

After she finished talking with me and getting to know me, she nonchalantly asked, "So, what's your story?" What's my story? The answer to that question can change on a minute-to-minute basis in recovery.

Yesterday my story was that I had an alter ego. Today I felt like saying my story is that I have become the girl in the fitting room whose pants don't zip up or button. But somehow I managed to say, "I am a journalism student about to graduate in December and I want to be a writer."

That definitely wasn't what I was feeling like in that moment at all, but my actions spoke louder than my thoughts today. Yes, I thought I was that girl who now can't fit into her old-size pants, who is having a hard day in recovery from her eating disorder.

I could have stayed in that dressing room, sat on the floor and cried, like I wanted to. But I didn't. I didn't let my thoughts drive my actions into doing that. Instead, I was sitting across from a wonderful professional woman, getting an interview for my story that will be published next week.

Regardless of my thoughts about myself today, that action speaks the truth about who I am, and I am going to do my best to hold onto that.

Hello Life!

******

Day 240: Donating My Sick Clothes

I had bought these pants on the day that I had reached my lowest weight. They were the pants I was wearing at a Friday night family dinner when my dad said to me, "You look way too skinny."

They were my sick pants; my pants I wore when I was sick in my eating disorder. More than that, they were my favorite sick pants when Ed was in charge. They had also been the one consistent pair of pants that I had continued to try on whenever I was feeling vulnerable in recovery.

I had worn them two weeks before when I knew I had a big family dinner to go to, hoping that the constant reminder of the buttons pushing into my stomach because of how tight they were would be a reminder for me to not eat 'too much'. And I had also worn them today.

Wednesday, September 18

I was feeling bad about the way my body looked today, and instead of being kind to myself, not only did I go and find those pants, I actually dug them out of the bottom of my drawer. I had put them at the very bottom of my drawer this week when I was putting away my laundry, because I already knew they were severely damaging to me and my recovery.

Ironically, these are the same pair of pants that I was wearing at my brother's MMA fight about six months ago, when he won, and said to the entire audience of hundreds of people, "This win was for my sister, Shira. She is more of a fighter than I will ever be."

So, needless to say, these pants have journeyed with me. They have journeyed with me through the lowest days of my eating disorder and through the most memorable and poignant moments of my recovery. And now it's time that they journey elsewhere, because they are no longer suiting me.

The thought of just throwing away my sick clothes, especially this particular pair of pants, is extremely hard for me to think of. It's a big reason why I have waited until now, seven months into my recovery, to even think of about it.

It's like throwing away a part of me ... a part of Ed ... and all the false lies of what he made me believe beautiful was. But if I think about donating them to a place where they benefit someone else, it's not so hard anymore.

Just because my sick pants no longer suit me, doesn't mean they can't suit someone else. So I have decided to finally donate my sick clothes, starting with these pants, to Hope of the Valley

Rescue Mission, a local shelter for homeless women and children near me.

On that note, knowing how hard a step this is for those of us in recovery, if you, or someone you know, would like to donate your sick clothes to someone in need and you need a pathway to doing so, you can mail me your sick clothes and I will make sure I donate them along with my own. If this is something you are interested in, contact me through my 'contact me' page.

Of course, I know that mailing things across the world can be expensive, as I know many readers are not even in the United States. If you find yourself wanting to donate your sick clothes, or even give away your sick clothes to somewhere near you, please feel free to take pictures of your experience and send them to me via my 'contact me' form.

I am going to set up a page on the blog explaining this, as it will be ongoing until the last day of this blog, not just for today. On that page I will say how to contact me to send me your clothes, and I will post any pictures of others donating their clothes on it as well, so we can show the world our journey to gaining our power back from our Eds and helping others at the same time.

I loved these sick pants, and Ed loved them too. They were his weapon to use against me. But I love my recovery more. And I love me more.

To my dear sick pants, may you bring someone else the comfort and happiness that I once thought I could find by fitting in you, that instead I found within myself during recovery.

Hello Life!

******

Day 241: Making the Front Page

I had picked up our university newspaper this morning to find out that my most recent story had made it onto the front page. I had no idea that it was going to be the cover story until I had seen it. It was the first time one of my stories had been the front-page story, and it gave me this feeling of success and of achievement.

Thursday, September 19

I am not totally used to these kinds of feelings when they are not tied to Ed. I know how it feels to be proud of hitting a low weight; I know what it's like to feel proud to starve all day; I know what it's like to complain to others about how hard it is to find tiny clothes, yet inside Ed is patting you on the back over and over.

I know those kinds of 'accomplishments' – those eating-disordered, twisted, false sense of accomplishments that only lead you to more loneliness. But this kind of accomplishment, the kind where I made it happen for myself through my dedication, my passion and my writing, is such a different feeling.

I have experienced it a few times in recovery, and every time it feels different. Sometimes I am proud of myself, other times I am embarrassed; today I felt shocked.

After feeling so bad about myself for NBC not giving me the job I wanted because my writing was "not up to par", I guess I was surprised that I still had enough talent to make it onto the front page of the newspaper. But that element of surprise quickly led to excitement, and that feeling of accomplishment that I keep referring to.

However, the difference between this kind of accomplishment and Ed's kind of accomplishment is that this one is not followed by, "Okay, good job, but now go harm yourself more and do better next time." This time it's followed by love, support and many congratulations from family and friends. But most importantly, it's followed by me taking a moment to let myself feel like a worthy writer again, something I haven't done since the whole NBC meltdown.

And on that note, I am off to get ready for a blind date, which could be a whole new post in itself. I really don't want Ed on this blind date with me, as I am already nervous as it is, and he will only make it worse. But even if he does happen to make an appearance, at least I can say that I am going.

A few months ago Ed would have been my one and only date. Just him and me basking in our misery. So even if he is there tonight, at least it's no longer just him and me. I have decided that if he comes, he will have to settle for third wheel, and I can settle for that too at this moment.

Hello Life!

******

Day 242: Let's Luncheon

Today I had spent the day covering an event for my university, where the alumni were being honored, specifically those who were celebrating fifty years since graduating.

I was extremely nervous for this event for two reasons: Firstly, because I had to go in there by myself and hope that people would talk to me; secondly, because half of the event consisted of a luncheon. A luncheon equals people plus food. Ed hated luncheons – actually, Ed didn't do luncheons.

Friday, September 20

Ironic as it is, the woman who I happened to be interviewing right before the luncheon began had an Ed of her own. How do I know that? Without saying anything triggering to anyone, I will just say that she had all the physically visible signs of it. Then when I told her we could continue to speak after the luncheon, she said, "Oh sweetheart, I don't need to eat. We can still talk."

And there was Ed's moment he had been waiting for – the green light to participate in an eating disorder along with someone else. I used to love those moments when I was so ruled by Ed, but today it wasn't going to happen.

I actually had to tell her that I needed to go sit at my assigned table, so I couldn't continue talking with her. I am the one who excused myself to go eat. I mean, wow, talk about a shift in the driver's seat –Ed wasn't even in the car at that moment.

I sat across from her table, and while she didn't touch any of her food, I knew I had to eat mine, and I was so glad I did. Had I not gone to the luncheon, I would never have met Rusty, my favorite person I met all day.

Rusty was sitting next to me, and he was telling me about how he used to protest on campus for things he believed in. Then he looked at me and said the comment that changed my whole day: "I always tell my kids to leave Negative Ned at home."

"Who?" I asked.

"Negative Ned. You know ... like a negative attitude. I tell them to leave it at home."

I had heard of Negative Nancy before ... and now I had heard of Negative Ned. It just made me realize, yet again, that everyone has some kind of 'Ed' of their own who they deal with on a daily basis, and just how Rusty said, I guess it really is our choice whether we want to leave them at home or not.

I can definitely say that I left Ed at home today. I ate that entire lunch and spent the whole time talking to Rusty and his wife, listening to their experiences and stories, and Ed wasn't there to distract me.

And as for my first fear about people not wanting to talk to me today ... I was proven so wrong. All I needed to do was go say hi and ask them for their story. Each and every single person, one *after the other, talked for at least twenty minutes about different parts of their lives they wanted to share with me.*

I guess it goes to show how we all have a story that needs to be told, and sometimes it just takes someone asking us about it to let it out. Those people, most of them in their eighties, were so happy to share their experiences, knowledge and wisdom with me.

Like E told me a few days ago, today was my chance to give someone else a platform to share their story, just how I am sharing mine on this blog.

Rusty left Ned at home today. I left Ed at home today. Now I am leaving him here again as I go to my family dinner.

Hello to luncheons, hello to leaving our Eds and Neds at home, and Hello Life!

******

Day 243: Isolating Ed

This day's post was very short. It had been a hard day for Ed and me. He had been very loud. He had been loud when I went running, loud when I ate, and loud when I got ready to go out.

I know why Ed had been loud today – because I had time alone.

Saturday, September 21

It's on days when I am alone that Ed tries to come and keep me company, because up until a few months ago I would always let him.

Ed wanted me to stay home tonight and isolate myself so he could have me all to himself and, really, I had every opportunity to do so.

But after my brother invited me to go out with his friends, and after my best friend told me to go, I decided I needed to isolate Ed instead of isolating myself. So I went, and I am so glad I did. Something about being around others makes Ed shut up.

Hello to isolating Ed instead of isolating myself, and Hello Life!

******

Day 244: Naming My Future

I had been totally obsessing over the food I had eaten at lunch on this day. Don't ask me why I had eaten what I did, because there was only one answer: I had just really liked all of it. Everything I saw happened to look good to me.

I know that Ed would say that was completely irrational and that it wasn't 'normal' to feel like that, but I felt as if he was wrong. Aren't there times where everything you see just looks good? Now that I thought about it, that had actually happened to me the previous night too.

So I went upstairs to watch Joel Osteen, knowing that listening to him usually gave me some sort of positive energy. As he was talking, he said something interesting:

> *"You need to name your future. Don't name it based on your past, name it based on what is destined for you."*

So it really made me think for a moment: If I could name my future anything, what would it be? Joel said we should name our futures "blessings, health and strength." While all those are beautiful things, they didn't resonate with me.

Sunday, September 22

If I could name my future anything, in one simple word it would be freedom. Freedom from Ed and his life-sucking grip on everything that he comes into contact with. Freedom from being mad at myself for eating foods that just happen to look delicious to me. Freedom from trying to change my physical being. Freedom from thinking that I as a person am not enough, all because I am not perfect according to some eating disorder's standards. Freedom to love, laugh and smile, just because we want to, not because Ed allowed us to for reaching some kind of unattainable or unhealthy goal.

Freedom, freedom, freedom. Recovery is freedom.

Looking back over history, freedom never came easy to any group of people, and it never came overnight. It came from years of fighting, years of speaking truth, and years of trying to create change over and over and over again, even after times of failure.

So I guess if I really look at these past eight months, I have already started the tremulous process of achieving freedom. I am fighting, I am speaking my truth, and I am going to continue to make drastic changes in my life, where I am in charge, not Ed, even if it takes me time and time and time again to do it.

Really, all of us in recovery have already chosen freedom. We have already named our future – and it's not called Ed.

Everyone has their own idea of what they would like their future to be called. If you could name your future, what would you name it?

Today I didn't name my future Ed. I didn't name it a number on a scale. I didn't name it a clothing size. I named it freedom.

Hello to one day meeting and embracing true freedom, and Hello Life!

******

Day 245: My New Favorite Picture

Everything in my day had been going pretty good up until about ten minutes before, when I was trying to distract myself from doing my homework by looking through old Facebook pictures that other people had tagged me in.

I had deleted all pictures that showed my body from my phone a while ago, but I guess I had never thought about Facebook.

So ... you know where this is going already.

Monday, September 23

Every time I saw an old picture of myself, my mind instantly became a human calculator and all these numbers just jumped right into sync with each other. Before I knew it, I had already established what I weighed that day, how the clothes fitted that day compared to how they fitted now (as I am still in the very beginning process of donating away my sick clothes), and what I ate that day.

I literally can recall all of that information for every single picture, including down to the crumb of what I ate. That goes to show you how much Ed took over me during those years.

Anyway, I didn't delete those pictures yet, because by the time I finished going through them right now, I realized how Ed-controlled it was and I stopped. Going back to delete them now wouldn't be smart, because I feel like I would be sucked right back into analyzing all those numbers again.

So, instead, I am making myself, all of you, and Ed very aware of what just happened, because once it's no longer a secret, it doesn't hold as much power, and it's now something I know I need to stay away from for now, and plan on deleting in the future, when the time is right.

So along with remembering all that information about what I weighed on those old pictures, I also remembered how I felt on each of those days. I remembered which days I felt trapped, which days I binged, which days I felt weak, which days I had fights with my boyfriend at the time. I remembered everything – every bad part – but for some reason I didn't remember any good parts.

When I look at my pictures that I have uploaded in the past few months, I see only one thing: The fun thing I did that night. My favorite recent picture is one of my best friend and me wearing some amazing heart glasses at a restaurant we went to.

I don't look at that picture and see my weight, because I don't know what it is and probably never will again. I don't look at it and see what I ate that day, because I honestly don't remember.

I do, however, remember that the restaurant we went to that night didn't have the chocolate cake I wanted for dessert and I was really upset and had to settle for monkey bread instead, which is a pretty awesome Hello Life moment in itself. I look at it and I see fun, life, freedom and change.

My previous favorite picture was one of my ex-boyfriend and me when I was at my lowest weight. Not anymore. Not anymore at all. Now my favorite picture is my best friend and me wearing heart glasses. What a change right? It doesn't even show my body, it only shows my smile.

Why did I even waste my time reminiscing on those old pictures anyway? To look at them and wish I still had my old body, that is the true answer. But the reality is that I have so much more than that now.

I might not have Ed's dream body for me, but I have my life, I have my laughter and I have my smile. And I have the hard-earned privilege of living in recovery and saying: Hello Life!

******

Day 246: Just Shut Up and Eat

From the minute I had woken up on this day, right up to the time I wrote my blog, my day had been extremely busy. I literally hadn't had one second to relax.

I went hiking with my sister in the morning, did seven different interviews for my story due that week, wrote my actual story, attended a three-hour class at school, and was finally able to sit and write my blog. It was safe to say I had been very much distracted all day.

Distractions and recovery can work very well together sometimes. There had been many times where healthy distractions, such as watching a movie, going out with friends, or being deeply involved with my schoolwork, had actually distracted me from listening to the mean things Ed was telling me.

But today it hadn't served that healthy purpose. I had felt it the moment I had woken up too.

Tuesday, September 24

I know how the cycle goes when I slightly slip and skip a meal or even a snack. I get so sucked back into Ed and his ways, then it makes it a hundred times harder to pick myself back up the next day.

I don't have time today to slip and fall a few steps back, because I am writing my biggest story yet (it will be my second front-page story) and I need to stay focused. I also want to continue feeling as strong as I can in my recovery.

Therefore, I literally had to tell myself today, over and over again, "Just shut up and eat." I could talk myself out of eating in one second, or actually Ed is the one who could talk me out of it very easily, so telling him to shut up was essential today, and it's worked so far. I just need to do it one more time after I write this blog so I can go eat dinner and I will have successfully stayed on my meal plan today and made it through another day in recovery.

My desire and absolute lack of appetite right now is making this last meal really hard for me, but I knew that if I wrote about it first and left myself accountable to all those who read this blog, then I would have no choice.

Sometimes there are days where you can't do something for yourself, so instead you do it for others, and that is what I am doing today, and I think that it's okay.

Hello to another day of making it through recovery, and Hello Life!

******

Day 247: The Hello Life Moment that Made Me Cry

This past Monday, I had read the little girl I tutored a poem called 'Hug O'War' by Shel Silverstein, which goes like this:

> *"I will not play at tug o'war.*
>
> *I'd rather play at hug o'war,*
>
> *Where everyone hugs*
>
> *Instead of tugs,*
>
> *Where everyone giggles*
>
> *And rolls on the rug,*
>
> *Where everyone kisses,*
>
> *And everyone grins,*
>
> *And everyone cuddles,*

And everyone wins."

I had read it to her because it teaches about loving others, being kind to others and being fair to others. It's a poem about love and kindness, and we had talked about what it meant for a good twenty minutes after I read it to her.

Tonight when I had come to tutor her, there was a piece of paper that she had written on lying on the table. I cried when I read it. She had taken those words that meant so much to me, and she had written them on paper for me, with nothing but love and kindness.

It was such a true Hello Life moment.

Wednesday, September 25

Sometimes when we are trapped by an addiction, our entire lives can become so consumed with the things bound by them. For example, with Ed and me, sometimes I can get so consumed by what I ate today or how my clothes fit that I tend to lose sight of life's undeniable truths that no eating disorder can overshadow, one of them being true love.

This picture was true love. I thought I was teaching her a lesson about love and kindness by reading her that poem, when in reality she actually taught me one.

Recovery was hard for me today. It was a struggle to eat, but none of that seems to matter to me right now, when I stare at that picture.

My life and our lives are so much more than the tiny obsessions we can get so sucked into, such as calories or numbers, or tangible things to fixate on, such as clothes money or jean sizes. It's about moments like these – moments where the love of others seems to find its way to our hearts and souls and has a way of bringing so much joy into our lives.

There have been only a few true Hello Life moments since I started this blog, and this is the first one that has ever made me cry. No Ed in the universe can give me that great feeling that I felt tonight when I walked in and saw that picture on the table. Ed can give me familiarity, structure or some image of an 'ideal body' but he can't give me love.

If I could only love myself half as much as this girl loved me enough to make this picture for me today, Ed would never stand a chance again.

I am on my way to making that happen. Hello Life!

******

Day 248: Time to Relax with My Dessert

I had just finished the biggest story that I had ever done. I had worked on it for the past week endlessly. Seven days and over twenty interviews later, I felt that I could finally breathe and relax.

Simply stated, I never could have done this story if I had been living by Ed's rules. He would have starved my body, which would have made me weak and unable to focus.

It was because of recovery that I had been able to stay focused enough to use my writing skills and my passion for journalism to finish this piece. It wasn't easy.

Thursday, September 26

This week has been the hardest week of recovery I have experienced in a while, because it would have been so easy to skip meals and blame it on being 'too busy', and it was so hard to take that time out to eat.

The black-and-white part of me still exists. Although there is a lot more gray now, I still tend to be extreme at points. If I am working on something, I work until I am done – nothing in between. But I found a way to shove recovery somewhere in between all those black-and-white moments this week, and it feels good.

So now I am giving myself one night to breathe and relax, until tomorrow, when I start my new story.

Ed is already telling me to work out tomorrow morning, but I won't. He is telling me to not go eat this frozen yogurt that is in my freezer right now, but I will, because I want it. It looks good, and who doesn't like to relax at home with some kind of dessert? It only feels right to complete my night like that.

Goodbye Edward, as my dad calls him, hello dessert, and Hello Life!

******

Day 249: Jean Sizes Don't Validate Me

I had started today by adding two more pairs of sick pants to my bag that I am going to donate. I hadn't tried them on first, even though I had wanted to. I had just put them straight in there.

It had been so hard. Both of those pairs of pants had true meaning to me. They, along with my scale, used to validate how worthy I was on a daily basis. At one time, one of those pairs of pants used to be so tight on me, and at the end of my time with Ed, right before I chose recovery, they were falling off me. I was literally pulsing inside, wondering how they would fit now.

I could have tried them. No one was there. But I knew, no matter how good I felt before that moment, I wouldn't feel good after trying them on. Not because I didn't necessarily like the way I looked today, but because I would have been stepping back into that place of letting those pants be my judge.

Instead, I dropped them into the donation bag. Soon, but not yet, I think I will be ready to donate my first bag of sick clothes to the homeless shelter I found.

Friday, September 27

I spent the day seeing E, then relaxing and sleeping. After such a crazy week, I just needed to rest. It felt weird, but it was necessary.

Ed doesn't like it when I rest, but he already lost his power today when I put those two pairs of sick pants in the donation bag. Then tonight I celebrated the birthday of one of my brothers, who turned eight yesterday. He was so happy, because my sister and I got him his first real pair of walkie-talkies. Seeing him smile and seeing him play with the new toy we got him just made me so happy.

Sometimes material items can have such a hold on us. My pants are just pants, but they meant the world to me at one point, because I trusted them to tell me whether I was skinny or not that day. But then there is something like this pair of walkie-talkies; so simple, so innocent, yet it brought joy to my brothers and their cousins for hours today.

But more than that, I didn't need to wear a pair of sick pants, or a certain jean size tonight to feel like I was valued. I saw it on my brother's face when he smiled and gave me a big kiss and said his walkie-talkies were the best present he got. No size jeans can do that.

Hello Life!

******

Day 250: Standing Tall

Simply stated, on this day I was celebrating two hundred and fifty days without a scale, so I dedicated my blog to this achievement and more.

Saturday, September 28

On this day ...
I celebrate two hundred and fifty days without a scale.
I appreciate two hundred and fifty days of living in recovery.
I gave up two more pairs of sick pants to donate.
On this day ...
I listened to my body when it was tired, to end my morning walk.
I listened to me more than I listened to Ed.
On this day ...
I remember where I was two hundred and fifty days ago.
I remember how I felt when Ed used my weight to tell me how good a person I was that day.
I remember those numbers. I felt like they were literally inked onto my body.
I remember carrying them around with me every day.
On this day ...
I close my eyes in sadness at the prison I once lived in, yet I open them to find I have begun to set myself free.
Sometimes my feet get tangled in some of the chains that are left behind, and sometimes I fall.
But on this day ...
I celebrate the two hundred and fifty times that I picked myself back up and lived each day in recovery.
I never thought that I could do this, and somehow I have.

Thank you to everyone, both old and new readers, followers, supporters and fellow fighters, who have given me the strength to make it to this two hundred and fifty-day milestone.

On this day ... we celebrate us standing tall without the confinements of our addictions.

Hello to two hundred and fifty days of beginning my journey to freedom, and Hello Life!

******

Day 251: Chocolate Cake for Breakfast

I had been feeling really sick the previous night and this day, so don't ask me why I had chocolate fudge cake both meals in a row. I hadn't even wanted it. I couldn't even really taste it because I was feeling sick, yet on this morning it had been my breakfast.

Sunday, September 29

Now I have been thinking about the chocolate fudge cake scenario in my head all day, so I am going to try to break it down for myself.

Part 1: Ed's voice.

When you live with an eating disorder, eating 'forbidden' things, such as cake, is not allowed. If you do eat something forbidden, you need to eat all of it, right away, really fast, then go and somehow 'fix' it later.

That is what happened today with the cake for breakfast. Ed couldn't handle it just being in my fridge. Usually I am okay with unsafe foods being in my house, because I am at the point where I can trust myself around them, but today just didn't flow like that.

So, Ed said if I was going to have this cake in my fridge, I needed to eat it all, right now, standing up, then not eat for the rest of the day to compensate.

And yes, I listened to him about eating the cake. Did it feel good to let him make that decision for me? No. But here is the second part.

Part 2: I really just like cake.

I was craving cake all week, so when I had the chance to order it yesterday, I did. It was bad timing, because I was sick, and maybe I should have waited until I could better enjoy it, but nonetheless, I got it.

This is the healthy part of this situation. You like cake, you eat it. No guilt, no over-thinking. It's one piece of cake, not the entire universe on a platter.

I did let Ed dominate the cake for breakfast situation more than I would have liked. I don't regret eating the cake because, like I said, I love cake, but I wish it was more on my terms – my way. Maybe sitting down, or maybe on an actual plate, or something of that matter.

But at the end of the day, although Ed would like to make me think that this one piece of cake completely morphed my body and that I need to go do some drastic extreme measures of exercising or restricting to fix it, I know he is wrong. Really, if you think about it, all that happened was that I had a piece of chocolate cake for breakfast. No exercising or restricting needs to follow that.

What needs to follow that is some self-compassion and understanding. Big deal Ed, so I ate chocolate cake for breakfast. I will live on, and you, one day, will not.

Hello Life!

******

Day 252: Breaking from Rigidity

The previous day, after I had eaten the chocolate cake for breakfast, I just hadn't seemed to fully recover from it mentally.

It had been a very long time since I had felt that I was locked inside Ed's prison again, banging my head on the bars, wishing to rip them out of the ground with my own two hands, only to find that my hands and feet are glued to the floor and it's as if I am not even moving an inch – just letting those bars stare at me, with Ed dangling the key far, far away.

I had spent all the previous night in that prison, watching Ed dangle those keys in front of my face. I had eaten dinner there. I had eaten even more dessert there. I had slept there, and I had woken up there this morning.

Somehow I had found it within myself to take E my bag of sick clothes that I was donating to charity. I knew the moment I got up that they needed to get out of my room, otherwise I would have been trying them on all day, over and over again.

Monday, September 30

When Ed is loud like he was today, I always turn to my plan – his plan – pure rigidity. Eat only safe foods. Follow the food rules – those that are the basic plan of rigidity.

Even though I gave away my seven-page list of food rules to E within the first hundred days of this blog, there are still food rules I abide by. I knew that if I stuck to all of them today, they probably wouldn't be broken again for a long time and, honestly, I didn't have the capacity today to fight it on my own.

I was planning on getting a salad with some protein for dinner, like I usually do on Mondays (rigidity, rigidity, rigidity), but my grandma decided to make us dinner. It's as if she knew that I needed to break some kind of food rule today in order to step out of that jail, but I never even told her. I haven't broken a food rule like this in months.

I even asked her whether she had made dinner for both of us or just for herself. What a dumb question, right? Why would she make it only for herself? So, of course, when she said she made it for both of us, it was clear that I was officially going to be breaking the salad for dinner on Mondays rule.

Here I sit, one hour later, and I can say I did it. Surprisingly, I feel really good about it. It was easier doing it with someone I love, but since I didn't say what I was thinking, I kind of battled with the experience inside my head.

But there we go, the rigidity has been broken. A part of me has been taken back from Ed. Am I in a better place than I was this morning? Yes, but am I in a good place? No, not yet.

Recovery ebbs and flows, and I know that I will have those keys back in my hands soon. But for now I apologize to those who emailed me asking for guidance or advice today. First off, thank you for sending all your love and support, because it keeps me strong on days like these. But the reason I haven't answered yet today is because I don't have advice to give at the moment, since I am kind of sitting in Ed's little house myself, and I don't want to say the wrong thing. But when I do know the right words to say, I will so happily respond, as I normally do.

I don't write today as an inspiration or as a form of guidance, I write today as another fighter who needs support.

Part of breaking the rigidity of an eating disorder is breaking the rules – food rules and all other eating disorder rules – one of the biggest ones being to never show you are weak, because that would mean you admitting that you are actually not perfect (every Eds worst nightmare).

Well, here I am admitting it and breaking that major rule. I need support today – there, I said it Ed. I am not perfect and I need some extra strength today.

If we are going to break away from rigidity, let's give it all we have got, right?
Hello   *Life!*

October 2013

Day 253: More Rule Breaking

THE previous day I had written about being stuck back in some of Ed's ways, and knowing that I needed to break a few of my rules that went along with that, so I had broken my food rule about only eating salad with chicken for dinner on Mondays.

I didn't feel great about it. I actually felt nervous and very anxious about it, but it felt good that I had taken some of my power back from Ed.

I knew when I went to sleep last night that today would be another battle like yesterday had been, as it was always so hard to unlock myself out of Ed's prison once I somehow get locked back in.

Tuesday, October 1

I don't work out with my trainer on Tuesdays, and I used to take Tuesdays off from working out, but for the past month or so I haven't. So as much as I wish I could sit here and tell you all that I vowed to myself that I would wake up today and not work out (since I knew I needed to take a day off to get out of Ed's hold), I can't say that.

I planned on working out. Even though I was still not feeling well from the weekend, even though I told E I wouldn't, and even though I told my best friend I wouldn't, the truth is I was planning on doing it anyway. Well, okay, Ed planned it and I was going to go along with it.

But when I woke up, before I could even get out of bed, I received a phone call to do an unexpected interview for the new story I am writing for my university newspaper. This interview took longer than I expected, and then it led to a slew of other interviews.

Before I knew it, the one hour I had set aside to go work out was now gone. If I went later I would be running behind on all my homework and tasks I had to complete before I had to leave for school. So I didn't go.

Had I not gotten that call for the interview in the morning, I would have worked out. By getting that call, it threw off my entire Ed-dominated schedule. And yes, I did make the choice after that interview to do homework instead of still work out, and it's a decision I am very proud of.

I broke another rule today. I broke Tuesday's rule about working out. It's scary to be breaking these rules right now. Throughout my recovery I have broken a lot of Ed's old rules that I used to have, especially around food, but in the process he has also created new rules, such as this working out on Tuesday thing.

I think it goes to show me that my work in recovery is far from done, and while I may be stronger than ever, Ed is certainly not done either. For every rule I break, he will create a new one, but that is where my faith and hope come in.

Somehow, my grandma knew to make that dinner yesterday that broke my Monday night salad for dinner rule. Somehow, that lady knew to call me today for that unexpected interview in the morning, right as I was planning to go work out.

On days that we can't always be 100% strong and 'perfect in recovery' (I hate the word perfect, but I can't think of a better word right now), I think it's okay to rely on faith in the world to get us through. When our hearts are fighting, like mine is for my freedom, I truly believe the universe will do what it can to help.

It has done it before at the doctor's office when I went for my check-up, and the nurse told me I could skip the scale, before I could even open my mouth to ask her to not weigh me. It also happened again today with that interview before I wanted to work out.

And you know what else happened today? I broke another rule. Hello to breaking not only the old rules but the new rules too, and Hello Life!

******

Day 254: Turns Out the Only Person Who Expects Me to Be Perfect Is ... Me

The previous night, the huge story that I had been working on during the last week for my college newspaper had come out online. Naturally, the first thing I did was read it, only to find three grammatical errors.

This may not sound like a big deal to most of you, but to me it was major. Three errors? Yes, three entire errors. I was so upset that the blood inside my whole body was literally heating up and wanting to spill out.

If I sound overly dramatic, it's because that was the first time I had ever seen any of my published work flawed.

Wednesday, October 2

As many of you reading this blog who struggle with eating disorders of your own already know, one of the major characteristics that make us such good candidates for eating disorders is the constant need to be perfect. We all tend to be on the perfectionist side of the spectrum, and that is where our Eds get to us. They tell us that in order to achieve perfection, we need to lose that last pound, or work off that last calorie.

Needless to say, my point is that I am exactly that perfectionist person, so when I saw those errors, it literally ate away at me. It was the same feeling I had when I failed my writing test for NBC.

Anyway, I was up until 3a.m. as I was so upset over it, only to wake up at 6:30a.m. to find that I had made one more mistake in the story. I had interviewed someone who had gone through a traumatic event in 2010, yet when I referenced to that event in the article, I wrote 2006. Don't ask me why I wrote 2006, because I clearly knew it was 2010; for whatever reason, I just did.

So the balanced and not black-and-white part of me would have thought this through, but I wasn't balanced this morning. I was black and white – the gray was totally not there. So what did I do? I emailed the guy who I made the mistake about, asking him whether he wanted me to correct the date. Then I decided that, of course, he would want me to fix it, so I sent another email saying I would.

Only thirty minutes later, my editor made the change online and it was all fixed. It was nothing for her to fix. Even she said it was such a minor error and not to worry about it. But I was worried. I would be worried until I heard back from the guy that it was okay.

So now I was on my fifth email to this guy in the span of an hour, saying that the error was now fixed. Had I waited and gone to my editor first, he wouldn't even have known there was an initial mistake.

Anyway, I waited all day for his answer. All day I was anxious. All day everyone told me it was no big deal, and most people said they didn't even notice the grammatical errors. But I didn't care. It wasn't a perfect story now and it bothered me.

As I was sitting in class falling asleep due to not sleeping because of all my anxiety last night, I got an email back from that guy. This is what it said:

"Hi Shira,

Thank you very much! I appreciate you going through all this effort. It's a great article. I showed it to my boss and he thought it was great!"

Yup ... all that worrying and anxiety, and he was actually happy with the article! And then it hit me. That guy didn't expect perfection from me. My editor didn't expect perfection from me. My friends and family who read the article didn't expect perfection from me.

It turns out the only one who expects me to be perfect is no one other than myself. It's a quality that assisted me in becoming so good at having my eating disorder. I had to become perfect in the eyes of Ed, and only then would I stop.

Starving ... exercising ... losing ... always striving for more and more 'perfection'. But the truth is, and it's a truth I have learned in recovery more than once now, there is no such thing as perfection. Believing that we can reach perfection, especially perfection to our eating disorder's standards, can actually be dangerous, since it can be deadly for those with eating disorders.

So along with the lessons I have already learned, such as that my recovery won't always be perfect, and my meal plan won't always be perfect, I guess today I learned that my writing won't always be perfect either.

Restricting wasn't the answer today to make me feel better. I think the answer lies right here in front of me on this blog. The answer is that I am not perfect.

Maybe it's more perfect to admit you are not perfect than to really try to say you are. Yes, I made some mistakes, and yes, maybe a year ago I would have let Ed make me ashamed of them, and have probably starved myself because of them. But not today. Today I post this article here in the name of imperfection.

If I can't be perfect, then hell, the least I can do is embrace the beauty in imperfection. Hello Life!

******

Day 255: Being a Part of Something Bigger and Better than Ourselves and Ed

Recovery had been good today for two reasons.

Firstly, eating had been easier today. I had played it safe, which wasn't bad, as safe meant the meal plan, but it meant that I hadn't broken any food rules either. But I actually thought this was okay, and I believed E would think this was okay too.

We step outside of our comfort zones in recovery, just to step into a land of the unknown, and sometimes we have to settle in over there before we go and step into the next unknown land. So that was what I had done today. I was settling into this first unknown land from breaking two food rules earlier this week.

The second reason recovery had been good today was because I was part of something greater than myself and greater than Ed.

Thursday, October 3

If you remember, I just had a huge story published yesterday for my university newspaper (yes, the one I not so mildly freaked out about over three grammatical errors), about undocumented immigrants in California soon being able to get a driver's license, once the governor signed the bill into law.

Well, today at 9:45a.m. the bill was signed and it was officially made into law. I know that I am not the one who made this law happen or anything even remotely close to that, but I felt like I was part of it, because through interviewing so many undocumented people for my last story, I had been able to get to know a few of the people who it will affect. It felt really good to be a part of this new law, and that my story gave them a chance to express their voices about it.

I know this doesn't necessarily have to do with eating disorder recovery, but in a way it kind of does, because when you feel like you are a part of something bigger than yourself, it means you realize that you are a part of something bigger and better than your eating disorder too, and that is what today was for me.

Hello to being a part of something bigger than our Eds, and Hello Life!

******

Day 256: Needing to Use Recovery Tools

I was really, really, really extremely uncomfortably full. Ed was telling me it was all my fault. It was late at night, I was stuck feeling like this, and I already felt my body becoming sore.

Friday, October 4

So, I am uncomfortable. I am kind of mentally spiraling just ever so slightly and I really don't want to talk about it tonight, which is unlike me, but for whatever reason it's how I feel in the moment.

What makes me feel even worse right now is that tonight at dinner my brother came and showed me that he made me two Hello Life bracelets. They are bracelets he made with this blog's colors (yellow and purple).

I feel so bad, because as I keep looking at them on my wrist right now, I wish I could just focus on that beautiful gesture of a gift, but instead I am focused on feeling so full and on my soreness.

I know that this is where the tools I have learned from E for my recovery really need to come in. What are the tools that I can use right now to help me make it through tonight?

- *Distraction – I can work on my new story or study for my upcoming test.*
- *Breathing – Every breath means a new second.*
- *Talk to Ed – Ah, what I would give to sit Ed in E's chair like I have done before and yell at him right now. I can still talk to Ed now, but I am not really mentally ready for that. (I know, it's crazy, but sometimes E and I let Ed 'sit' in her chair, and I tell him how I feel about him. Seriously, it works).*
- *Do something that evokes a positive emotion – Okay ... what makes me feel good? It's too late for a massage. I don't want anything to do with food. It's too late to watch a movie. Sometimes reading people's comments on this blog makes me feel better, so I guess I can do that.*

Well, I guess I now have four things that I can spend my energy on that will replace me sitting here and talking about how terribly consumed I am by Ed. I feel that if I write about it, it will only give him more power. Or maybe it's that I am so consumed by him right now that I don't even have the energy to vent to you all about the kinds of thoughts he is putting into my head. But by now you all know Ed just as well as I do, so you can pretty much imagine what he is saying to me in this moment of extreme fullness.

I think I will try the breathing thing. One breath at a time ... morning will come. I can sit here and get all anxious about the soreness that I will feel when I wake up but, really, what is the point? It's already here and I can only deal with things once they come to me.

And as I am taking my breaths, I am also going to keep glancing back at my wrist to stare at those Hello Life bracelets my brother made me.

Any hard day in recovery is still better than a good day at an eating disorder. I will leave it that for today.
Hello to one breath at a time, and Hello Life!

******

Day 257: And ... Action

When I had written my blog the previous night, I was partially writing and Ed was partially writing. We were in a dark place together, where we both were unreachable to anyone else, other than to one another – a feeling I knew all too well.

I hardly slept because I kept waking up to feel how sore my body was and whether it was getting worse, as it usually did overnight. Thankfully, at 6a.m., my mom had told me to go back to sleep and, for whatever reason, once I had heard someone say it was okay to sleep and let go, I was able to rest for a few hours, but when I had finally woken up, I decided to take action.

Saturday, October 5

In the book I have just finished about eating disorders, Eating Disorders: Decode the Controlled Chaos, *it talks about the stages of recovery. The second to last stage is the action stage. So, just like it says in the action stage, you take action. It's when you break the food rules and essentially step outside the chains that Ed tries to hold you down with.*

The last stage is the maintenance stage – a stage where you maintain recovery. Every time I think I have made it into the maintenance stage, I am quickly reminded that I am still in the action phase, and I am okay with that. I like the action phase because it's proactive. Action creates change.

So today I could have stayed home like I have done many nights before when my body feels sore after eating, but I didn't, and I am not going to tonight.

I went to get my hair done today, which is like self-care 101. A little bit of self-care can go a long way, and once I did that I felt ready to take action and go out tonight. Soreness and all, I am going out with my amazing best friend tonight, and even my sister.

Just like they say in the movies, "And ... action!" Here I come Saturday night.

Hello Life!

******

Day 258: The Story of the Too Tight Jeans

This day's post was the typical 'my jeans were too tight on me today' story. I know it was nothing new and it was a topic I had written about many times before, but this blog was my daily journey to recovery, so today was another day of the tight jeans.

The question that I sat there asking myself wasn't why the jeans were too tight, or why they were tighter than they used to be, because that was part of my recovery and I was open to that idea. The question that I was asking myself right then was why did I continue to wear those too tight, uncomfortable jeans, once I had tried them on and seen that I didn't feel good in them?

I mean, seriously, what was the point of that?

Sunday, October 6

I walked around all afternoon and evening, and even ate dinner, in a pair of jeans that made me feel terrible about my body and, therefore, myself.

There is no logical reason why I made the choice to wear them. Honestly, I was secretly hoping that, deep down, they would stretch out and maybe they were only tight from being in the dryer, since I wore them only a month ago and they fitted perfectly fine then. But it's been about eight hours now and they still fit exactly the same, so I am going to take it that they are staying this way, which means only one thing: Get rid of the jeans.

How many pairs of jeans will I need to get rid of in recovery? When I started recovery last December it was winter season, so all my jeans that used to fit me then no longer really fit now. It wasn't as much an issue over summer because I wore dresses and sweat shorts that didn't really correlate to a size. But now that the colder weather is coming and it's jeans season, I think I need to start buying some new ones.

Every time I try on an old pair of jeans, I hope they will fit the same. Umm ... they are not going to fit the same. Eight months in recovery, of no longer starving my body will cause that, and rightfully and deep down, happily so. But that still doesn't make this any easier.

So, I guess my point is that today I have another pair of pants to take to E tomorrow to add to my donation bag of sick clothes that I am donating. If this continues, which it will because I won't keep these sick clothes around, I honestly need a new wardrobe. I guess maybe that is not such a bad thing.

It won't be easy to do, but I would rather donate my sick clothes and buy myself a new healthy wardrobe instead. I am not sure when that will happen, but as my clothes collection is slowly dwindling every time I find a pair of sick pants to donate, it kind of has to happen sometime soon.

Anyway, so yes, I wore the too tight jeans today and I felt bad in them.

But I went out in the world and lived my life anyway. I still saw my best friend, I still studied for my upcoming test, and I even had dinner with my aunt and cousin, all while wearing the too tight jeans.

But where the story of the too tight jeans used to end in me crying and tearing myself apart alone in my room for hours, tonight it ends with me carrying on with my life anyway.

Hello Life!

******

Day 259: Putting Others in Front of Ed

Today had been going fine in terms of recovery, until I got to one of the girls I tutor, and her nanny had made me food. It wasn't a salad or some chicken or something we in the eating disorder world would consider 'safe', it was these hand-made chicken dumplings tossed with a lot of butter.

She had only made this for me because I had told her once before that they were my favorite Russian dish. They were a Russian family, and since my ex-boyfriend was Russian, I had really got into Russian food.

I had just finished telling E the same day that I wasn't ready yet to break any more of my new food rules and that I was feeling like I needed to just stick to my meal plan. Well, life obviously didn't really care that I wasn't ready to break any more rules, because this situation was totally breaking a rule – many rules in fact. It broke the snack rule, the safe rule – I mean I could give you a list of the rules it broke.

I had already had my snack, and this was a heavy meal, yet it wasn't dinner time, so it put me in a really hard spot with Ed. I tried telling her I was full. I tried telling her I wasn't hungry.

"But I made it just for you," she kept saying.

Monday, October 7

Living in an eating disorder can often cause us to unknowingly and unconsciously think only about ourselves – our calories, our food, our schedule for eating – and sometimes we can push others aside because of it.

I know that I used to do this many times when I was living with Ed. I wouldn't even let my little brothers choose a restaurant they wanted to go to because it wasn't one I was comfortable with.

Anyway, today was a chance to break that habit of sometimes being a little self-centered while living in an eating disorder. I have done this many times before, but it didn't seem to make this time that much easier.

I could have insisted on saying no, and it would have really hurt her feelings, knowing that she made them just because she knew they were my favorite. Or I could have said yes, because sometimes it's worth it to go out of the Ed comfort zone to make someone else happy.

And yes, she was so happy. Of course, she wasn't happy when I only ate six of the twenty dumplings she put on my plate but, for me, even eating that amount was a huge step.

It wasn't even about the amount of food I ate, it was about the gesture and meaning behind it. Eating those dumplings meant that I was putting someone else's feelings in front of Ed's, and even my own discomfort.

I still ate a decent dinner, considering those dumplings were a heavy mini meal, so for that I am also proud of myself. But mostly I feel proud of myself that not only did I go with the flow when life decided to break my food rules for me, but also I was able to put someone else in front of Ed.

I am still uncomfortable with the whole situation, but it was honestly worth it to see the nanny smile.

Hello Life!

******

Day 260: Taking a Leap into Recovery

The previous day I had written about how the nanny of a girl I tutored had made me a really yummy yet heavy and very 'not safe' food that I loved. I had also written about having to choose between eating it to make her happy and putting myself in an uncomfortable spot with Ed, or saying no to her and letting her down.

Through the comments and emails of my blog readers, I had seen that while it was a big step in recovery to put Ed aside to make the nanny happy, I also didn't have to do that if it meant making me uncomfortable. Listening to what was comfortable with me at the time also could have worked, and I also could have made the nanny happy by maybe asking to take the food home with me.

I was glad about what I had done, and I was glad I put her in front of Ed. However, knowing that the other option of listening to my discomfort would also have been okay for that moment was something important to acknowledge too.

Before I had even received any those comments or emails recommending I used that method to approach a situation like that in the future, my mom had told me the same thing right after she had read my post. She had said that it was major that I had taken that step yesterday and put Ed aside, but that I didn't always have to make others happy. It would also have been okay to say no, if I was uncomfortable at that moment.

Of course, we both recognized the ultimate goal in my recovery would be able to sit and eat the food the nanny made me because, at the end of the day, I did really love it. But it would also have been okay to honor where my discomfort was at that time.

Tuesday, October 8

Tonight my mom made dinner. It was very yummy, yet it was something I would never typically eat on a weekday. It would be more of a weekend meal because it was heavier.

I tend to give myself more leeway with food on weekends than on weekdays, a similar pattern I used to have with restricting during the week and binging on Sundays when I was with Ed, and it's not a pattern I intend to keep. But for now I follow my meal plan during the weekdays (no restricting), and on weekends I tend to let myself eat a little more (but no binging).

My mom had told me earlier what she was making and she was totally understanding of the possibility that I might choose to eat something different. I knew I wouldn't offend her if I chose to eat something else that was more safe for me, because she even advocated for me to honor those feelings yesterday.

But tonight was different to the situation yesterday. Tonight I didn't want to eat the dinner she made to make her happy. I wanted to eat it because I actually wanted to. It was something I wanted to do for myself.

It wasn't a decision that I came to right away, and it's one that I thought about for a few hours in school. I went back and forth between deciding whether to eat her meal or to get my own, and I was left with one memory that is just etched into my mind: Me sitting at a table, any table, whether it be out with friends, at work or with family, with everyone eating something almost the same, and me eating nothing, me eating my safe food, or in those days, my Ed-approved foods.

Sometimes I still need to be that person with her safe food if that is the place in recovery I am at on that day, and that is totally fine. But today I didn't want to be her. I wanted to be the one at the table eating the same thing as everyone else.

How many times I have spent being the odd one out, eating 'my food', is a number I have lost count of and I just didn't want to add to that today. So, my mom, my grandma, my sister and I sat down to eat dinner together. I don't remember the last time it was just the four of us.

I sat with them, ate with them, and ate the same food as them – maybe not the same amount as them, but nonetheless, the same food. Now that right there was more than a step in recovery. It was a leap. And it was a leap because it was a brave act of courage against Ed that I wanted to do, not because I wanted to make someone else happy.

While flying in the air and taking that leap was scary, the momentum and little taste of freedom that came with it prevailed more than the fear of it. I am not saying I could take that leap every day, because I can't right now, but I did today.

One day, one leap, one taste of freedom at a time, I am doing recovery, and that is really more than I could ever ask for of myself.

Hello Life!

******

Day 261: Dancing to the Beat of My Drum

This was the first day that it had rained in Los Angeles during this season, and being that I really don't like water, I really don't like the rain either.

My professor for my class on this day had made the mistake of telling me on Monday that she wouldn't be in class today, so there would be no quiz and we would have a guest speaker instead. "Don't tell anyone else in the class or else they won't come," she had told me.

I don't think she thought that I, knowing this information, would be the one who wouldn't go to the class, but turns out I was. It was just the perfect opportunity to spend a day with me, myself and I.

Number one, it was raining, and I didn't want to drive. Number two, she was gone, so why not?

Wednesday, October 9

Typically, the straight-A student in me would never do this, but today I just needed a mental health day. At first I thought I would just use the time to work on my new article and relax, but it actually turned into a lot more than that. It turned into a day of self-care and a day to challenge and beat Ed.

Oh yes, Ed came marching in right away, literally playing drums and trumpets because I now not only had no school to go to, so I could skip the snack I normally get at school, but I also had the house to myself at night too, so dinner could just be a little snack or something totally not on the meal plan.

And when I say marching with drums, he really was that loud, and it really did come off like a party inside my head, like being able to skip these meals was some kind of celebration. But I didn't want to miss my snack and I didn't want to miss dinner. I got hungry and I wanted to eat. It was just that simple.

It's hard for me to even say and write what I wanted versus what Ed wanted, because the line is so blurred. At one time, Ed's line was my line, and there was no blur. I saw what he wanted and I thought it was what I wanted and I obeyed. But now there is a line between Ed and me, which is a huge step for me in my recovery, but it's still always blurry, and I had to keep reminding myself today of what I wanted, not what Ed wanted.

In the end, I actually sat down and made myself a really nice dinner, complete with a salad for an appetizer (Ed wanted it to be the main meal but that didn't happen) and the food my mom made for me last night. I didn't watch TV, I didn't go on my phone, I just sat with me, myself and I ... and InStyle *magazine. It was actually really nice. Ed was there too, but I just let him watch. By that point I already had control over the steering wheel.*

He is still marching right now, but without drums or trumpets, yet with more of a sad depressing symphony that I have let myself down because I had the opportunity to restrict and I didn't. It's not easy sitting here, challenging those thoughts, and that is the truth. Ed is wrong. Me, myself and I are right. We were right to eat. We were right to take a mental health day and not go to class, and to work on other projects and relax. We are right, we are right, we are right.

I wish Ed would march his way back out of the space he is currently taking up in my head, but if he doesn't, the least I can do is make him feel as uncomfortable as possible.

How do I make Ed feel uncomfortable? Easy – I expose him. I am exposing him and his drums and his sad symphonies all on this post. By exposing him, and by saying he is wrong over and over again, he might not be quiet, but he will eventually lose some of his credibility.

I would rather sit here and be the only one dancing to the beat of my own drum in recovery than sitting here feeling like I am being forced to dance to Ed's drums, like a puppet with no control over themselves.

So, me, myself and I were right to not listen to Ed today. We were right. He was wrong. We will dance to the beat of our own drum, uncoordinated and maybe not knowing the right steps for as long as it takes, until our beat is louder than Ed's.

I am not sure how long that will take, but I guess we have another one hundred and four days to figure it out. Hello Life!

******

Day 262: Ordering Coffee at the Coffee Shop

So there I was, ordering a cup of coffee before getting my nails done, because it was really cold on this day, and I hate the cold, when the lady asked me whether she could put in the half and half for me.

I asked her whether she just had milk, not creamer, and that it would be totally fine for me to do it myself. But there was no milk, only cream. Creamer is a huge 'not safe' food for me, and it would be the ultimate rule to break on my list of food rule that still exist.

Thursday, October 10

For people with eating disorders, I am sure you will feel the anxiety build in you as you read this. For those readers who don't have an eating disorder, let me explain how I felt today.

It's like when you drive to work on your usual route, only to come to your freeway exit and it's closed for construction. Now you have to make a quick decision as to what detour to take. You don't know which is the fastest way, or whether you will even make it on time now, but either way, you are stuck.

This was me and the coffee place. Okay, so there was only cream. I probably stood there like a deer in headlights, thinking of what to do for a good five minutes. The lady probably thought she had offended me or something.

Do I walk out? Do I drink it plain? (This for me is not tasty.) Or do I just drink it with the cream?

So, I added the cream. Also, let me add, there are no measuring spoons at a coffee shop, so you don't know how much you are adding. Woah, talk about disobeying Ed.

I sat with the coffee for a while as I was getting my nails done, and I tasted it really slowly. It was delicious, yet at the same time it was so uncomfortable, almost as if I was sinning in secrecy in front of all these people at the nail salon and no one even knew. It was as if I was committing a crime in front of their faces and they didn't even see it.

I forced myself to drink that coffee, even though it meant being uncomfortable, because I know that change only comes from action. To throw the coffee away wouldn't be action, it would be escape. I don't need any more escapes from Ed.

There is a time and a place for everything in recovery, and I am the first one to say to take our time to break our Ed rules, and each person has their own path. But today I knew inside myself that I was ready, and needed to break this rule.

E told me yesterday that recovery is literally like re-learning how to live. It's like teaching a baby how to walk. And she was so right. In recovery we have to re-learn everything. We have to re-learn the basics, such as eating and resting our bodies. We have to learn how to socialize again, we have to re-learn how to not be afraid of food.

However, we also have to re-learn the things that seem so remedial and small to others without an eating disorder, such as ordering coffee at a coffee shop; such as getting dressed in the morning and not doing body checks; and such as learning how to choose a restaurant to meet someone for lunch.

Isn't it kind of crazy how recovery works? I have learned to live without a scale, my most prized possession, for eight months now, and one of my most uncomfortable and scariest moments in recovery so far has been re-learning how to order a coffee with cream at a coffee shop.

I don't just mean to write about the food part. I mean to say that we are re-learning how to live our entire lives. I have thought about this all day, and I have decided that I can look at that in one of two ways:

One: Oh my God, how annoying, frustrating and terrifying that I need to re-learn how to live all over again, and even re-learn how to order something as small as a coffee.

Or ...

Two: How lucky am I that I get a chance to re-learn how to live my life in freedom? How lucky am I that I get to re-learn how to live my life for me, on my terms and my standards, not Ed's or someone else's? How lucky am I that I get to create new norms for myself, such as even ordering a latte one day, not just coffee?

Choice one is easier, as those emotions tend to be more natural. But choice two, while it's so much harder, uncomfortable and scarier, is what will make this process of recovery turn into a journey, as opposed to just 'something' I have to go through.

So, choice two is my choice.

Here is to the journey of re-learning how to live my life my way, not Ed's way.

Hello Life!

******

Day 263: Cheers

Yes, it was that kind of day. I was drinking wine, but not alone of course. I was at dinner with a friend for her birthday, which is why this blog had to be kind of short.

Friday, October 11

Today wasn't even that kind of day because of recovery, although there were the typical body issues, but it was just one of those days in life where you kind of need a glass of wine.

So regardless of the day I have had, sitting here now with my friends and my wine, I think tonight will be just fine.
To anyone else who had that kind of day today, here is to all our glasses of much needed wine tonight.
Cheers and Hello Life!

******

Day 264: But Ed, it Was a S'mores Cheesecake!

The previous night, for the first time ever, I had ordered a s'mores cheesecake. It was the newest cheesecake added to the menu at Cheesecake Factory, my favorite restaurant.

Now, I don't even like cheesecake, not because of Ed reasons, but because I just don't like it. But last night, I had just needed to try it, because I love s'mores.

Well, not only had I tried it, but I had loved it, and I had eaten almost all of it, which had led me to the result that always happened when I ate anything with a lot of salt or sugar – body soreness.

Saturday, October 12

Oh ... my dear body soreness. I could honestly write an entire blog about my experience with this body soreness in recovery. It happened to me last Friday and last Saturday too, both times because I ate food with either a lot of salt or sugar.
So, of course, I spent today with Ed telling me to be 'careful' of what I ate today (in Ed's world, meaning to restrict), since I ate that s'mores cheesecake last night. And as if Ed talking to me is

not already draining enough, I have the physical discomfort in my body to constantly remind me of it.

Sometimes, on days like today, I let Ed win. Sometimes I do listen. But today I was just so annoyed at him already. I literally kept telling him over and over, "But Ed, it was a s'mores cheesecake!"

I don't know why I keep thinking that Ed would care that the fact it was the coolest cheesecake in the world would justify me eating it, because to him it doesn't, but it does justify it for me.

I was telling one of my friends today about how my body was sore, and he said, "Well, at least the cheesecake had vitamins H and T."

Vitamins H and T? I had never heard of them. I had heard of vitamins A, C and D, but never H and T.

"Yeah, it stands for happiness and taste," he said.

I just loved that statement so much that I had to write about it, because it goes along with what I have been telling Ed all day. It wasn't anything more than the most delicious cheesecake, filled with vitamins H and T – happiness and taste.

I am not saying that our happiness should come from food all the time, but sometimes, and especially with desserts and for those of us in recovery for eating disorders, happiness from food every now and then is allowed, I think.

So, regardless of my soreness, I am still having my friends over for dinner tonight (and yup, with more cheesecake), and if Ed continues to bother me, I am going to keep saying the same thing: "But Ed, it was a s'mores cheesecake!"

Can't that just be enough of a reason to overlook the body soreness and move on with my day? I think so.

Hello Life!

******

Day 265: One Hundred Days Left … I Am No Longer the Person I Used to Be

Today marked the two hundred and sixty-fifth of the three hundred and sixty-five blog posts that I would be writing to document my year without a scale and my journey to recovery, meaning today started the official countdown of the last hundred days of my blog.

More than anything, today was a day of reflection for me.

Sunday, October 13

I still remember celebrating my hundred-day milestone. I remember writing that blog post. I remember the cake I ate and I remember the family I ate it with. It was significant of me truly starting this journey, and knowing that if I had reached one hundred days without my scale and of recovery, that I could go all the way for an entire year.

I don't know how I am sitting here one hundred and sixty-five days later, now entering the last closing phase of this blog, now not celebrating one hundred days in, but actually celebrating one hundred days left.

I know, from the deepest place within me, that I couldn't sit here and write today's post if I had to do this journey by myself. Thank you to all my family, my friends, my readers, my followers, my supporters and E for being my strength during these eight months.

Of course, this doesn't mean that in one hundred days I will take back my scale; it's actually the opposite of that. Giving up my scale meant making a decision. It meant choosing recovery. It meant choosing that I needed to re-learn who I was without that number. It meant choosing to learn how to completely relive my life, and rediscover who I was without my eating disorder and without my weight to define me.

Reaching that one-year mark in one hundred days will be the ultimate prize to myself that no number on a scale could ever give me. It will mean I have stuck to my decision; it will mean that I will have fought my way through this journey, through the tears, through the physical pain, and through the fear, because I told myself I wouldn't turn back; and it will mean that I am one step closer to freedom.

Will I be completely free of Ed by the time Day 365 comes in a little over three months? I really don't know. Had I asked myself that question eight months ago, I would have said yes, in a heartbeat. But if there is one thing that I have learned so far in recovery, it's that my journey is not about setting black-and-white goals and expecting myself to reach them; it's not about saying goodbye to Ed forever. It's about growing. It's about learning. It's about walking, dancing, turning and gliding through this process of creating a new life for myself. It's not about reaching some certain specific goal.

When I had my eating disorder, every day was about reaching some number on a scale. My life is not like that anymore. I am more dedicated to growing and journeying through my fight with Ed, through my struggles, through my pain and through my insecurities.

Lastly, I am not sure whether I will ever be forever done with Ed. I used to think recovery meant totally killing Ed, or crushing Ed, or suffocating Ed. But the more I grow in recovery, the more I see that, again, Ed is not black and white, and I won't hold myself to this expectation of either getting rid of him completely or living with him completely, because that is how I got so sucked into him in the first place.

"If I can't get rid of this eating disorder, I guess I will give it all I have got," I used to think. No. Not anymore. I am learning to navigate my life on my terms, and walk in the path of freedom, not in the path of numbers and restrictions. But I am also learning

that Ed might come and he might go, and it might be like that forever.

He is a part of me. We all have people or characteristics or flaws that are a part of us that are not always good. But we learn to become stronger than them, we learn to conquer them, and we learn to rise above them. We don't always have the option of expelling them out of our lives.

So, my point is, looking back on two hundred and sixty-five days ago, I am not that black-and-white person I used to be. I am not even gray. I am not a color. I am not a number. I actually don't even know who I am yet, and I am actually excited to continue to find that out.

For today I am a twenty-two-year-old girl, counting down the days to my birthday this Friday (first birthday in recovery), choosing what I will wear, and I am celebrating being a person, just like you or someone else who made a decision to fight for a better life, and actually stuck with it.

I am celebrating walking the road that is taken by few, yet wanted and desired by so many – the road to finding true self-acceptance, happiness and freedom.

Hello to the last hundred days of this blog, and Hello Life!

******

Day 266: All of a Sudden My Calories Became My Judge

Earlier this day I had received one of the biggest compliments that I think I had ever received. The publisher of our university newspaper that I wrote for, who was also my professor, and also someone who I really looked up to, told me that I was talented.

Not only did she say that I was talented, she said that I was smart, and that I was a great reporter.

I was sitting in her office looking at her, thinking, "Does she know who she is talking to? Does she really mean these things about me?" And I saw it in her face that she was sincere.

At that moment, the pants that I was wearing that felt so tight that morning no longer mattered. The fact that I had skipped the gym that day didn't matter. The only thing that mattered was that I was talented.

I left her office feeling like I was walking in another universe, where I was almost invincible to anyone, including Ed.

Monday, October 14

Hearing someone I admire tell me that I am talented gave me a satisfaction that no number on a scale could ever have given me. And now, fast forward to about thirty minutes ago when I was eating dinner, when, for some reason, the human calculator inside of me decided to calculate all of my calories that I ate today.

Why did my brain do that? I honestly can't tell you. I didn't want to. Yet somehow there I was, doing it, eating my food and counting calories inside my head, both at the same time, the count going up as the bites increased.

By the time I was done calculating, I discovered that the count was far higher than I expected or wanted it to be, and all of a sudden the fact that I was talented no longer existed. Everything I had felt earlier today when I received that compliment vanished, and now the only thing left to define my day was this calorie count. Yet again, another day in my life being represented by a number.

How did that switch happen so quickly? One minute I was feeling like this untouchable talented young woman, and the next I am nothing more than X number of calories, and not even a good X number at that.

This is the part of recovery that I hate to talk about, because it's so unbelievably draining, disheartening and discouraging. I apologize to anyone who it could possibly trigger, but to avoid writing about it would be avoiding my truth, and that is something I refuse to do in recovery.

I would rather sit here and admit to everyone on this blog that I let this calorie count label me today, instead of sitting here writing a dishonest post about how great I am still feeling that my role model called me talented today, because I am not feeling like that anymore.

However, I do have to acknowledge the fact that being aware that this calorie count is defining me today, and being aware that it's something I am not okay with, speaks volumes to me.

At one point not too long ago, I would have actually thought that it was totally justified to judge myself on how many calories I ate that day, and I would have thought it was acceptable. Today, although it's still happening, I am not okay with it, and it's not acceptable to me.

I accept that I feel lessened as a person because of it, but I know that feelings are not facts. Feelings are feelings, they just come and go like the tide in the ocean.

Feeling judged by this calorie count today is a feeling, and it's a bad, worthless feeling that I hope will trickle away soon. But, no matter how worthless I might feel right now, there is one fact that remains clear: My professor did indeed call me talented today. It wasn't a fantasy, it wasn't a dream, and it's not a feeling. That actually happened.

Feelings can be misleading, but facts don't lie. I am talented, and that fact has the ability to preserve itself and stand strong, even against the loudest, harshest and meanest Ed remarks ever, and it will be what I hold on to tonight until I feel strong again.

With hope that tomorrow will end in a better light: Hello Life!

******

Day 267: Forget Yesterday – It Has Already Forgotten You

"Forget yesterday – it has already forgotten you. Don't sweat tomorrow – you haven't even met. Instead, open your eyes and your heart to a truly precious gift – today."

I had read this quote earlier and it completely resonated with me today for a number of reasons.

Let's start with the first part: "Forget yesterday – it has already forgotten you." Yesterday had been a difficult day in recovery for me. I had allowed the number of calories I had eaten to act as my judge, and it had overshadowed one of the greatest compliments I had ever gotten – I was a talented writer.

Today, that day had gone, and the quote was right in saying that yesterday had forgotten me. It had forgotten me, my calories and Ed. So the only one walking around with its burden was me, and there was nothing fair about that.

Tuesday, October 15

Right now in this moment, after I have had not only a successful day in recovery, but a quiet day with Ed, I am letting go of yesterday and I am moving on to tonight.

I can't even say that I am moving on into tomorrow, because that feels so far away, as night time is a time for me to do my homework, a time for me to think and a time for me to reflect. But at least tonight I won't be sitting here obsessing over calories like I did last night, and for that I am grateful.

And just like the quote says, I am not going to sweat tomorrow. Tomorrow is tomorrow. Who knows what it will be? I can sit here and say that I won't let myself add up my calories again tomorrow, but that goes back to the black-and-white thinking that I try to avoid.

So we will just say that tomorrow will be tomorrow, and somehow, someway, I will roll with the flow of life and the flow of recovery and, no matter what, I will see something positive in it.

As for right now, my eyes are very much open to the precious gift in front of me, and that is today. I know it's cliché, but it really is true right now. Today is a gift because I didn't judge myself based on calories today; I didn't restrict today; I lived in a little bit of freedom today.

Because I know what it's like to live in the chains of an eating disorder, it makes me appreciate what others may consider just a 'normal' day that much more. I know this is not anything new or very insightful, but it's where I am at today. I am simply at this place of expressing pure gratitude for the tiny bit of freedom that touched my world today.

With gratitude and appreciation, Hello Life!

******

Day 268: My Two Worlds Coming Together

A few weeks previously I had written about how I was working on a big story for my university newspaper, and that I was getting so involved in writing it that it made my recovery very difficult.

I was having a hard time between letting the writing of that story become a distraction from eating and making it a motivator for me to eat, so I could keep my mind clear and focused.

I had made the hard choice to use that experience as a challenge in recovery, and I used it as a lesson in learning how to still nourish myself and eat on the meal plan, even during times of chaos and busyness, because that was bound to happen often in life and it was something I wanted and needed to get comfortable with.

Well, I couldn't have been more proud that I had chosen to stay dedicated to eating and keeping my mind clear during the writing of that story, because today that story had run on the front page of the newspaper and had a four-page spread, as well as getting over fifty Facebook shares in just one day. It was incredible.

Had I not made the choice to eat during the writing of that story, there is no way it could have been as beautifully written as it turned out to be, so for that I was grateful for my recovery.

Wednesday, October 16

A lot of times I get conflicted because I feel like I am two different people. One part of me is the part you see me on this blog – a girl in recovery, who I guess has turned into a blogger about my experience. The other part of me is this reporter and aspiring journalist, which is so different from my blog, because as a journalist I have no views and no opinion, I just give the facts. The blog, on the other hand, is purely my views, feelings and opinions.

They are two separate worlds, but today I saw how both of those worlds came together to work in perfect harmony. The recovery girl in me helped the reporter in me write the greatest story I have ever written.

I was thinking about how crazy it is that I have chosen a profession like journalism, where every great article is not only great because it exposes the truth, but because it has balance.

Any good journalist will find a perfect balance to a story – the equal amount of pros and cons. The story that ran today was in perfect balance, but how ironic is it that I chose a profession that deals with balance, the one thing in my personal life, especially with Ed, that I have lacked and I strive so hard to achieve?

For every negative comment in today's story, there was a positive one to offset it, or vice versa. If only I could apply that to my recovery and to Ed, I think I would win many more battles. Sometimes all it takes is one comment to change an entire story, view or situation.

What would it be like if every time Ed said something negative to me, I offset it with a positive comment back? Just like my stories, to keep everything in balance. Would that one positive comment completely tear Ed down and discredit him? No, not at all, just how one positive comment doesn't discredit a negative comment in my articles either. But it would add balance. It would add another view to think about. It would add my own voice to Ed's voice, and maybe mine just might be the one that stands out.

I am not saying it's easy to offset every negative Ed thought with a positive one, because it's one of the hardest things in the world to do – it's rewiring the brain of those of us who have eating disorders. But the idea of creating balance within my own life, the way I do for the stories I write, is one that is intriguing and exciting to me.

Overall, today was significant in my two worlds of recovery and journalism coming together to create a small step of success for me. No number on a scale, no calorie count and no clothing size could ever amount to the same level of success as a four-page article in a newspaper does, and the fact that I am able to realize and appreciate that is why I am thankful I chose the journey to recovery nine months ago.

Hello Life!

******

Day 269: My First Wish in Recovery

Tonight I had been celebrating my aunt's birthday with my family at a really incredible restaurant with really incredible bread. I had known that we were going to this restaurant for a few days and I had been thinking about this bread the whole time.

Should I eat it, or should I not? Maybe I should not eat it, because it was my birthday the next day, and I knew I was going to be celebrating with a lot of food. Maybe I would only have half.

Okay, well, the big moment came when the waiter put the bread basket in the middle of the table. All of my cousins took one. I just sat there thinking, and I decided to have half. Ed was satisfied with this half.

Me on the other hand ... I was done with that half within five minutes and was definitely not satisfied. I wasn't sure what clicked, but something within me had said, "Just go for it! Eat the other half."

I looked at the almost empty bread basket, and the only thing in it was my sad half, left there the first time around. It reminded me of so many nights that I had taken bites and bits from other people's food instead of ordering my own, or nibbling off something in the kitchen and only leaving a little half left, because finishing it was too much to handle.

So, I went for it.

Thursday, October 17

For the first time in a long, long time, I enjoyed the bread from the bread basket at dinner.

I know it may sound like nothing, but this was something. It was breaking another huge Ed rule. Ed never ever lets you eat appetizers or bread, especially if he knows there is a meal coming. But Ed was a tiny little miniscule thing on my shoulder tonight. He was so powerless and he knew it.

And since my birthday is tomorrow, we celebrated my birthday along with my aunt's too, and when I got the ice-cream sundae (most delicious one ever by the way), I could only wish for one thing.

I know they say that you are not supposed to say what you wish for to anyone, but this wish was important, because it was the first time I had ever wished for something in all of my recovery so far, and it was my first birthday wish in recovery.

I would have thought that I would have wished to not gain any more weight. I would have thought that I would wish to kill Ed. I would have thought that I would wish to get some incredible job when I graduate. Or I would have thought that I would wish to not eat too much this weekend. But I didn't. The only thing that came to my mind when I blew out that candle was this image of myself smiling and laughing.

I am not even sure if that is a wish, because it's more of an image, I guess, but it's an image that was almost showing me what I wanted my future to look like. So, essentially, I wished to smile and to laugh more often.

When I think of me on the other side of recovery, that is what I see – me smiling and laughing. I didn't even see a body when I made my wish. I didn't see a scale. I didn't see a number. I saw happiness. And if that doesn't speak for how far I have come in recovery, then I don't know what does.

Hello Life!

******

Day 270: Happy Twenty-Third Birthday to Me

Today I was celebrating my twenty-third birthday – my first birthday in recovery.

The difference in my birthday this year to how my birthday had been the previous year, when I was locked in my eating disorder, was as if I was two different people living two different lives.

Friday, October 18

A year ago today, on my last birthday, I woke up at my boyfriend's (now ex-boyfriend) house, and the very first thing I wanted to do was go get a scale and weigh myself. Actually I don't think I even wanted to do it, but I remember feeling like I needed to do it. It was a necessity at the time, like air is for humans to breathe.

The scale was tucked away in my boyfriend's mom's closet, something that usually wasn't an issue, because she normally left for work before I woke up. But for some reason, on my birthday last year, she was still home in the morning.

I remember wondering what in the world I was going to do. Do I take the scale from her closet and go weigh myself in the kitchen like I always do, even though she already thinks I am crazy about my weight anyway? Do I not weigh myself, and try to have a day without it?

I couldn't. I needed to get that scale. I can remember that feeling I had when I walked with my head down to that closet and pulled out that scale, set it down in the middle of the kitchen, and stood on it to weigh myself.

"Shira, why are you doing that?" I remember her asking me.

"I just have to," I said.

I can remember the humiliation I felt as I stepped on that scale in front of her eyes. I can remember how ashamed I felt, how defeated I felt, and how controlled by Ed I felt. And after all that, I hated what that number showed that day. I remember exactly what it was.

That day I let myself have one chocolate for breakfast. It was a huge deal. It wasn't a Sunday (my binge days), and the fact that I even let myself have that was almost unimaginable.

At my job at the time, I didn't tell anyone it was my birthday, because I didn't want anyone to bring me cake or cupcakes. I met my grandma and mom for lunch at a deli, where I knew I could order egg whites. They sucked. And that night, before my boyfriend took me out to dinner (which I hardly ate or enjoyed), I made his mom take a picture of us, telling her I wanted it as a memory, when I knew deep down that all I wanted to do was see how my body looked.

As I started this first birthday in recovery this morning without a scale, without a number and with many different yummy chocolates, I sat with E over coffee and I almost cried.

I have given every single ounce of my inner strength to make it to this birthday in recovery. I have fought, I have cried, I have been in physical pain, and I have walked through the mental chaos in my head that only those with eating disorders or addictions can truly understand. All for one reason: Because I finally know that I am worth fighting for a life of happiness and freedom.

Today I celebrate that life. While I have a long way to go in my recovery, it's important that I sit back and acknowledge how far I have come since a year ago today.

I was surrounded with so much love today. I hugged my sister last night as we blew out a candle on a cupcake together right at 12a.m. I had lunch with her today. I am going to have dinner with my family later.

I was able to truly start this day feeling loved by others, not because of what I weighed, and not because I looked a certain way, but because they love me for who I am as a person.

Even last year, people around me loved me for who I was, but because I was so busy only conditionally loving myself based on what number I attached to myself that day, I couldn't even enjoy it.

I didn't need a scale to tell me my self-worth today. I didn't need a number. All I needed to do was reflect back on the chains that were shackling me a year ago, and now see that they lie broken on the floor beside me, and that I am the one that broke them.

That right there shows my worth. It shows the fight I have within me. It shows the love I have for myself and it shows that, deep down, despite what Ed might say, I know I am worth living a life of true self-acceptance and love.

I cry as I write this post right now, because I look back and I know that I will never have to go through that humiliation of standing on that scale in the middle of the kitchen ever again. No eating disorder, no Ed, no nothing can ever bring me back to such a hopeless and dark place, and it's my deepest hope and wish that no one reading this ever does either.

On this twenty-third birthday of mine, I celebrate my life. I am celebrating my hard-earned life in recovery.

I also need to say that today wouldn't be the same without my twin sister. She was brought into this world next to me, and she can truly see into my soul. She has been a huge source of strength during my recovery, and I am blessed to share this special birthday with her.

When my sister and I were born, she was twice my size, because she ate all my food – ironic right. I was really tiny and had to fight really hard to get to be a healthy baby. My dad once told me, "Shira, you were born a fighter. From the minute you came into this world, you were fighting."

And on top of that, I was born on the 18th (obviously), which in the Jewish religion, stands for the word 'chai', which literally means life. The story of my life literally translates to: Fighting for life.

But today I am not fighting, I am celebrating. Hello to my first birthday in recovery, and hello, hello, hello to my beautiful life. Hello Life!

******

Day 271: This Party Doesn't Stop for Ed

Today I needed to thank everyone for the beautiful birthday wishes left via comments and emails. I couldn't express how much love and support they had given me, and I was so grateful for them.

Moving on to today, I would have been lying if I had said that Ed wasn't there. I wish I could have said he wasn't, because I had had such a beautiful first birthday in recovery the previous day, but the truth is that he was there today, and he had been since I had woken up in the middle of the night and I felt my body sore again.

And then he had been there again when I got dressed and hadn't liked the way I looked in the mirror. And he had been there when I took a picture of myself with my phone right after that (which I deleted right away afterwards). And lastly, he was there right at that moment, asking me what people would think when they saw me tonight.

Saturday, October 19

Tonight I am going out to celebrate my birthday with my sister's closest friends. Some of them I haven't seen since I started recovery. Ed loves this because it just amps his voice up as if it was being projected through a megaphone.

But here is the bottom line: This is my birthday, not Ed's. This is my first birthday in recovery, so Ed can seriously just find his way out the door, because my party is not stopping because of him.

On that note, I am going to get ready to have the greatest first birthday in recovery celebration ever. I will only experience my first birthday in recovery once, so I am doing it right. So, Ed, you can now leave, and the party can now continue.

Hello to keeping this party going with or without Ed, and Hello Life!

******

Day 272: Let Me Tell You About My Birthday Cake

My party the previous night hadn't stopped for Ed, and my birthday celebration hadn't stopped for Ed today either.

Today had been my final birthday celebration (I guess it was about time, being that my birthday was two days before), and it was by far the best one, because it was truly symbolic of everything I had been writing about during the previous few days in terms of where I stood in my recovery.

Sunday, October 20

My best friend and her boyfriend took me out to a beautiful brunch, which in itself is symbolic of how food has the power to be such a bonding experience. Then at the end of it they brought out my birthday cake.

This cake was so special, thoughtful and symbolic that it truly deserves an entire blog post of its own, so here it is getting one.

It showed my favorite picture taken during my recovery. It's my favorite picture because it's with my best friend and it was a night that I remember was filled with laughter, fun and food – all worlds of recovery coming together.

It also showed my newest article that ran on the cover of my university newspaper last week. The fact that this article is on a cake means so many things.

This cake is sweet, it's bright, it's delicious and it's self-indulgent. It's everything Ed would never let me have, and my article is the result of where recovery can take me, not just with my perception of my body, but with my entire life, such as with my career.

I wrote a post earlier this week about how my recovery and how eating and nourishing myself kept me focused and was a big reason why this article was so well written.

Finally, this cake was ... a cake! The word cake is like a forbidden word to Ed, but this cake was all for me, with my name on it, my picture on it, and my successful article on it – three things that Ed can't take from me. Rather, they are three things that recovery gave back to me.

Recovery has given me that smile that I wore in my picture, it has given me the tools to stay focused to write that story, and it has made me proud to own my name, my story, my life, and all that goes with it.

So now, even though I am looking at all the pictures that people posted on Facebook from yesterday, feeling really full, and thinking about how I don't like my body in each one, I sit here and remind myself that those things, while they might seem so important in this moment, are really nothing.

The way my arm looks in that one photo is not important. The way my leg looks sitting down in another photo is not important. What is important is this: I am blessed with the love and support of the greatest family and friends, and I am blessed to have celebrated my first birthday in recovery that I worked so hard to get to with E.

I want to say a special thank you to my beautiful best friend for not only making my birthday incredible, but for literally being my rock and, so many times, my sanity during this process of change and recovery.

What is important is everything that I listed that my cake symbolized to me. And if that is not enough, then the fact that a huge birthday cake got an entire post dedicated to it on an eating disorder recovery blog definitely is. Hello Life!

******

Day 273: Today Was Worth the Fight

Today hadn't been an easy day in recovery for me. It had been one of those days where you wake up and you don't know how you are going to make it to the next hour, so you just go minute by minute.

Between waking up bloated from all the food the previous weekend, my body feeling sore from all of it, and the mental distraction of replaying what I had eaten over and over as I kept looking back at the pictures that had been taken of me on Saturday night from my birthday and hating on each one, today had kind of started out belonging to Ed.

And then as I was walking into the gym, the scale there had literally haunted me the entire time.

Monday, October 21

It was exactly this time last year after my birthday that I decided to start weighing myself every day again, and it's when my eating disorder took a turn for it's all time low. I never turned back after that. I couldn't stop – until I got into treatment.

I knew that if I stood on that scale today, Ed would literally become who I was again, and there would be nothing anyone could do to pull me away from him. And as much as I would like to say that I didn't step on it because I love my recovery so much, I wasn't in that space today. Today recovery was hard and it was hard to remember even the incredible things I wrote about it a few short hours ago last night on this blog.

The honest reason why I didn't step on that scale today is solely because of this blog and the commitment I made to be scale-free for a year – that and only that. And, you know, maybe that is not so bad. Maybe that is okay for today, and maybe it's okay because it was enough to keep me from stepping on that life-sucking machine.

All day I kept looking at the pictures that were posted of me from the weekend, thinking about how I can change my body in all different kinds of ways.

I don't know why, but sitting there and almost fantasizing about the many ways that Ed could come in and save me from recovery was almost something that I was locked in a daze by. I couldn't get out of it for a little while.

But after I looked at those pictures so many times over and over, I realized that my answer to becoming happier with the way I look in them doesn't come from change and it doesn't come from Ed. My answer doesn't lie in stepping on another scale. My answer is acceptance.

A big part of recovery is learning to flow with changes and learning to embrace change, but what happens once those changes have set in? Then change is no longer the answer. The answer then moves into acceptance.

The question is how to get to that acceptance, and I don't have an answer for that right now, other than what I know from these nine months of recovery so far, and that is if I set some kind of special *goal about how and when I want to fully accept myself, I will epically fail. The only thing I can do is give myself time and go with the flow of this process called recovery.*

I need time to accept the changes, time to accept that I will never be who I once was, both physically or emotionally, and time to accept that it's okay to give myself time, I don't need to be the hero right now.

On that note, at the same time that I am embracing this opportunity to give myself time to master acceptance, I am also going to accept that today wasn't easy, and that is okay. Not every day needs to be a great day. All every day needs to be is one worth fighting for.

Considering the fact that every day leads me one step closer to freedom from this eating disorder, today was definitely worth the fight.

Hello to knowing our lives are worth the fight, and Hello Life!

******

Day 274: If She Can Go Two Hundred and Nine Days Without a Scale, I Can Go to a Basketball Game

My newest article was due in two days. I wouldn't have time to work on it later that night because a friend was taking me to a basketball game for a belated birthday gift and Ed said I needed to go to the gym that morning.

The facts that remained that morning were that I needed to write my article because I wouldn't have time later, and that if I went to the gym I wouldn't have time to do my article. So, that was when I had to prioritize.

If I had put Ed first, he would have got first priority, and my article would then have been last priority, making my recovery kind of last too.

At that stage in recovery I was too aware that the consequences of doing that could be to suck me back into Ed.

Tuesday, October 22

I was blocking my grandma's car in the driveway this morning, and I knew she had to leave by 11a.m. If I left my car there, it would have been my motivation to leave by 11a.m. too, and to go to the gym, so I wouldn't block her in.

I literally had to go and move my car right when I woke up so I couldn't use that as an excuse to go work out. I don't know how I got myself to go do it with Ed yelling in my ear, but I did. But I am glad I did, because I sit here six hours later with my article pretty much done.

However, the idea of not working out and now having to go eat unsafe food is overwhelming me at the moment, and it's giving Ed a lot of fun material to tease me with.

But right before I wrote this post, I was reading some comments that other bloggers left me on some of my posts a few days ago. One person said that my blog was part of the reason she gave up her scale, and has been scale-free for two hundred and nine days now.

It just made me think for a second, that if she could give up her scale for two hundred and nine days, and I have given up mine for two hundred and seventy-four days now, then can't I go to this basketball game and go through the motions of maybe eating some different or unsafe foods?

I don't know why, but knowing someone else gave up their scale for two hundred and nine days is a lot more motivating for me today than to look at my own accomplishment of two hundred and seventy-four days without a scale, so I am going to focus on that.

Sometimes all it takes is knowing that if someone else fighting the fight can do it, so can you. That is what those two hundred and nine days of her being scale-free are for me.

If she can go two hundred and nine days without a scale, then I can go to this basketball game, unsafe food and all. Hello Life!

******

Day 275: What Made Me Smile Today?

Earlier this day I had posted a tweet that said, "Fighters, what made you smile today?" and it was accompanied by a picture that said, "I hope you always find a reason to smile."

I had seen that picture and it had made me think about one of the biggest lessons I kept learning in recovery, and that was to always try to embrace the small moments of freedom that we find, and sometimes just being able to say we smiled today is a huge moment of freedom in itself.

As I drove to school after tweeting that, I started thinking that I posted that question for others, yet I hadn't even answered it myself, and being that I was the one who posted it, I figured I should have an answer to my own question.

Wednesday, October 23

I sat in my car driving and I sat in class for three hours trying to think of some big 'recovery' moment that made me smile. Did I smile when I did my body check this morning? I thought maybe I smiled today because I was a little bit more accepting of what I saw, but no, I didn't smile at that. Did I smile when I ate any of my meals? No ... not today.

So I was feeling kind of like this 'recovery failure' because there wasn't some big aha recovery moment that made me jump for joy today. Then I remembered that the minute I woke up today I shared something on my Facebook page for my ten-year-old brother, Edaan.

He has started a website, where he is making bracelets and giving all of his proceeds to an organization that helps people who are fighting cancer. It blew me away that such a young boy can have such a huge idea and go as far as to create an entire website for it, complete with an online store and 'about me' page. I actually think his website is better set up than my blog.

I shared his website on my Facebook account, and I remember that, as I was sharing it, I was smiling because I felt so proud of him. On that Facebook status I wrote, "Please show some love and support to this incredible young man as he tries to make a difference in the world." It made me smile that someone as young as him is trying to create change and trying to help others.

So then it hit me that I don't need some huge aha recovery moment in order to smile. It's okay to smile at other things that don't have to do with recovery, and it's okay to not find 'recovery' things to smile about every day.

I really realized today that maybe along with celebrating the victories in recovery, such as eating unsafe foods or breaking some Ed rules, maybe recovery can also mean smiling about something that doesn't have to do with food, weight or calories.

So, to answer my own tweet: What made me smile today was knowing that my ten-year-old brother wants to help other people.

What made you smile today?

Hello to smiling about our aha recovery moments and our not so aha recovery moments, hello to finding the happiness in both of those situations, and Hello Life!

******

Day 276: Maybe Having a Little Faith Is Not Such a Bad Thing

I had suffered from road rage today. A drive that would normally take me only twenty minutes had taken me almost an hour and a half, meaning that I would be done tutoring the kid I was driving to an hour and a half later than planned.

As I was stuck in my car, I needed to pee and I was really hungry. I don't know why I was hungry, because I had eaten all my meals and snacks, but for some reason I just was.

Thursday, October 24

So there I am sitting in my car getting so frustrated with both of these uncomfortable situations (having to pee and being hungry, such a bad combination) on top of the fact that I am running late for work (my perfectionist self doesn't approve), and I couldn't help but realize that two hours before that I was upset at the way my arm looked in the mirror, and now I am upset that I am hungry and can't eat for another two hours.

I mean, talk about recovery's ups and downs. It never ceases to shock me how quickly my perspective on myself and on food can change so quickly. And just like that, the way my arm looked in the mirror this morning didn't really matter as much. And yes, it was just one arm.

I don't know why I only looked at my left arm today. But, being that it's one arm fewer to criticize than normal, I am going take that as a good thing and be appreciative of it. I have learned that being appreciative of even the smallest or weirdest things, like the fact that I only looked at one arm in the mirror today instead of both, or instead of my whole body, can go a long way, so for today I am going to go with that.

The arm didn't matter. The fact I had to pee didn't matter. And even the fact I was late didn't matter. What really mattered to me was that I could feel myself getting in a bad mood because of hunger.

Does this ever happen to anyone else? When I was really locked in my eating disorder, I was disconnected from my hunger cues so I didn't even feel those hunger pangs as much. And when I did, I tried to numb myself with the scale or with other Ed thoughts to distract me. I didn't ever get upset at it. I was just numb. Sometimes I even liked feeling hungry, but now that I can feel my hunger, I have to say I don't like it. It's really not a good feeling, and in this case it put me in a bad mood.

Anyway, I finally got to the house of the kid I was supposed to tutor, apologizing and feeling really sorry, and the first thing this seven-year-old boy said to me was, "I was so happy you were late. I got to play football while you were driving." Umm ... what? Yes, all of that frustration, annoyance and road rage was all for nothing.

Actually, it wasn't for nothing. It was all working in favor of giving a little boy extra time to play football. I was so worried that I wouldn't eat on time and that he would be upset I was late, and the entire time everything was already taken care of.

I ended up finding an extra granola bar in my purse (true indicator of someone in recovery, right?) and our lesson went really well.

And now I sit here in bed and write to you, with my chocolate banana tea latte, already having forgotten about the road rage, already having forgotten about my left arm, and already having forgotten about my hunger putting me in a bad mood.

All I know is that everything worked out today, and that maybe having a little bit more faith in days like today wouldn't be such a bad thing.

Hello Life!

******

Day 277: Talking to Myself in the Bathroom Mirror

The title of this day's blog kind of explained everything in one sentence, but it wasn't as crazy as it may have seemed. Or maybe it still might have looked crazy, but that was okay.

I had just finished getting dressed on this morning, and I was standing in my bathroom attempting to do my hair, when I caught myself just staring at myself in the mirror, thinking about how this sweater didn't fit me the way it used to last winter.

At first I was thinking these thoughts in my head, like why the material was bunching up on part of my arm, or why it looked a certain way, then before I knew it I was talking to myself out loud.

It was kind of funny when I came to I write about it but, honestly, in that moment it wasn't funny.

Friday, October 25

I couldn't believe that I was standing in front of my bathroom mirror having a conversation with myself about why my arms look too big in my sweater. This explains only a small fraction of the crazy-making things that an eating disorder can do to you.

All by myself I went through all of the reasons why I don't think I look good anymore – out loud. I was actually trying to be kind to myself and justify why it's okay to not look the same as I used to. I am not saying it worked, but I did try.

And Ed was watching this the whole time, because I could feel his presence around me, laughing at me, thinking how ridiculous I am for trying to convince myself that these were actually legitimate reasons to not look good. For Ed, there is never a legitimate enough reason to not look absolutely perfect.

Is this really that crazy, or don't we all have conversations with ourselves on a daily basis? Those conversations might stay inside our heads and not always be verbalized, but I know I have conversations with myself about the way I look in the mirror almost every day. Sometimes they are good conversations and sometimes I tell myself how great I think I look.

Today just happened to be not such a great conversation and it happened to be out loud. I am thankful no one was home, although I guess that doesn't matter much anymore, now that I am telling you all about it here.

Then later in the day I found myself having the same conversations with myself in yet another mirror, but this time it was at my dad's house and I was looking at the way my jeans looked on me. This time I didn't talk to myself out loud because my little brothers were there, and I would never let them hear the kind of negative thoughts that Ed taints my mind with sometimes.

So, there you have it. I talked to myself in my bathroom mirror today, out loud, about why I didn't look good in my sweater. Was it the greatest day in my recovery? No, but it also by far wasn't my worst.

At least with this experience I can kind of look back on it as I write this and laugh at it. Sometimes laughing at even the things that hurt us the most can help speed up the time it takes us to heal.

Hello to laughing at talking to myself in my bathroom mirror, hello to not judging myself for it, hello to moving past it, and lastly, Hello Life!

******

Day 278: It's Days Like Today that Keep Me Going

It was days like today that kept me going. They were the days that reminded me why I had chosen recovery in the first place.

Saturday, October 26

It's days like today, where I only did one body check, that keep me going.

It's days like today, where I ate birthday cake frozen yogurt in the middle of my day for no reason at all, other than the fact that I just wanted it, that keep me going.

It's days like today, where I was able to study and get homework done without being so preoccupied by how I look or what I ate, that keep me going.

It's days like today, where I didn't encounter another conversation with myself in the bathroom mirror about why my arms don't look good, that keep me going.

It's days like today, where I didn't go shopping at the mall because I knew I wouldn't be accepting of any new clothing sizes, and I see how I have learned to have compassion for myself, that keep me going.

It's days like today, when I am reminded that when I gave up my scale to my therapist, the first words that came to my mind were, "Hello Life", that keep me going.

It's days like today, where I didn't have a number to define me, that keep me going.

It's days like today that I ask you all what keeps you going in recovery?

It's days like today, where recovery is on my side, that I humbly say: Hello Life!

******

Day 279: Oh Yes, I Ordered the Chocolate Chip Pancakes

Every year for my birthday, my aunt took my sister and I out to brunch – just the three of us. Every year we went to the same place. This place was very well known for their pancakes, and every year for the past three years that we had gone there, Ed had come with me.

I remembered going the previous year and wanting to order these chocolate chip pancakes, but there was just no way Ed would approve of that, so I had ordered egg whites.

The year before that I had ordered the same egg whites, but my sister ordered the chocolate chip pancakes, and I remembered the one bite I let myself have. I think I went home and binged that day, because I thought that even one bite was too much, so I had punished myself for it by bingeing.

Needless to say, that restaurant was always Ed's restaurant, not mine – until today.

Sunday, October 27

I knew that we would be going to this restaurant for brunch today, and I even talked to E about it on Friday. "I really want to go and take this brunch back from Ed and make it my own again. I just don't think I can get the pancakes, not yet," I told her.

But when I walked into that restaurant today, I was determined. I was doing it. I was going to take back my birthday brunch with my aunt from Ed. He had had it all to himself for three years, and now it was my turn to take it back. I mean, after all, it's my birthday brunch, not his.

So I was staring at the menu, still kind of nervous, and still thinking how I would actually get the words "I want the chocolate chip pancakes" out of my mouth to the waitress, so I decided to tell my aunt and my sister about what I was going through.

My sister, knowing what an incredibly hard thing this was for me, helped me conquer Ed, and she helped me take back this brunch. Together, she and I not only ordered and shared the chocolate chip pancakes, but eggs and bacon too.

We divided everything equally and we each had our own plate to ourselves. I made sure we did this, so I could feel mindful of what I was doing. Eating off plates with other people is often really eating-disordered behavior, and it's become important to me to have my own plate at meals.

I remember spreading the chocolate chips around on the pancakes before I took the first bite and I was just thinking to myself, "Oh yes. I did it. I ordered the chocolate chip pancakes."

I felt like a mini hero in that moment. This was the first time that I had had my own plate of chocolate chip pancakes in many years. And wow, had I missed them. I don't think I can go years without them again.

Ed lost today – majorly lost. I, on the other hand, took back my birthday brunch with my aunt and my sister, and I took back this restaurant from Ed too.

Hello to eating chocolate chip pancakes, hello to being my own mini hero today, and Hello Life!

******

Day 280: Somehow, Some Way ... I Will

Today I had to keep telling myself, "Somehow, some way ... I will." I was still telling myself this as I wrote my blog.

Sometimes, "I will" is all you can say, and it's all you can do. Today, I had made many "I will" statements to myself.

Monday, October 28

When I woke up stressed out because I had so much work to do, meaning I had to cancel going to the gym, I had to literally sit, take a deep breath and tell myself, "I will be okay. I won't work out today, and I will be okay."

There came a point in my day where I was so overwhelmed that the only thing I could tell myself was, "I will, I will, I will." It wasn't even followed by anything, because today was so chaotic with life being life that I couldn't even put in that next word. I just knew that somehow, some way ... I will.

And now that I am sitting here after not having my greatest day in recovery in terms of eating, because when I am stressed out my hunger cues are the first thing to go, I remind myself of the saying I have been telling myself all day:

"I will. I will have this last meal. I will get done what I need to get done. I will take tonight one minute at a time if I have to. I will put one foot in front of the other and move forward. I will let myself cry again if I need to, then I will move on. I will carry my head high into tomorrow, even though I know I have had better days in recovery. I will make tomorrow better."

Whatever your "I will" statement is for today, I hope it brings you hope, strength and courage as mine have to me.

Mini crying sessions and all, I will get past today and I will give tomorrow all I have got. If Ed can't be the one to comfort me today, then who will?

I will. Hello Life!

******

Day 281: Raised Spirits

I didn't know what it was about this day, but after a day like I had been through the day before, someone somewhere must have known I needed a little extra support. Not only was I lucky enough to receive it, I was overflowed with it.

From private emails, to comments, to tweet messages, to Facebook messages, and a special phone call from my mom, there had been a beautiful person sending me a positive and inspiring message at the end of every media outlet.

Some had given me words of encouragement. Others had told me how my blog had touched their lives. One girl even told me my blog had saved her life.

But what no one knew is that, deep down, getting everyone's support is what had lifted my spirits back up from my hard day and brought them into the place of hope that they were now in.

Tuesday, October 29

Because of your love and support, I had a good day in recovery today. I didn't have a good day because I worked out, because I didn't work out today, yet again. I didn't have a good day because I didn't think about calories in my food, because I most definitely did do that. And I didn't have a good day because my newest story for my university newspaper ran on the front cover today.

I had a good day because something so much stronger, bigger and more fulfilling than Ed could ever make me, surrounded me all day and all night, and that was the support from all of you.

A year ago I was the girl who would have said that I could handle everything on my own. I was the one who never needed help. I was the one who helped everyone else. And even though I still tend to feel that I am expected to be this superhero all the time, I am no longer afraid to say that I can't do this alone. I can't do recovery alone, and I don't want to do it alone.

I am not afraid to admit that it's because of other people that I made it through today with a sound and hopeful mind. Ed was the one who was afraid of other people, not me. And now I get to embrace the love and support I was missing out on for so long when I was letting Ed rule our lives.

This blog is truly no longer only my journey, but the journey of an entire community – leaning, encouraging and supporting one another. Thank you for being the reason I sit here tonight with raised and hopeful spirits.

Hello to the beautiful souls who have made today's recovery a gift, and Hello Life!

******

Day 282: Excuse Me Ed ... I Have Something to Say

The previous few days had been extremely chaotic, hectic and stressful for me, and had really tested my recovery for all that it was worth.

When I was stressed out pre-recovery, I would turn to Ed for support and guidance anytime I felt anxious. I used to think: "If I have to be stressed out about life, then the last thing I need to do is stress about gaining weight, so I won't eat, and it will be one less stressor for me." Well, recovery wasn't like that, and that mindset was no longer an option.

Wednesday, October 30

To say that I haven't listened to Ed at all while being stressed these past couple of days would be a lie, because I have listened to him.

Usually, I am more open and flexible with myself in terms of letting myself eat what I crave or what I feel like having, even if it's an extra chocolate here or extra frozen yogurt there. But these past few days I have stuck exactly, and I mean exactly, to the meal plan. Nothing less, but definitely nothing more.

Even though I was eating what I needed to, it still kind of felt like restricting, because I wanted foods that Ed wouldn't let me have, and I listened to him. I just didn't have the energy to fight him at the time. But today I told myself that I had to put my armor on and become a fighter. If I couldn't fight Ed as being Shira right now, then I would fight him with a coat of armor, pretending to be some kind of warrior.

And oh, did we fight ... all day long. Finally, at 5:30p.m., I had a break from class and I really wanted some M&M's. I wanted them, but Ed didn't of course. At first, I sat there in the classroom and told myself I wouldn't get up to go get them, because it was too far to walk to go buy them. Um ... it's a three-minute walk at most, and I know that. I had a fifteen-minute break, so time wasn't an issue.

In that moment, I had enough. I want some M&M's and Ed is not letting me? Excuse me Ed, but I have something to say: "I am getting my M&M's!" And I did get them.

I didn't eat all of them; not even half of them. Okay, so I actually only ate five of them, but the point is I got them. It was symbolic of me gaining my power back from Ed.

And to set Ed straight, I got what I wanted for dinner, not what he wanted, and I ate it in bed with him while watching one of my favorite TV shows. It was the best thirty minutes that I have had all week.

Ed was there for all of it. He was there when I threw away the rest of the M&M's. Yes, that is true, but he was also there to witness me buying them in the first place, and that is a victory in itself. A small victory but, nonetheless, a victory.

Having him watch me actually enjoy my dinner tonight (and finish it) is also a victory. Sometimes it's the small victories in recovery, or even in life, that deserve some recognition to remind ourselves how far we have come. Hello Life!

******

Day 283: Halloween: The Recovery Edition

Today in the US it was Halloween. For any international readers in countries that don't celebrate this day, it's a day when all the kids dress up in costumes and they go from house to house and collect candy. It's called trick or treating.

I had been surrounded by Halloween all day. It had been in the kids who I tutor, when they showed me their costumes; it had been in the picture of my little brothers all dressed up; and it had been at school, with even college-age kids dressed up.

So, needless to say, it made me reflect back on my Halloween experiences.

Thursday, October 31

Halloween for me as a child was a bitter-sweet holiday. It was sweet because I got to eat all the candy I wanted for one night, but it was bitter because I was always the overweight girl in my group of friends and siblings, and I always felt that people were watching me and my candy because of that.

My pediatrician at the time told my parents that they should follow this rule for Halloween: Let your kids eat all the candy they want on Halloween night, then throw it all away the next day. That way it's not lying around the house for them to keep eating.

Of course, at the time, the pediatrician was only trying to do her job and keep me as healthy as she could. My parents, who obviously didn't have a manual on how to treat Halloween with three kids, two who were overweight and one who was skinny, adopted that rule into our home. I don't think they or I could ever know the implications that rule would bring me about Halloween or the feelings associated with it.

Now that I am in recovery, I look back and see how that rule was the most black-and-white rule I have ever seen. Eat everything in one night, then throw it all away. It's like Ed telling you to binge, then restrict the next day to fix it.

So when I think of Halloween as a kid, I think of this one year in particular. I was eight years old and I was dressed up as butterfly barbie. I wore this big puffy blue dress with sparkles. I don't know why, but for some reason that was the first time I ever remember feeling subconscious about myself and my weight on Halloween.

I don't know the reason for that. I just saw a home video one week ago of me on that exact Halloween, and I was eating pizza with everyone else on the floor and getting ready to go trick or treating just like everyone else. But even at that age I knew pizza was bad, and eating it on a night like that was a treat for me. I guess Ed was just a baby then, but now looking back, he was there with me.

Anyway, I can still remember coming home after trick or treating, spilling all my candy out on the floor with my brother and sister, and eating as much of it as I wanted. No one said anything. No one stopped me. We just watched TV and ate our candy on the floor in our costumes. I love that memory. I was truly a kid in that memory.

I don't remember what I felt when I knew my Halloween candy would be gone the next day, but I do remember my twin sister always hiding hers somewhere and me going and stealing some whenever she wasn't around. This candy was so forbidden after that one night, that eating it afterwards was like a rebellious act that no one could know about; an act I did in secret.

So today, when the eight-year-old girl I tutor offered me some Halloween candy, I froze. I didn't know what to say. I had planned that I wouldn't eat any Halloween candy today, not even one, to protect myself from bingeing. Or maybe Ed made this plan; I am not sure. But then this innocent little girl offered me some, and how could I say no? I told her we could share.

I drove home just thinking over and over again about how I am no longer that eight-year-old girl in her butterfly barbie Halloween costume who needs to feel self-conscious that people are watching her. I am not her anymore. Where at one time that Halloween candy held so much power over me, I see now that it doesn't have to be like that any longer. There is no longer the rule of eating all my candy in one night and throwing it away tomorrow, and I think I speak on behalf of my parents when I say that too.

As a family, we all have evolved since that Halloween when I was butterfly barbie. We have grown to understand and learn that black-and-white thinking is not the answer to everything we face. And now, as I am an adult, I am not that little girl who should feel lucky or rewarded to eat pizza and candy. I can have Halloween candy now. I have the right to enjoy it, and not just for one night, but for as long as I please.

Baby Ed may have left his mark on some of my childhood Halloweens, but now Ed and I are both grown, and I am stronger than him. Today is my chance to take back Halloween from Ed.

So am I going to go eat a whole bowl of candy? No. Did I even eat an entire piece of candy today yet? No, and I most likely won't tonight, but I did share some candy with the young girl I tutor. I did enjoy that, and maybe that is all I can do for Halloween in this first year in recovery – sharing a piece of candy with a little girl who I love.

Maybe next year I will eat one whole candy all to myself. Maybe next year I will be the one offering the candy to someone else. Who knows where I will be next year? For now, sharing a piece of Halloween candy was a good enough start for me.

To all of the recovery soldiers like me who celebrated Halloween at work today, who are taking their kids trick or treating, or who are passing out candy and are faced with the many eating disorder challenges that go along with all of that: May your Halloween be a positive experience that belongs to you, not to your Ed.

Hello *Life!*

November 2013

Day 284: Sorry Ed, I Am Cutting Myself Some Slack

AFTER having woken up at 7a.m. to answer a bunch of emails and work on my two stories that I had submitted to my editor on this day, I had planned to get up to go running.

Planned is the keyword, because I guess my body didn't want to do that because it kept falling back to sleep. Finally, when I did manage to wake up, I just knew that I couldn't go today. It was the typical daily battle of Ed versus Shira.

Friday, November 1

If you remember, on Monday I wrote about how hectic and stressful a day I had. I couldn't see how I would make it to today. But, not only did I make it to today, I made it with flying colors.

Two completed news stories later, many blog emails later, and many tutoring and class sessions later, I sit here feeling accomplished. So in honor of that, when I finished my work today, I literally told Ed:

"Okay Ed, my dear friendemy, I am plopping myself down right here on this bed and I am watching Law and Order *until I have to get up and leave for work."*

And that I did. It wasn't an easy task to do with Ed reminding me every time I ate something that I didn't work out today. But seriously Ed, cut me some slack.

Actually, maybe it's not Ed who needs to cut me some slack. Maybe it's me who needs to cut me some slack. So I didn't work out today ... big deal, I will live on. Unfortunately, so will Ed.

So I ended up eating chocolate peanut butter ice cream last night with my sister after I very seriously told myself I wouldn't even eat one single piece of Halloween candy. So what, Ed? So what?

I feel like I need to take a moment and give myself some credit today because up until now, I have let Ed tell me to feel terrible about myself because I didn't work out and I still ate what I wanted.

But you know what? I worked hard this week. I was productive this week. I enjoyed ice cream last night. And I sat down in bed and watched Law and Order *for two straight hours. Good job me. I deserved to do that today.*

I mean ... don't we all deserve to cut ourselves a little bit of slack every now and then? Even if Ed says the answer is no, I am doing it anyway.

Hello Life!

******

Day 285: Let's Make a Toast

I had been thinking about what to write about on this day, thinking that I had nothing to say, until I read a saying in a positive thinking book that said, "If you could make a toast to yourself today, what would you raise your glass to?" So, of course, you can see where this post was going ...

Saturday, November 2

It took me about an hour or so to go through my entire day thinking of what positive thing to toast, when I realized I actually had way more positive things to cheer to than I thought. Some of them may come off as small or insignificant to someone else, but to me these things are worth toasting.

So here we go onto my virtual non-alcoholic toast to myself for today. And please feel free to share any toasts you have for yourself as well.

Today I make a toast to ...

- *The laughter I experienced when talking to my sister about me sleep talking last night.*
- *The two more spoons of chocolate peanut butter ice cream I had.*
- *The cream (yes cream, not milk) that I totally didn't measure and used in my coffee this morning.*
- *The delicious piece of black-and-white cookie that I got for my sister, yet ate some for myself anyway.*

Today I make a toast to ...

- *The two hundred and eighty-five days of hard-fought recovery that led me to be able to even acknowledge these small victories today.*
- *The fact that my voice, while maybe shaky during hard times like eating today, was stronger, louder and more definite than Ed's.*

Today I make a toast to ...

- *Another day without a scale.*
- *Another day without a number to define me.*
- *Another day that reminds me of why I chose recovery.*
- *The fact that these good days seem to be coming more often than not.*

Today I toast to ...

- *Another day of hope.*

- *The fighters, warriors and souls who are all on the journey to self-acceptance just like me. It's your strength, perseverance and commitment that inspire me every day.*

And, of course, Ed is trying to interrupt my toast right now and that is okay. I will continue anyway.

Lastly, I toast to another day of living in recovery and I toast to being able to say: Hello Life!

******

Day 286: The Odds Are in My Favor

Have you ever internalized something so deep within yourself that it has made its way into your subconscious and hasn't only taunted you during the day, but has followed you in your dreams as you sleep?

That is what had happened to me the previous night. I had a dream about my body hurting and aching from the food I had eaten and I had dreamt that I woke up in pain.

To no surprise, when I had woken up this morning feeling totally unrested and worn out, I had felt exactly how I felt in my dream – sore and in pain, and mentally exhausted from having to deal with the lies that Ed was feeding me every time my body hurt from somewhat overeating.

Sunday, November 3

Sometimes this physical pain doesn't bother me, but today it really does. It's one thing for Ed to whisper things to me about food or about what I am eating or doing to my body during the day, but to have dreams about it is truly a battle where I have no armor to defend myself.

Every time I try to think positive today, I move my body one inch and I am reminded of the physical pain that I am still dealing with during recovery.

It's the pain that my body has to go through to heal itself from the torment that Ed put it through. It's the pain that he tries to use against me week after week. It's the pain he tries to use as a strategic tool to get me to restrict, which doesn't work, but nonetheless, it's still something I need to fight.

Today is just not my day. I don't feel good about the way I look. I don't feel good about eating, which has made it an extremely mentally hard task to do today. And I don't feel good about the homework I still have left to do, even though I have spent six hours working already.

I know that everyone has bad days – eating disorder or no eating disorder, people have bad days. I know that a bad day doesn't have to mean a bad night, or even a bad week. I know all of that, but for this one exact moment as I write this post, I don't have it within me to say the right words of inspiration or encouragement today.

Truly, all I can do is sit here and write to you all about my honest feelings. My feelings are that today really sucks. But on the other hand, yesterday was a good day (prior to coming home and dreaming about my body soreness), and the day before yesterday was overall a good day because I cut myself some slack.

So in the bigger picture, a 2:1 ratio of good to bad days is actually not that bad. It doesn't make today any easier, but it gives me hope that tomorrow my ratio will work in my favor and it will be a good day again.

Of course, there is nothing guaranteeing that, but the odds are in my favor.

Hello Life!

******

Day 287: The Little Boy Who Made Today a Better Day

I had said yesterday that the odds were in my favor that today would be a good day. While today hadn't necessarily been a good day, it had been 100% a better day.

There would have been a point where only being a 'better day' wasn't good enough for me, and I would have strived and wished and desired for more. But I had come to learn to be accepting of things in recovery and in life, just the way they were.

So if better was what I would get today, then better it was. Yes, it would have been nice if it had been a good or great day, or one of those days where I was just in love with recovery, but for now better was what I was going to be accepting of and grateful for.

In all honestly, better was better than having another bad day, right?

Monday, November 4

Today was better for pretty much one reason only and it had nothing to do with how I feel about my body or food, because that is kind of at the same status that it was yesterday.

The reason today was better is because I was able to be of service today and to make someone else happy. When I do that, it helps all those terrible things that Ed tells me about myself slightly lessen because it reminds me that my self-worth is based not on my physical being, but based on my inner soul.

Today I was able to give the 2nd-grade boy I tutor a certificate for completing his reading comprehension workbook that he has been working on with me for months. He was so happy that it was officially signed and dated, and he felt so accomplished that he went and taped it up on his bedroom door and yelled for his mom to come see it.

To know that I was a part of making that boy's day that much brighter reminded me that I am not this undisciplined and worthless person that Ed tells me I am because the way my body looks is not what I am loving right now.

It reminded me, that to this kid at least, I was worth enough that signing this piece of paper made him feel validated and proud of himself.

So if this is what a better day looks like, then actually I don't even need a good day at the moment. Imagining him smiling as he taped that certificate on his wall, not caring at all about what I looked like, but only caring about the fact that I, his smart tutor who he respects, acknowledged his hard work and therefore made him so happy, makes this better day pretty damn close to good.

Hello Life!

******

Day 288: The Dinner that Put Everything in Perspective

I had been sitting at dinner this night with my grandma and my sister, totally over-thinking about what to order and how to work it off the next day at the gym ... blah blah blah ... all those Ed-related thoughts. Then out of nowhere I had seen the older man at the table next to us stand up violently and pick up the table where his wife was sitting at the other end. (I assumed it was his wife.)

"I wish I could beat the living hell out of you right now," he told her. Then he picked the table up once more and walked out of the restaurant for a cigarette.

Suddenly, the major problems that I thought I had two minutes before about what food I was about to eat, were not so major anymore. They were gone. They were nothing.

I looked at my sister and my grandma and we sat there in silence. We were all equally disturbed. I didn't even know how I would eat when our food came because I had literally lost my appetite watching that. I wanted to go and steal that woman from her table and have her sit with us and come stay with us.

Both she and the man were in their late 60s, and to think that she possibly had endured that kind of treatment for so long ate away at the deepest part of me. She just sat at that table and waited for him to come back – so trapped and so stuck.

When her husband had come back and they had acted like nothing happened, I tried to ignore it.

Tuesday, November 5

Now that I write this, I can't ignore the parallel that was being presented to me at that moment at dinner tonight. I had just witnessed someone being a prisoner in their own life to someone treating them so inhumanely, and there I was, sitting at a dinner table with my family ordering food I never would have ordered eight months ago, living in the act of freedom that recovery has slowly brought me.

So that leaves me with two things on my mind right now:

1. Stupid, stupid, stupid Ed.

I am angry at him for letting me think that his issues, such as what I ate today or what I looked like, are what matter in life, when the woman across from me at a restaurant is being told by the man she is with that he wishes he could beat her up.

2. I am sad for this woman.

She very obviously is not getting a new life. This is her life. And me ... I am on my way to creating a new life for myself. I get to continue on my journey to self-acceptance and true happiness and she gets to live the rest of her life like that? Why? Why is it that some of us get the blessing of fighting for a better life for ourselves and some of us don't?

If my biggest issue is dealing with how I will get over all the unsafe foods I ate today, then, honestly, I am grateful. These are issues that I am dealing with so I can win back my freedom – something that woman will probably never get to do.

I don't even know the right way to end this post with "Hello Life" when the life I am thinking about right now is that woman's life and how sad for her I am.

Ed, truly, you may burn me with your taunting words about what I eat, but you will never make me your prisoner again. You will never own me again. And guess what Ed? At least for today I have realized that you are a small tiny problem compared to the things I saw at this dinner, and for that realization I am grateful.

And this is not to minimize any of the heartache or pain that Ed causes for me or anyone else, but it helped put things in perspective for the moment.

Hello to putting things in perspective, hello to continuing to fight for a life of freedom, and Hello Life!

******

Day 289: She Is Living Proof that Hope Exists

Today's post had nothing to do with food, calories or scales. Today's post was to do with hope.

Wednesday, November 6

As part of my senior project in one of my classes this semester, I have to present someone's history to my class. So today I had the honor of sitting down with the woman who I chose to present and hear her story.

I have known her since I can remember, as she was my neighbor when I was growing up, and over the years she became family. During my entire journey of this year without a scale, she has been an undeniable source of strength and wisdom for me and she has come to know my entire story as I am writing it every day, yet I never knew hers.

I could write pages about the things I learned from her today, but to sum it up for this blog post's sake, I will leave you with the most important elements.

This woman is truly the definition of a fighter and a conqueror, and let me tell you why. She experienced an extremely unfair and unjust childhood, she didn't have an easy adulthood and she never had anything handed to her. She could have let life defeat her. She could have let her own Ed (whatever kind of monster he may be ... doesn't have to be with food) defeat her. But she didn't.

She told me that it took her until the age of fifty to learn a lot of life's major lessons, such as that everything happens for a reason and that there is strength behind that. At the same time, she told me how happy she was for me that I am getting my life together at the age of twenty-three, at the very beginning of it.

Lesson One: It's never too late to change your life. It's never too late to change your destiny. And it's never too early to start either. Regardless of the place in life anyone reading this is at, it's never too late to strive for the changes we know we deserve.

At the age of seventy (how old she is now) she has signed a book deal where she will publish three books, and on January 7, 2014, her first published book will be hitting bookshelves. She said that this is the most accomplished she has ever felt in her entire life, as well as the most proud of herself she has ever felt.

Now, keep in mind, this book is partially a memoir about herself, tied with a mystery story. It was her way of using her hard life experiences and turning them into something for other people to read, learn from and enjoy.

Writing this book, along with quilting that she also does, gave her a chance to reflect back on the hard things she endured as a child and as an adult, and it helped her turn those negative experiences into something she learned from, something that healed her, and into something that inspired her.

This woman is hope. She is living proof that hope exists.

Lesson Two: She is living proof that regardless of the fight each of us is fighting, whether it be an eating disorder or any other fight that life has told us we need to become warriors for, she is proof that it's possible to not only use our suffering and pain as a way to grow, but proof that it's possible to find self-acceptance and happiness at the end of it all. Above all, she was a fighter turned conqueror.

I left her house, the house that I once sat in every Wednesday afternoon and quilted dresses for my dolls, leaving truly inspired. One day I will be a conqueror too.

Hello Life!

******

Day 290: Bon Appétit to Me

I only had two things to say today. Ed had been really quiet. He had let me eat in peace for the majority of my day and I hadn't been too absorbed in him and his lies.

Secondly, I was about to go to a friend's house, who was cooking me some delicious Russian food – one of my favorite foods. May I add that it was a very unsafe food as it's made with many delicious calorific ingredients that Ed hated, but I was going anyway and I was actually excited for it.

Thursday, November 7

Who would have thought that nine months ago I would have said that I am excited to go eat some unapproved Ed food?!

I don't take days like today where I get to live in a few breaths of freedom for granted. I am grateful, I am appreciative and I am excited to tell you all tomorrow about my dinner that I am heading out to right now.

Bon appétit to me (no Ed, you are not invited).
Hello Life!

******

Day 291: So I May Wear Leggings All Weekend

My dinner the previous night had been delicious. It was so yummy and it had been truly a great time – absolutely free of Ed. It had been truly a night of freedom and I was so deeply grateful for it. It was nights like last night that reminded me of why recovery was so worth fighting for.

So moving on to today ...

Friday, November 8

You all know the drill by now when I indulge in food or eat a little too much ... my body gets sore and I get bloated. Usually this only happens to me after my Friday and Saturday night dinners with family and friends, but this week I guess I started one day early.

Actually, I kind of started a few days early because I ate out at a restaurant on Tuesday night too. Let's just say I had an early start to my weekend indulgence.

When I woke up today and felt the soreness and bloating, I had two options:

1. I could freak out over it, go to the gym instead of going to see E, really, really eat very safe today, be worried about my dinner tonight and all the food that would be surrounding me this weekend.

Or

2. I could just accept what is and enjoy my weekend with the food, bloating and soreness as best as I can. One way to do that is to wear clothes that I know I will feel good in and clothes that will be forgiving. So leggings it is.

I wore leggings today. I will wear them tomorrow. I will probably wear them on Sunday and maybe even Monday (thankfully I have multiple pairs).

They don't have a size on them and they don't have tight waistbands, therefore they can't make me feel worse on days like today.

I am not saying it's been easy to live in the moment and to stay positive today when it's inevitable that I am sore and bloated and when I know I have many more encounters with food coming up, but it beats cuddling up with Ed.

So if wearing leggings for a few days is the worst thing I have to deal with this week in terms of Ed, then I can do that.

Hello to my stretchy, no size, comfy leggings, and Hello Life!

******

Day 292: Staying in the Moment and Still Wearing Leggings

It hadn't been easy to stay positive and in the moment for various Ed reasons today, but the point is that I did anyway.

Saturday, November 9

I apologize in advance for this post being so short, but my brother just had another MMA fight tonight and won, and I am now waiting to celebrate with him and my family at home. So because I don't want to take away from his night, this post will be rather short.

Tonight is not about me, it's about him and his hard-fought earned victory. It's not about Ed and what he wants. And when that pizza gets delivered in twenty minutes, Ed has no say.

So because tonight is about staying in the moment, which is also a part of recovery, I am going to leave this post at that.

And for the record, I am still happily wearing my leggings.
Hello Life!

******

Day 293: The Day I Totally Forgot that Fitness and Food Magazines Exist

I had woken up early this day to my neighbors doing some kind of construction work, making it impossible for me to sleep in or to study, so despite my body still feeling sore and uncomfortable, I got out of bed and decided to go to the library.

I had to wait an hour and a half for opening time, only to see a lady post a sign on the door that said the library was closed for the holiday weekend.

We all have these kinds of days, right? The days where everything around you seems to be going against the current that you are trying to travel by.

But instead of being discouraged, I had decided to walk around in the bookstore nearby. I used to love books as a kid. I was the ten-year-old who asked for books for my holiday presents; they were a way into someone else's world.

Sunday, November 10

Today, as I was walking around in the bookstore, I was just overtaken by this feeling of joy. I got to see so many different books about so many different things. I saw one about tattoos and their hidden meanings, I saw one about all the front-page covers of Time Magazine *and I even saw one on some of the world's greatest motivational speakers.*

It was a total escape out of my world. It was an escape from my body soreness. It was an escape from the things that had gone wrong that morning. It was an escape from Ed and thinking about food and what to eat. It was an escape from the stories I am writing or the homework I have to do.

It was this sense of joy that our world is truly filled with so many more stories than just our own. It was this realization that there is passion in things that don't just have to do with food.

There were times when I would spend hours online just looking at recipes and saving them. I would spend hours looking at cookbooks in bookstores and never buy them.

When I was locked in my eating disorder, food was the only thing I had an interest in. It sounds ironic, but it's true. I would only read cooking magazines or, if I was at the bookstore, I would sit at Starbucks and get a big huge stack of health and fitness magazines.

But today wasn't like that. Now that I think of it, I didn't even go to the magazine section. I was so in awe of all the books about art, dreams and hidden meanings that I forgot those cookbooks and fitness magazines even existed. I mean, really, I can't believe I forgot to go check those magazines out. It doesn't even seem like me.

It's a beautiful thing to be reminded of the other stories that exist; of the stories about art, people and history, that Ed just has nothing to do with.

Now that I write this post, I think that the library being closed today was a blessing in disguise. Had it been open, I would have sat in there and studied all day. But instead I had the chance to venture around in a bookstore and be reminded of all the things that interest me and intrigue me that don't have to do with Ed.

Life has a way of surprising us sometimes, and the more I learn to accept what is, the more beauty I see in that. I even had someone ask me today where she can buy a Hello Life bracelet, another beautiful surprise.

Hello to the small blessings in disguise that we sometimes don't see until later. Hello to being able to escape from Ed while in the bookstore. Hello to still wearing leggings today (well, jeggings, but it's the same). Hello to not even thinking about the food or fitness magazines. And Hello Life!

******

Day 294: Today's Scorecard: Shira 3, Ed 0

Because today was Veterans Day, a federal holiday, a lot of the US had the day off work and school.

Before I began writing about the day, I had to thank any veterans reading my post, as I knew there were a few who followed my blog. I thanked them for their service, courage and bravery.

Monday, November 11

Because my university was closed today, it didn't feel like a typical Monday. To begin with, I didn't work out today, which is something I usually do on Mondays after I indulge over the weekend. But the truth is, I did my hair yesterday and it still looked really good this morning, and I knew if I went to work out it wouldn't look good anymore, then I would have to redo it after I showered. I know this may sound crazy, but today Ed was just not worth ruining my cute hair, so I decided to not workout.

Scorecard: Shira 1, Ed 0.

Not working out was just the start to my mini Monday vacation that I had today.

After seeing E, I came home and my grandma and sister were going to lunch, then going shopping. Needless to say, I really wanted to go with them. So, despite my usual type-A controlled personality, I cancelled both my tutoring sessions for today (and let's hope the parents never find this blog and find out I lied about being tied up in an interview for a story I am writing), and I decided to go with them.

Part two of my Monday vay-cay was lunch with my grandma and my sister. Yes, lunch. On a Monday and not on the weekend, and not even on a day that I worked out.

Scorecard: Shira 2, Ed 0.

Part 3 of my Monday vacation was shopping. I didn't go for my old 'sick' size. No, I went for my new healthier size.

It wasn't easy. There were one pair of pants that didn't even go up my leg. There was one shirt that could have ripped off me had I turned one wrong inch. But it was okay. I was okay. The moment passed.

And, to my pleasure, my sister's pants didn't zip up on her either, and while she doesn't suffer from an eating disorder, so that doesn't affect her in the same way, she was able to look at the pants and laugh about how poorly made they were. So I did that too. Stupid, poorly made pants. Them not fitting me doesn't mean anything.

How ironic is it that last time I was in this store was the day that I weighed least in all of my eating disorder, only to go back now *walking in there with recovery on my side. And walking out laughing at the pants that didn't go up even a quarter of my leg. Scorecard: Shira 3, Ed 0.*

So, yes, even after five days of pretty much eating what I have wanted, three days of body soreness because of it, and four days of not working out, I still gave myself a Monday vacation.

And Ed got a vacation today too. Well, okay, not a vacation he wanted, it was more of a lay-off or firing, but I just didn't want him around today.

Hello to the scorecard being 3-0, and in my favor. Hello to Monday vacations. And Hello Life!

******

Day 295: Being a Recovery Olympian

I normally used to go the gym if I was going to work out, but this day I decided to go running outside on a hiking path that I really liked.

As I was running, I was reminded of how I felt when I ran cross-country in high school. I had initially joined the cross-country team for Ed, because he told me to find some kind of exercise, but once I started it, it wasn't about Ed anymore. It became about my team. It became about beating my best time. It became about learning how to listen to my body, how to fuel it, and how to make it run as efficiently as it could.

Tuesday, November 12

When I was running today, I could literally hear my old coach telling me from the sidelines, "You are tall, you are strong, you are beautiful."

I was honestly not thinking about calories, numbers or miles today. I was stuck back in the 11th grade, with my other cross-country girls, just trying to enjoy the feeling of running. And just for the record, I wasn't even one of the fast runners on the team who won us any titles. I was the one who came in second or third to last, and truly pushed myself for even that. But I was known for my perseverance, a quality that I think has gotten me through a lot of rough days in recovery.

So there I was today, running, imagining that I looked like some kind of Olympic superstar, while we all know we never look like that while huffing and puffing as we run hard, but it was nice to imagine. Then, out of nowhere, I tripped and fell over a rock and landed right on my face.

The Olympian moment was over and now I was back in real life. My real life where, yes, sometimes I start to feel like I am flying, then I fall. But isn't that everyone's life?

Anyway, as I limped my way back to my car with my two scraped and now severely bruised knees, and two fake nails broken in half (most painful part), I realized something. And no, I am not about to use the metaphor, 'when you fall, pick yourself back up', although that did cross my mind too.

I realized that for the first time in a long time, when I was done exercising (obviously I was very done after my fall), I wasn't even mad that my run was cut short because I fell. I wasn't mad that I couldn't spend more time burning calories. I wasn't mad that my one hour of running turned into thirty minutes.

I was mad that my nails broke, that my phone fell in the dirt and that my knees hurt. Don't get me wrong, those are not fabulous things and in no way am I happy about it, but I am actually really happy with myself that I was mad at that, instead of being mad that my exercising got cut short.

That is recovery. To care more about myself and my body (from my knees to my nails), is recovery. That is self-care 101 and it's something that Ed knows nothing about. However, it's something that I know about now.

And now that I write this, I honestly still think I was like a mini Olympian today. I finished my own race. While it might have been flat on my face, it was my way, and it was without Ed judging me for it.

Who knew I would ever be more upset over some broken nails and cut-up knees than about not being able to run and burn more calories? That sounds like a recovery Olympian to me.

Hello Life!

******

Day 296: Hello Dear Ice Cream

What did I have to say today? Truthfully, I didn't really know when it came to writing my blog.

I could have sat and thought of some inspiring quote I had found online or something of that sort, then relate it to recovery in some kind of way. But my blog was a daily journal of my daily life in recovery so if I had done that just in the hope of writing an inspirational post, it wouldn't have been authentic.

So today's post was boring and uneventful, yet authentic.

Wednesday, November 13

I honestly felt huge today. I really did and for various reasons. I haven't been eating that healthily and I haven't worked out as much lately, so this is not a surprise to me. I think even people who don't have eating disorders have days like this.

And, for the past two days, I have been hungry all the time. And I mean all of the time. But instead of being mad about that, as at one time I would have been (I actually remember a time in the beginning of recovery where I was mad at myself for eating five extra almonds because I was extra hungry), I have learned to kind of laugh at it and to just go with the flow.

Over time, I am slowly learning to trust my body. So, if it's hungry, it's hungry. If it wants to eat two snacks instead of one, which it did both yesterday and today, I will have to let it do so. And if it wants to eat ice cream for dessert every night (a reoccurring theme for the past three days) then I guess I am going to let it do that too.

At first, when I woke up this morning feeling huge, I told myself that I am not eating any sweets or any ice cream today. But that didn't last for long, because I love chocolate, and now that I am writing this I really want that ice cream again.

We have two really amazing flavors in the freezer too (thank you to my sister). So, knowing myself and my sweet tooth, I already know I am going to end up eating it.

And while my day is still uneventful and maybe hasn't led me to writing the most inspiring of posts, it did leave me with two things to be grateful for: I felt huge today, yet I continued on with my day and ate what my body asked for anyway, and I am giving myself permission to eat ice cream for the fourth night in a row.

Hello dear ice cream, and Hello Life!

******

Day 297: It's Just a Day, Not My Life

What a day it had been today. The previous day I had said I felt huge, yet I had been able to kind of push it aside and not let it bother me as much. Well today it was bothering me a lot more. A lot, lot, lot more.

Thursday, November 14

I had a job interview today, which meant I needed to go find my nice work clothes – clothes that I haven't worn in a very long time. But ironically, I actually used to wear those clothes when I wasn't in my eating disorder, so I thought that they couldn't be triggering. But they were.

Naturally I had to try every single thing on; every skirt, every pair of pants, every shirt – just everything. And when the pants that I tried on that used to fit snug on me when I was X weight, now fit me the same way, it made me wonder whether I weigh the same now as when I last wore them (not a number I like).

I don't need to describe this whirl wind of events that occurred after that because I am sure by now you all know what happened. I stood in front of the mirror and tried to think of what I weigh now, what I weighed last time I wore them, and how big I look.

What can I say? I thought about it for quite a while, then I had to go get ready and leave, so I just left the thought where it was. I am still not sure what I think about it, but I don't like it.

Moving on to my job interview, which took place an hour after my mini guess the weight game with myself and Ed. I was grilled in this interview. Four people interviewed me, asking me questions as if I wasn't qualified for the job that they had called me in to do the interview for.

No small enough weight in the world could have saved me from that hard interview today. I left there wondering whether I wasn't up to par with what they wanted in a candidate for this job.

Combine not feeling up to par with people's expectations of you with feeling huge and trying to estimate my weight a few hours earlier, and it's safe to say that today hasn't been the most fabulous of days.

However, it's just a day, not my life. On to tomorrow. On to the next interview (okay, well wishful thinking, but let's hope there will be other interviews). On to another day where even if I spend all day trying to guess my weight, I will never know it. On to another day of hard-earned recovery.

For anyone else not having the greatest of days today, on to tomorrow we go. Hello Life!

******

Day 298: Is This Real Life?

I had to apologize for writing such a late post, as I had just been so busy and was late home.

Despite all my negative feelings about the way I looked, today had been a big stomp on Ed day, as I explained in my blog.

Friday, November 15

There were three particular moments where I stomped on Ed today.

Moment number one: I went to lunch with a friend, and my friend wasn't Ed, it was my friend Anna. We had lunch together, then we went to a bakery and shared a piece of cake with some coffee.

Moment number two: I ate cake ... as a dessert ... after lunch. This is pretty much a self-explanatory moment and one of my favorite moments of the day because I love cake.

The best part about this moment is that when I tasted the cake and found that it actually wasn't that good, my friend and I went to a liquor store nearby and picked up a chocolate bar to make up for it.

Moment number three: I was at a basketball game with my grandma, cousin and sister, when it came time to get food. For years now I have either taken my own 'Ed food' to the basketball game, or I haven't gotten anything to eat all.

My sister always gets pizza from California Pizza Kitchen at the basketball games, and sometimes, just sometimes, I used to let myself eat a bite of her crust that she didn't want.

Today I shared a pizza with my grandma and had some other snacks. I had an entire two pieces of pizza to myself. This was the first time in years that I can remember eating the same food as everyone else at a basketball game.

While I have learned that recovery is about far more than just food, today food was a big part of it. It was a big part of it because it gave me a social life.

Lunch with a friend was part of being social. Eating cake together was part of being social. Eating pizza with everyone else at the basketball game, that wasn't only social, but that was feeling like I was just like everyone else – it was comforting.

Are these moments scary? Yes. Oh, yes they are. Am I loving how my body feels right now? Nope. Not at all. But I had three moments of recovery today. Three moments of freedom. Three moments of Shira in charge, not Ed. Three moments towards the rest of my new life in recovery.

I mean ... cake, candy and pizza in one day? Is this real life? I guess in recovery it is.

Hello Life!

******

Day 299: I Cried Today, but Not Because of Ed

Today had been low key. I had almost cried two times today ... well, one a half times. One time I really had cried, the second time it was just me hyperventilating with that knot in my throat, but I didn't cry again. So let's just say I had cried one a half times.

Here is the recovery niche of that statement: I hadn't cried over my body, or Ed, or what food I had eaten, or the food I had eaten the previous day, or what I looked like in the mirror. I had cried because I honestly had so much homework to do and so many things to fix on the latest articles that I was writing and absolutely not enough brain power or time to do it all at once.

Saturday, November 16

Sometimes, when I get overwhelmed, Ed comes to comfort me. But today he didn't. He didn't because I didn't let him, and I didn't let him because having him come into the picture will only make me cry more tomorrow.

Not to sound totally crazy here, but having a day where I am stressed out, or a day where I even cried over something totally not related to my body, to calories or to food, is kind of refreshing.

Those readers who are struggling with eating disorders may understand this a little bit better. When I was locked in my eating disorder, everything revolved around it. Everything from food, to weight, to what I wore that day, to how I felt that day. My emotions were once (and sometimes still are) regulated by Ed and what he told me to feel that day.

If I weighed a 'good enough' number, he would tell me I could be happy. If I weighed a 'bad number' he would tell me to be stressed, angry and sad. And that was pretty much the entire range of emotions I ever felt when I was in my lowest point with Ed.

I never cried though. And if I did cry, I cried alone at night, by myself in bed, when my heart would beat really slow and I would get scared about what I was doing to my body.

So the fact that I cried today not because of anything Ed-related, but because I was stressed out about something absolutely not related to him is actually a great thing. I am moving on to new stressors that are not about my eating disorder.

No stress is ever fun, and I am in no way happy that I cried, because obviously I am having a mini freak-out about how I will handle all this work in such little time, but I am able to see what this means. This means life after Ed.

Also, I just want to say thank you to everyone who emailed me and told me they received their Hello Life bracelets today. I haven't had a chance to respond, because as you can tell by this post, I have been stressing out today, but I promise to respond soon and I really appreciate you taking the time to let me know you received them.

I guess it's not really low key that I cried anymore because hundreds of people now know, but I don't care. You are the same people who know that I have cried because of Ed, so why not tell you when I cry because of other things not about him?

It's kind of refreshing to read, right? For what it's worth, it's refreshing to feel.

Hello Life!

******

Day 300: Impossible No Longer Exists

Today we had celebrated our last milestone together until sixty-five days later, when we would reach one entire year without a scale and my very last blog post.

Today we had celebrated three hundred days of being without a scale. Three hundred days of hope, inner strength and self-acceptance. But most importantly, today we had celebrated three hundred days of humanity. Three hundred days of people coming together from all around the world to support, love and encourage one another.

I say 'we' had celebrated today, as opposed to saying just I, because this blog had become the journey of so many. It had become my journey, my readers' journey, my struggles and their struggles, all wrapped up in one online community who had come together to support one another.

Today, we had celebrated doing the impossible.

Sunday, November 17

If someone had told me three hundred days ago that I could go even one day without my scale, I would have never believed them. There were days where I couldn't even go one hour without my scale, so to now make it to Day 300 of being without it and of being in recovery, I can honestly say that we have defeated the impossible.

Ed was my impossible. With Ed, living was impossible, laughter was impossible, close relationships were impossible and, mostly, loving myself was impossible.

Three hundred days of fighting for my freedom from this eating disorder later, and I can truly say that those things haven't only become possible, but they have become my reality.

Obviously, you know by reading my posts, that not every day is a happy reality and not every day is easy. I actually think it's safe to say that there are more hard days than easy days. But without suffering and without hardship, there is no growth.

So here is to all of us fighters, not just those with eating disorders, who are learning to grow through our pain. Here is to three hundred days – let me repeat, THREE HUNDRED DAYS – of believing in myself enough, that even on my hardest days I never turned back to Ed.

Here is to three hundred days of you all believing in me enough to never stop supporting me, even on the days that I didn't know how to support myself.

Here is to the beauty of humankind, to the love of strangers who have now become friends through this blog, and to the strength in numbers that we all get from supporting one another.

Here is to the last sixty-five days that we have to journey, grow and learn from one another. Here is to the next sixty-five days of finding our paths to self-acceptance, self-love and self-compassion.

If you are reading this blog post right now, thank you for being a part of my journey.

Three hundred days of fighting for freedom from Ed. Three hundred days of defeating what I once thought was impossible.

I don't know what else to say. Three hundred days guys. Impossible no longer exists.

Hello Life!

******

Day 301: It's the Little Things

I don't know what had brought this on, but I really had been able to appreciate the small gifts of recovery on this day. And it was nothing big or major like 'I am so happy that I finally accept my new healthy body' (because I was far from that point), but it was more of those small moments of joy and simplicity that I knew I would never have even noticed before I started recovery.

Monday, November 18

Before I started recovery, I still tutored; however, I would always mentally prepare myself for how I would get through the session with refusing food from the parents/nannies who would love to feed me.

Today I enjoyed two amazing chocolates that one of the nannies gave me. It was small, but so liberating, so yummy, so me and not Ed.

Last year I only let myself have a chocolate one time at this girl's house and that was on my birthday. So to enjoy those two chocolates today was really empowering and the fact that I could realize that is a beautiful thing to me that speaks volumes about my recovery.

I also used half and half in my tea today because Starbucks didn't have milk out. Before, I would have gone up to the counter to ask for some alternative, but today I used the half and half. Half and half! Cream! Deliciousness – all for me, and none for Ed.

Today I found one of the nicest girls at school, who let me interview her for a story I am writing. After twenty students walking away from me, finding her was more than just a little thing, it was a major gift.

Today I didn't even get to do cardio, yet I ate my chocolates anyway.

Today taught me that it's truly the little things in life that sometimes force us to step back and realize how far we have come. It's the two little chocolates during a tutoring session. It's the half and half in a cup of tea. It's the nice girl who offered to take her time to interview me. These moments make up freedom.

You know who else was a little thing today? Ed. Yup, Ed was a tiny, little, minuscule thing today.

To all the little things that make recovery worth fighting for ... hello to you all, and Hello Life!

******

Day 302: Figuring Out Self-Acceptance

Before I began the day's post, I needed to address something that I had gotten a lot of emails and a few comments about recently. There had been a lot of people emailing and asking about what was going to happen after we reached the one-year mark of my blog.

While I didn't plan to continue to blog daily after my journey came to a close, and a new one would begin, I wanted everyone to know that my blog would remain active, meaning the blog would still be available online, anyone would still be able to comment or contact me, and I would send updates to let everyone know how I was doing in terms of recovery. I would never want anyone to think that because I no longer blogged, it meant I had gone back to Ed.

Another blogger and fighter had given me the idea of creating a page explaining what would happen after we reached our one-year mark, and I really loved that idea. So I had decided to create a page about it in more detail once the blog was a little more towards its one-year end and once I had figured out the little things, such as how often I would update, etc.

I also mentioned that I would like to put a poll up asking my readers what to do with my scale once the year ended. Even though I would no longer be blogging every day, I for sure would never go back to my scale. However, E had my scale and I felt as if I needed to do something with it. I wasn't sure if I wanted to bury it, smash it, or have some kind of ceremony for it, so I was going to let everyone vote and decide.

Tuesday, November 19

Today I gave a presentation in my class that was worth 50 percent of my grade and it went along with an entire research paper. I chose to present about the negative impact that media has on children's body image. I know, no surprise that I chose this topic.

As I was doing my research, all the studies showed how so many kids at such a young age are starting to feel insignificant and worthless because they think that they don't look like the people they see in the media.

It broke my heart to not only think about us as adults who are struggling with eating disorders, but to think of the small kids who I was presenting about that research showed were dieting and exercising, trying to look like these airbrushed celebrities.

I wished I could go and find all of them, hug them and tell them they are just exactly right the way they are. I don't want to use the word 'perfect' because I no longer believe in perfection. But knowing how horrible it feels to compare myself to others around me during my eating disorder and even now, it made me so sad to think of kids doing the same thing.

But this was a crush for Ed. Stupid, stupid Ed. Eds all around the world are born from these kinds of thoughts. The thoughts of "I don't look good enough," or "I am not enough." It devastates me to know that kids are having these thoughts too.

I used to have these thoughts as a child, so I know how it feels. I don't think there is a solution really to any of this other than spreading awareness, and I don't mean awareness about the media or about eating disorders, but about loving ourselves. When will it be acceptable to love ourselves just the way we are? I am three hundred and two days into my journey of figuring that out, and I still have a while to go.

I guess all we can do in the meantime is keep trying to fit all the pieces of self-acceptance together into the crazy puzzle that we call life.

Hello to another day of figuring it all out, and Hello Life!

******

Day 303: I Am Only Human

By today I had added the two pages I had been talking about the previous day. I was very excited to say that I had added a page that had the poll about what to do with my scale after we reached the one-year mark.

The voting would be open until January 21, literally until the moment I wrote the last post, so I asked everyone to please share their opinions with me as I was really looking forward to seeing what the end result would be.

Wednesday, November 20

If you all remember, I wrote a post last Thursday about how I went to a job interview where they grilled me pretty hard. Let me just start by saying that even though I didn't want this job, because it was on Saturdays and Sundays from 3p.m. until midnight, I still had high hopes for it.

So you can imagine my disappointment when I found out today that I didn't get it. Actually, maybe you can't imagine it, considering I just said I didn't even want it, because, truthfully, I didn't even understand myself why I was sad that I didn't get it. I mean ... I told everyone who knows me I didn't want it, so why was I sad to not get it?

While I am happy to report I didn't spend two whole days crying over this rejection like I did over NBC, I still cried a little. I don't know why, but lately I am like a little ball of emotions. But I guess that is better than being numb and only seeing, tasting and breathing Ed – a world where emotions don't even exist.

So anyway, as I was kind of pathetically crying in my car, I realized I wasn't crying over this job. I was crying for two reasons: Because this leaves me back in the unknown, and because I feel rejected.

Whether you have an eating disorder or not, being in a transitional phase in life where nothing is known for sure is very scary. Me struggling with Ed only makes it that much harder because I have to fight to not use him as my coping mechanism for those fears.

For me, the worst part is being rejected. I am starting to feel like those litters of cats you see in boxes on the sidewalk who just want someone to pick them up but instead people just keep walking by. What if no job wants me? On top of not having Ed, now I have to think that I might not have a job. Okay, I am being a little dramatic with my cat metaphor, but what can I say, it's how I feel at the moment.

With NBC, we were all able to sit here and say, "Stupid NBC, you are better than them, Shira." We had tons of comments and emails saying that, and I really loved it because it made me feel much better. But can we really say this employer was dumb too? Is it them or is it me?

While I was driving and slightly still crying, I was able to have this epiphany that even if I was a size 000000 today and even if I weighed my lowest weight yet, I still wouldn't have gotten those jobs. I realized that Ed can't fix everything – actually, he can't fix anything. All he can do is be a temporary mask for me to wear while I blind myself from life.

Well, I didn't turn to Ed today, therefore I am not blinded. I can very clearly see that I am about to embark on a whole new journey of its own, far past just recovery. It's transitioning into a new part of my life, graduating college and starting my career, and doing it without Ed. It's a lot to take on.

I can also clearly see that this won't be my first job rejection, and that I might just have to be okay with being a little wrapped-up ball of emotions for now. If I cry, I guess I will cry. I am entering the unknown yet again, and this time without Ed by my side. I am entitled to some tears, to some fears and to some anxiety, right?

Ed doesn't let anyone feel entitled to any kinds of feelings; he only lets you feel undeserving. But I am deserving of all of those emotions, and I am also deserving of giving myself a little bit of compassion.

Today was only my second rejection. Yes, it sucks. Two rejections in a row suck. And yeah, maybe I cried over it. But hey, I am only human, right? Despite what our Eds all tell us, does anyone really expect us to land the first job, or the second, or maybe even the tenth job?

It's just like recovery. Does anyone really expect us to do it perfectly the whole time? Although we might want to, I think we quickly learn that it's impossible to do that.

Ed doesn't believe in human error, because how could he? He lives and breathes perfection. I don't live like that anymore. It's a hard pattern of thinking to break free of, but I am on my way.

On to the next job interview. On with life.

Hello Life!

******

Day 304: The Best Breakfast Break Ever

I had woken up on this morning at 6a.m. to do an at-home workout that my trainer had given me to do. I had it all written down, it was all planned and I was ready to go.

I had even put a picture of the written exercise plan on my Instagram and personal Facebook page. I don't know why I had done that, because I later deleted it because this 'gym rat' vibe that picture gave off was far from who I was or who I wanted to be.

But, anyway, I was tired and hadn't felt like doing it, but I guess Ed had kind of partially told me to.

Thursday, November 21

When I tried to do my at-home workout in the living room, I felt so closed in. I needed to be outside. Only when I went outside, it was raining and wet. So what did this mean? It meant I was over this whole at-home workout and Ed could just get over it too.

And I was hungry. So I told myself I would take a breakfast break and then finish the workout after.

Well, the breakfast break turned into a shower and nap break, which then never led back to the workout. It was the best breakfast break ever, because it kind of stayed a break for hours.

I still went on to eat foods very much out of my comfort zone today, which doesn't physically feel so great right now, but I am alive, I am breathing and it will pass.

On top of this breakfast break turned nap break, I also got my new shipment of Hello Life bracelets today. Almost half of them are already gone, which is insane because who knew it was possible to truly form such a strong community through one blog?

Also, so far from the voting about what to do with my scale, it looks like the majority of people are ready to smash it to pieces. But I guess we will see in time.

Today I say hello to the best breakfast break ever and to another day of recovery.

Hello Life!

******

Day 305: Just Me and My Brownie Pop

I had been having lunch with my sister on this day, when right after we were done, I really wanted something sweet and she didn't have the time to get dessert with me. So I had tried all the alternatives, such as chewing gum, eating an orange, having a tic tac ... nothing had worked.

Ed had been practically shoving those things in my face, telling me that they counted as dessert, when really, let's be honest, they didn't count for anything but boringness. Pure and utter boringness.

Friday, November 22

I sat in my car for about ten minutes thinking about what to do, then I just decided that I was driving myself to the bakery to get a dessert, hopefully a brownie because that was what I was craving.
It didn't matter that it was after lunch, it didn't matter that it wasn't a Saturday or Sunday and it didn't matter that it wasn't part of my meal plan or that it wasn't snack time yet. I was just going to do it.
So I walked into the bakery and, to my surprise, all the good stuff was nearly gone. I really wanted a brownie but I didn't see any left. Maybe this was because it was 3p.m. on a Friday, I am not sure.
But then I saw this perfectly beautiful brownie pop covered in edible flowers and it was just asking me to buy it. So I bought it. No box, no bag necessary – I was going to eat it right then.
I am not ready to eat dessert alone out in public yet, and I even told the cashier the brownie pop was for someone else ... why I did that, I am not sure. That was most definitely Ed talking. So, needless to say, it wasn't a perfect bakery visit, but it was 97% there. I am okay with that.
Anyway, I went back to my car, put on the radio and sat and ate that delicious brownie pop. By the way, a brownie pop is a brownie on a stick. I am not sure about other places in the world, but here in LA, anything on a stick is the 'it' thing right now.

Brownie pops, cake pops, rice crispy treats on a stick ... we have it all.

So it was just me and my brownie pop, happily enjoying each other's company. And the best thing is, while Ed might have been with me while I was talking to the cashier in the bakery, he was definitely not with me when I was eating that brownie pop. I think this was actually the first brownie pop I had ever had.

Today was a great day in recovery because I listened to myself instead of Ed and I didn't let Ed guilt trip me after I was done eating. This doesn't happen often, so when it does, I am truly grateful. I mean ... I drove myself to a bakery because I wanted a brownie ... how much more recovery can one day have?

Hello to many more brownie pops, cake pops and whatever other pops that I may want to try, and Hello Life!

******

Day 306: The Power of Good Company and Chocolate

I had had one of those days where I was stressed out with work and people around me were just really annoying me ... basically just a typical day of stress.

I thought I had complained enough during this week on my blog about me not finding a job, being stressed out with school, etc., and I just didn't feel like complaining about it even more.

Sometimes it helped to write about things that bothered me, but other times it gave them more power, so for that reason I didn't want to write about them on this day, and I also was just sick of my own complaining.

Saturday, November 23

I was going to stay home tonight, but my best friend came to my rescue and invited me for dinner. Some awesome food, delicious chocolate-covered almonds, chocolate bars and vanilla tea later, I sit here a happy camper again.

The power that some good company and chocolate can have on a person never ceases to amaze me, especially when they are more powerful than Ed.

I saw a picture and it reminded me of myself tonight, just happily eating my chocolate and drinking my tea with my friends. That picture pretty much summed up my night. It was a picture of a toy bear and the caption, 'It's the weekend! Enjoy life's simple pleasures.'

I am that happy satisfied little bear right now, simply enjoying life's pleasures.

Hello Life!

******

Day 307: Sorry that I Am Not Sorry

I had been helping my aunt cook for the upcoming holidays this week, one of which would be Hanukkah. I am Jewish, so while I am not big on religion, Hanukkah is more of cultural and family event that happens every year, and it was always, always, always surrounded by lots of fried and delicious yet not Ed-approved food.

The main food you eat is potato latkes, which are basically fried potatoes, pretty much like hash browns. So that was all my aunt and I had made today – over one hundred potato latkes.

Not only did I try the first one we made, I tried the second one, I tried probably the twentieth one and the thirtieth one, and all the super-crispy fried pieces that had broken off in the frying pan while cooking. I also had a lunch in between, and then later on tried some more latkes.

I later came home and had pizza for dinner, with bread (carb overload) and then realized that over the past few days I had pretty much eaten an entire loaf of bread myself.

Sunday, November 24

I would be lying to you if I said there wasn't a slight mini freak-out moment of anxiety after I realized I had eaten almost a whole loaf of bread over the past few days. This after eating fried potatoes all day and eating pizza and bread for dinner (not to mention all my chocolate from yesterday).

Ed wanted me to be sorry. He still does want me to be sorry. But honestly, can't I just have a few days where I eat whatever I want – chocolate, fried potatoes, an entire loaf of bread? Don't people deserve that sometimes? Am I not entitled to eat the food I worked so hard to cook today?

Even though I might not be happy with the idea of it all and I might be thinking about how much weight I have gained from this, especially with Thanksgiving coming up this week, I am not sorry. So Ed, I am sorry that I am not sorry.

You know Ed? It's the holidays – a time where people eat and actually enjoy it. Somehow, they all move past it and don't blow up like a huge balloon like you are trying to make me think I will. You are really just not that credible a source anymore.

Again, sorry that I am not sorry for what I ate today and these past few days, and sorry in advance for not being sorry about the food I will eat this week.

I see that Ed is not going to cut me any slack, so I am going to have to work extra hard this week to be extra kind to myself. It won't be easy and I know I won't succeed every minute of the day, but I will try.

It's funny how the holiday season is about giving to others, but we so often forget to give to ourselves. How amazing would it be if we could all give ourselves and others the gift of kindness this year?

One person who is for sure not on my gift list is Ed – and I am not sorry for that either.

Hello Life!

******

Day 308: Welcome to Recovery Ed – the Land of Cocktails and Restaurant Dinners on a Monday

A day that had started out totally consumed by Ed, was now ending totally not consumed by him.

At the beginning of the day, I had been telling E how I had some extra time today because my class and my tutoring had been cancelled, and that instead of enjoying it, I wanted to spend it at the gym. I had been almost in desperate need of being inside the gym, as if I was thirsting for it.

Monday, November 25

I went to the gym, but only for twenty minutes, then after I hit that twenty-minute mark, my body was just done. And I am still done. Done enough that I don't even think I will go tomorrow, even though Thanksgiving is on Thursday.

Ed, my body and I are done and we need a break. And today we took that break. Instead of living inside the gym today, or living inside my room looking over and over again at the pictures I took of myself in the mirror this morning (which are now deleted), I decided to go to a movie with my grandma.

The movie actually ended up being kind of sad, as there was a lot about death centered around it, but it also made me think of the death I have seen in my life, and I have only truly seen and felt one death that touched my life directly, and that was my grandpa.

When you think about losing people you love, stupid pictures of the way your body looked this morning after eating a little extra the past few days is just not as important.

You know what is important to me now? The fact that I spent time with my grandma today; that quality time together is important.

You know what is important now? The amazingness in her and me going to dinner after the movie to one of my favorite restaurants and ordering cocktails.

Cocktails with my grandma, guys. Let me repeat: Cocktails ... with ... my ...grandma! Is she cool or what? I mean, how awesome and rare is that? And how incredible is it that it actually happened?

I used to only see my grandma on Thursdays, at one particular restaurant, where I only got exactly one kind of salad. No dressing, no nothing on it, just plain, boring and Ed-driven. Here we were, on a Monday, seeing a movie together and eating at my favorite restaurant – with cocktails.

Ed can kiss my cocktail and amazing dinner from The Cheesecake Factory's behind, because they were far more important than him and his pictures from this morning, and his deep desire to stay at the gym all day.

Welcome to recovery Ed – the land of cocktails and restaurant dinners on a Monday. We are here to stay.

Hello Life!

******

Day 309: Whatever Enough Means ... I Am It

I had had another story run on the front page of my university newspaper today.

I hadn't worked out because I needed a break.

One of the top officials at school had approached me, wanting to do an interview with me for a story.

I had found out I got an A on my presentation in one of my classes that I had done last week, that was 50 percent of my grade.

The beautiful woman whose oral history I had documented on video was actually proud of the work I had done.

Yet, for whatever reason, none of it had been enough for me.

Tuesday, November 26

I found myself sitting here in bed right before I started writing this post, adding up the calories I ate today. Like, really? Really? I had all these great accomplishments today, and that is what I am sitting here doing? Adding up calories?

Why can't I sit here and brag about all those little victories that I made happen for myself today? I did try to put my cover story on my Facebook page, but that didn't help.

All because I ate today, none of my accomplishments seem to matter. I didn't even eat 'bad'. I ate totally on my meal plan – maybe some extra sweets but nothing that should logically make me feel guilty.

It's days and moments like these where I need to stand back, close my eyes and give myself a reality check. And if I can't see the reality check, that is fine, but at least I need to try.

Reality check: All my accomplishments today had nothing to do with Ed.

Actually, maybe that is why Ed was so loud today, because he sees me succeeding in my life without him and he is trying to hold onto me. I honestly don't want to be held by him anymore. Let me go, Ed. Some days you are nicer, some days you hold on tight, like today.

To sit here and not let myself feel proud of my accomplishments because of calories pains my soul. I don't deserve that, and I know it. What I know and what I feel are two different things right now, but that is okay. Like I always say, feelings come and go, but facts stay.

Maybe none of the things I did today feel like enough, but maybe tomorrow they will. Maybe this post will reach someone who is going through the same thing today, and maybe knowing that will be enough. Maybe just realizing that I am not in the happiest mood, that it's okay, and that it will pass is enough.

Maybe enough is not about amounting to anything or achieving some kind of accomplishments, maybe enough can start with just being honest with myself.

If I am honest with Ed ... well, there is no honesty with Ed ... if I let Ed pull me in to his lies, then my honesty with myself is gone and that is not an option.

So here is my honest moment with myself: We didn't have the greatest day with how we feel about ourselves today, but we are okay. I got through the day being honest with myself instead of honest with Ed, I ate on the meal plan, and I am still able to see that tomorrow is a new day.

I mean, sometimes making it through the day is enough in itself right? Whatever enough means, I would like to think I am it today.

Hello Life!

******

Day 310: Then So Be It

I had got out of the shower today and got dressed only to find that it was really difficult to get my pants on. I don't know if it was because I had just got out of the shower, because the jeans were just out of the dryer, because they had shrunk, because I had got bigger, or maybe because my perception was off and they really had fit the same.

There was a good possibility of the latter but, nonetheless, it had been a hard situation to get through. It was a situation I had never had to experience when I was locked in Ed, and the more often it happened, it never stopped having its impact on me.

Wednesday, November 27

Sometimes it's easier and sometimes, like today, it's a little bit more difficult to handle, especially when you do what I did and try to figure out all the reasons why these pants or jeans were so hard to get on.

I was feeling discouraged and not in the greatest place, and then I saw a picture on Pinterest and it made me laugh at Ed. The picture said:

~ How to put on skinny jeans ~

Grab belt loops

Jump around like a bunny

Twerk for a few minutes

Lunge left

Lunge right

Assuming that this was posted by someone who doesn't have an eating disorder, it made me laugh for two reasons. Firstly, because assuming the person who posted this doesn't have an eating disorder, it just made me realize that I am not the only one who has a hard time fitting into my pants. While mine are not skinny jeans, it's the same idea.

Secondly, this was so exactly me this morning, and to think of myself jumping around like a bunny (let's totally not include the twerk because I have no clue how to do that), and I was definitely lunging into my pants, I thought it was pretty funny. I was able to take what could have been a really Ed-dominated situation, change my perspective on it and laugh at it instead. Whoever posted this picture has been in the shoes I was in this morning and I am sure many of you reading this have too.

So what if we have to jump around like a bunny, maybe break some belt loops or lunge a few times when we get dressed? I am not saying to squeeze into our sick clothes, because that is so far from what I believe in, as these pants are new and for my healthier new size. I am saying that if there are times that are difficult, like for me today when I got dressed, if we could sometimes find laughter as a remedy, I think it helps.

If we need to jump, lunge, dance or even throw the damn pants away, then so be it. If we need to laugh, cry, smile or be sad to make it through a hard situation, then so be it. If we need to spend time looking for inspirational pictures on Pinterest to lift our spirits, then so be it. If we need to name our eating disorders and talk to them like they are a person and show them who is in charge, then so be it. Whatever it is we need to do to become the strongest and most hopeful and healthiest versions of ourselves, then so be it.

So to my dear Ed: If you are going to try to tell me that it was hard to fit into these new pants because I am wrong for what I ate, or any other lies you are telling me, that is just fine, then so be it.

I happen to think they just came out of the dryer and it's as simple as that. And if I have keep telling myself that line over and over until I really believe it, then so be it.

Hello Life!

******

Day 311: Thankful for the Gift of Kindness

Today I had wished everyone living in the US a happy Thanksgiving. Today's post had been my first Thanksgiving in recovery.

For those who don't know, Thanksgiving is a holiday that is totally centered around food. The whole point is to have a huge dinner with a lot of yummy food with your loved ones. But it's also about taking a moment to realize what you are thankful for.

Thursday, November 28

During my time in recovery I honestly feel like I have learned how to become thankful for life's smallest gifts every single day.

Sometimes just making it through the morning without checking my stomach out in the mirror is something I am thankful for. Sometimes having a day of peace and quiet from Ed is something I am thankful for. But today, because it's Thanksgiving, it was more of a time for me to be reflective.

Last Thanksgiving I weighed myself in the morning. I then weighed myself in the afternoon at my aunt's house before dinner, and I weighed myself at home after dinner. That number was my Thanksgiving.

Who cared about the food, the family and the dessert that I helped make? Ed didn't care, therefore I didn't care either. I cared about my number, my one and only number. It's weird to think that I saw that exact same scale today and yet just walked past it. I had my power back.

This Thanksgiving, my first Thanksgiving in recovery, while I sit here uncomfortably full, I also sit here and smile because recovery and I rocked this Thanksgiving. We took over this Thanksgiving and we let Ed sit back and watch. There was no meal plan today, there was an eat whatever you want because it's Thanksgiving plan.

Today I am thankful that I was able to bake with my aunt and get to experience and enjoy tasting everything along the way. I am thankful for being able to see the smile on the face of the girl I tutor when I surprised her at her house and gave her a birthday present. I am thankful for the text messages I got from my family and friends that were so beautiful.

I am thankful that I was able to save the day when our apple pie fell onto the floor right before we put it into the oven, and I decided that the ten-second rule would turn into the two-minute rule, and I put the whole pie back together with my cousin. It was the best pie I ever had.

I am thankful for my family, but mostly I am thankful for the gift of kindness. I can truthfully say that I was able to be kind to myself today. I don't know if that many people can understand why this is such a big deal, but let me try to explain.

Being kind to yourself means giving yourself permission to be proud of yourself. It means giving yourself permission to taste the food you worked so hard to make. It means loving yourself enough that even though you are physically uncomfortable from eating, you hug yourself tight and know that deep down you put yourself first, not Ed.

Being kind to yourself means eating the food at Thanksgiving; it means being part of your family and being present with them. It means hopping onto a plane to Las Vegas tomorrow despite the fact that Ed will try to tell me I don't deserve it because there is food there and fun there, and things that I don't deserve because I ate what I wanted today.

Being kind to yourself means even through your physical pain from fullness, you smile, laugh and almost cry out of happiness because, hell yes, you didn't listen to Ed.

Above all, being kind to yourself ultimately means that you are learning to love yourself, even on days where strong forces, like Ed, tell you not to.

Ed never appreciated my soul, and that is why he is so hollow, so empty and so void of warmth. But me, the more I love myself, the more kind I am to myself and the more I value myself, based on internal things, not based on my body or how I look, the more I am able to not only appreciate my soul, but the souls of others.

Kindness is the best gift I can be thankful for this year. Kindness to myself. Kindness to others. Kindness to my body.

Ed doesn't know how to be kind because he only knows how to be self-deprecating, and for a long time I didn't know how to be kind to myself either. But now I do know how to be kind to myself, and instead of fighting Ed along the way, I am going to teach him how to be kind to me too.

Today's lesson to Ed for learning how to be kind to me: It's Thanksgiving, therefore I am allowed to be like every other American and eat the yummy food – oh, and also, you don't get to stop me from having fun in Vegas.

Hello Life!

******

Day 312: Las Vegas Checklist

Before starting this day's post, I just needed to say how grateful I was to be a part of this journey with everyone. The previous day, Thanksgiving, had been an extremely challenging day for a lot of people in recovery, and there had been so much support and so many inspirational comments and emails following my post that I was just blown away.

I thanked everyone for not only being a part of my journey by reading my blog, but for sharing about themselves and their journeys with me. Hearing about how my words were helping others and hearing about their daily journey to recovery was beyond the gift of kindness. That was the gift of support, and it's one we all deserved to have.

Friday, November 29

I am officially in Las Vegas, guys. The land of lights, alcohol, shows, Elvis and no clocks or sense of time – aka the land of fun.

I woke up today so sore from the food yesterday, and I will be honest with you and say that today wasn't an easy start for me. Ed wasn't being kind to me at all – no surprise – and I had to actually reread my own blog post from yesterday to keep me present and in a positive mindset.

But fast forward from waking up and flying on the airplane to a few hours later in this amazing city with my family. I knew if I needed to make this experience an enjoyable one I needed to do it right.

So here is my Las Vegas checklist:

1. Pack only leggings. No jeans or anything that can somehow fit remotely tight or in any kind of way trigger Ed to feed me his lies. After all, I am in post-Thanksgiving dinner mode. Also, did I mention, Vegas has amazing restaurants, not to mention a restaurant all devoted to chocolate? So, leggings are the only acceptable pants I will be wearing, and my suitcase had exactly that – three pairs of leggings and some long-sleeved shirts.

2. Hide the scale from the hotel bathroom. For whatever reason, hotels here love to give you a scale in your bathroom. The minute my sister and I saw it, she asked, "Do you want to hide it?" At first I said no, because I know I am not going to step on it anyway, but after passing it a few times, it was just staring at me and it made me uncomfortable, so into the closet the scale went. Bye-bye hotel bathroom scale.

3. Make sure to buy chocolate for my hotel room. This is self-explanatory. I mean, what happens if I have a chocolate craving late at night or something? Of course, Ed told me what a non-disciplined and careless person I am for buying it, but I don't care. It makes me happy to have my chocolate here, and while I am not so happy it's almost half gone, I am on vacation, so I am living a little.

4. Check where the gym in the hotel is. Okay, so this was a little Ed and a little me. I like to work out because it makes me feel strong, but today I didn't want to. Ed and I checked where the gym in the hotel was, and when we saw that it wasn't only in another hotel, but I felt like I would much rather take a nap, the working out situation didn't go as planned.

I am not sure where Ed even went after that. I did a few body checks and went to sleep. Somewhere along the way between the body checks and telling me to work out, I must have found kindness to myself, because the only thing I did was take a two-hour nap. Sorry Ed, working out didn't make the checklist, but taking a nap did.

5. Last thing on my Vegas checklist is to remember to be kind to myself, and when I am forgetting how, to reread my post from yesterday and everyone's comments that came with it.

Leggings – check

Bathroom scale hidden – check

Chocolate in my possession – check

No workout today and nap instead – check

Self-kindness – check ... well, check in the making

Last time I was in Vegas, it was about a year ago, and it was a trip for three – me, my ex-boyfriend and Ed. Ed dominated my whole trip. I remember he let me have two bites of pizza on that trip. Two bites that he never let me forget the entire time. I was so trapped.

I think it's safe to say Ed has experienced Vegas enough. Let's make this my trip.

Hello Life!

******

Day 313: 90% a Victor

I was in Las Vegas for the weekend. Although I had been there many times before and I had seen every hotel and every shop, I decided that today I wanted to go walk around and look at them yet again.

No one else in my family had wanted to see the same hundred thousand shops for the hundred thousandth time, which was totally understandable, so it was an adventure I took by myself, and I was so glad I did.

Saturday, November 30

In short, this is what my shopping trip looked like:
- Walked to the hotel that all the amazing shops are at, a perfect coincidence that it's the same hotel that has an entire restaurant devoted to chocolate.
- Stopped and bought myself a chocolate truffle from that restaurant.
- Ate the amazing truffle in peace.
- Went shopping and only tried on some very cute loose 'recovery style' shirts and another pair of jeggings. You can't have enough of those in recovery, right?

Then after I was done shopping and I was halfway back to my hotel, I hit my first Ed dilemma of the day. I had about a half mile left to walk to reach my hotel, but my back hurt and I was tired.

It just so happened that the hotel I was passing had a tram that was going back to my hotel. I can't even begin to write down all the reasons why Ed told me I should continue walking instead of taking the tram.

"You know you want to eat some chocolate and get Starbucks later, keep walking," he said.

"You already had that chocolate truffle Shira, keep walking," he said.

"You had a big breakfast, keep walking," he said.

The list could go on and on.

It wasn't that I wasn't listening to Ed, because I was, it was hard not to. But somehow I ended up plopping myself down inside the tram. I feel like sometimes I am able to just do the right thing even when my mind is telling me not to, like I am on autopilot. My mind told me to keep going but my feet took me to the tram. Actually, it's more like Ed told me to keep going, but I guess I took myself to that tram.

Anyway, a tram ride, a Starbucks Frappuccino and some more chocolate later, I sit here feeling like the victor for today, not a victim of Ed.

I wasn't the victor 100% of the time. For example, trying on clothes was still hard. Ed was still there. New sizes were still hard to accept. The fact that I walked a lot today is still in my mind. But I was the victor 90% of the time and I am good with that.

Some days I am only the victor 10% of the time, but I remember the days where I was never the victor and only Ed's victim. To be in a place where I am the victor now, whether it's 10%, 50% or 90%, is a place I am grateful to be.

So hello new jeggings, hello to my chocolate from the chocolate restaurant, hello to sitting on that tram, and Hello Life!

December 2013

Day 314: I Came Home to Recovery

IN Vegas the previous night I had heard a song that made me think of my ex-boyfriend, and since that moment I had been thinking about my last trip to Vegas, which was a year ago with him.

I had just started treatment, and while I hadn't given up my scale then, I was really motivated to succeed in recovery. At that time, our relationship was falling apart, and I thought a getaway to Vegas would somehow be our answer. At that time, I still didn't realize how being in that relationship was part of the reason I was in a relationship with Ed.

Anyway, how ironic that the same hotel that I had taken myself shopping to the day before was the same hotel that my ex-boyfriend and I sat in a year ago at a bar, where I had found the courage to explain to him who Ed was. For sure, I thought he would think I was insane, naming my eating disorder and treating it like a person. But he didn't think I was insane. We actually ended up sitting at that bar and cheering to the death of Ed.

I remember not wanting to leave Vegas that weekend because there wasn't a scale in my room, so I hadn't had the option to weigh myself even if I had wanted to. I had even eaten two bites of pizza. While I was still trapped, I had also partially experienced a moment or two of freedom and I wasn't ready to go back to my world of imprisonment with Ed at home.

Sunday, December 1

I am not sure what it was about yesterday, whether it was the fact that I was thinking about the last time I was there, and how I was cheering to the death of Ed with a person who is no longer in my life (for the better, but still not an easy thing to realize), or if it was the fact that last time I was there I didn't want to leave because I was so happy to be in a place that was free of my scale, and now I am so far from there.

Or maybe it's the fact that I was thinking about what my part was in the reason my ex-boyfriend and I are no longer together, and how much of a part Ed played in that. Was I really more devoted to Ed than I was to love? Or were they both just that toxic that in order to get healthy, it meant leaving them both?

Whatever it was, I sat up late last night with my sister and just cried. Part of me was sad about letting go of that part of my past, and part of me was just in shock about all the changes that have happened since then, in a beautiful positive way, but I guess I was so filled with emotion over it that tears are what came to me.

Since then, almost a year ago now, not only have I let those relationships with my ex-boyfriend and Ed go, but I am no longer cheering to the death of Ed. I have learned through my recovery, while I don't want to admit it all the time, Ed is not going anywhere. He is a part of me. My recovery is learning how to rise above him, to become stronger than him, and to quieten him down, but to say he will forever die is not realistic, nor is it really my goal. How can something die that has played a big part in who I am?

The last thing that has changed since last year, and the most beautiful thing that has changed, is that I was no longer afraid to leave Vegas today like I was a year ago. I wasn't scared to leave a world in Vegas where I once felt so free without a scale, because I was happy to come home to the new world I have created for myself here – recovery.

I am not coming home to a scale this time. I am not coming home to a house where I am living with someone who is not healthy for me, or with someone who I felt I had to go on vacation with to try to repair our wounds.

I am coming home to a world where there is not a number waiting to define me; a world where, while the man with whom I once cheered to the death of Ed is no longer here, in his place Shira is here. Shira – strong, confident and healthy. My new world and my old world couldn't have lived together in harmony.

Vegas was more than just an opportunity for me to spend time with my family and not pay too much attention to Ed; it was a time for me to realize where I was a year ago and where I am now.

That place I was a year ago looms heavy in my heart. I can still feel every emotion I had. I even remember what that pizza tasted like, I remember how sore I was after, and I remember the number I weighed when I got home. I also remember how desperate I was to hold onto this fake world in Las Vegas where I could pretend I was happy with my unhealthy relationships, both with Ed and my ex-boyfriend.

But this year in Vegas I didn't need to pretend I was happy because I actually was happy, even without my ex-boyfriend and Ed by my side. Did you hear that Ed? I was happy without you.

Recovery is not fake. Everything I have worked for is real and present, and it's beautiful to me that I came home today not being scared to leave Vegas because I didn't want to face life with Ed here. I came home to recovery.

Hello Life!

******

Day 315: A Tribute to a Fighter and Recovery Warrior

Today's post was a tribute to one incredible fighter that I had met along this journey.

Monday, December 2

Today, after months of waiting, and after a tragic family event two days ago that could have stopped her, this fighter walked into an eating disorder clinic in London and she bravely went through an intense eating disorder treatment assessment. This will be the deciding factor in what kind of treatment for her eating disorder she will receive – a decision she will find out next week.

Essentially, she chose recovery today. She could have not gone. She could have cancelled. She could have let her family event a few days ago stop her, and it would have been understandable. But she didn't. She walked in there, as strong as the definition of strong can mean, and went through that assessment.

I remember that it wasn't long ago that I went through a very similar assessment when I started treatment – blood tests, blind weigh-ins, blood pressure, blood work and EKG scans, not to mention having to verbally say out loud how many calories you eat, how much exercise you do and expose the things that are so private. Things that were between just you and Ed; things that the thought of anyone else knowing is bone chilling. It was one of the hardest things I ever had to do in recovery. It made everything so real.

As I woke up this morning and was Facebook chatting with my dear friend as she was in the waiting room in between her tests, I was just in awe of her strength, courage and bravery. She was my strength today.

When she wrote to me after it was over and said, "I couldn't do this without you," I almost cried. I know it seems like I cry a lot lately, maybe because it's true, but it is what it is. But these were tears of happiness.

This whole time I was looking at her as this incredible fighter, yet she was looking at me the same way. I don't know if I even deserved for her to say that she couldn't do it without me, but it's important to me that she knows how much strength her saying that gave me. I was part of someone else's recovery today, and she was a part of mine.

Today's post is a tribute to my dear friend, fighter and recovery warrior, and while I won't say her name, she knows exactly who she is. In honor of her and her courage and bravery, I say, Hello Life!

******

Day 316: Ditching My 6a.m. Work Out

At 12:30a.m. the previous night, when I should have been sleeping, it had looked like I was packing for a weekend vacation. I had three bags on my floor ready for the morning: My school bag, my gym bag and a bag that held all my clothes in it so I could shower after the gym.

I had a phone interview for a story I was writing at 8:30a.m., followed by an appointment with E at 9a.m., and a whole day of things to do after that, meaning if I wanted to work out, it literally had to be at 6a.m., before any of that happened, and it meant showering and getting ready at the gym.

Because I knew I was going to dinner this night for my cousins birthday, and still being slightly in the post-Thanksgiving state of mind, Ed and I had packed those bags the previous night with the stone-cold intention of using them for their purpose – to go work out at 6a.m. today. But when I had woken up, tired and exhausted, I had looked at all those bags on the floor and thought to myself, "What are you doing?"

Tuesday, December 3

I knew if I went to the gym at 6.a.m, Ed would just take over me for the day.

I couldn't go. Going would mean choosing Ed over recovery. Going would mean sacrificing my need of sleep in order to work out, and that is not in the recovery guidelines.

So I didn't go, and I ditched my 6a.m. workout for sleep. I went back to sleep for an extra two hours.

When I woke up again, hated my body check in the mirror, then realized I still have to of course eat today and go to dinner later, Ed was wide awake with me.

I walked into E's office almost not able to spit out my anxiety fast enough. Ed was in charge for a little while.

But as I sit here now writing this, I write to you after not only enjoying that dinner with my family, and the dessert that we had with it, but also writing to you and about to tell you that I had a really great day.

When I was at dinner, I got an email from this top official at my university who is going to do an interview with me. This interview will give me what I need so I can write the final cover story for my university newspaper for the fall semester, a huge honor in itself. He chose to interview with me; he asked to do the story with me. This was a huge moment.

That dinner with my family, celebrating my cousin's birthday, and eating the yummy dessert with everyone, was already me outshining Ed, but getting this interview is the sweetest icing on top of this cake ever. It made me almost forget that I didn't work out today.

So, long story short, I survived today. While Ed told me I would have a breakdown all because I didn't work out, I didn't – so far from it. Instead, I studied in the library with my friends (let me not forget to mention the social eating aspect of that, which includes studying junk food, but nonetheless, a social part of recovery), I had dinner with my family and celebrated a birthday, and I got this final interview so I can write the last cover story of the semester.

Ed didn't have any part in that. If I had listened to Ed today, I probably wouldn't have gone to the library and bought snacks for my friends and me. I wouldn't have gone to the dinner (and trust me, I was thinking about it). And I probably wouldn't have even cared that I got this interview.

But I didn't listen to him, therefore I am able to feel proud of myself for these mini accomplishments today.

There will be no more episodes of multiple bags sitting on my floor to go work out at 6a.m. anymore. I come first.

Hello to ditching the 6a.m. workouts, and Hello Life!

✶✶✶✶✶✶

Day 317: Bad Days Don't Last for Ever

I called this day the day of the sweets, because that is pretty much what it had been.

I had been sitting there not too long before writing my blog listening to Ed telling how horrible a day today had been because of it, and it was hard not to listen to him. He knew how to mesh his voice with mine so well, almost to the point that I couldn't tell them apart.

But honestly, after I had added up all those calories from today and almost had an anxiety attack over it, I realized that I was letting him win.

Wednesday, December 4

Really and truly, is it really that bad that I had M&M's today? Is it really that bad that I need to have something sweet after every meal? Is it really that bad that I had a few bites of ice cream today, and also some chocolate ... okay, and maybe also some little cookies?

Well actually, yeah, I guess it does look bad – really bad – at least in Ed's world. In Ed's world, eating what I ate today is the same as me lying down on the floor and wearing a sign around my neck that says, 'Kick me, I have no self-discipline'. That is what he has me thinking I am looking like right now.

I won't sit here and write that I am happy about all the sweets I ate today because I am not, partially because they were a bunch of little bites here and there, and that is really eating disordered-like behavior. Ed takes bites, he doesn't eat. Recovery tastes, eats and enjoys.

I am also not happy because, well, for the obvious reason that sweets equals calories. Ed hates calories. But on the other hand, aren't there worse things in life that I could have done today or yesterday than eat sweets?

While Ed is busy making me feel like I should be wearing that sign around my neck for not eating the healthiest of foods today, I have been exhausted. I don't even have the energy to deal with him. Part of the reason I even ate these sweets was to help me stay awake. I fell asleep twice before being able to wake up and write this post.

These are the kinds of days where I am envious of people who are able to eat the M&M's, the few bites of ice cream or the cookie after lunch and think nothing of it. They just go on with their day. How peaceful and calm that must be. I have experienced that kind of peacefulness too, but it just seems far away right now.

For the moment, I am not feeling the greatest. Even though I know Ed is wrong, I still feel like I am kind of wearing that invisible sign around my neck right now.

So maybe I am a little left behind in Ed's world right now, but the part of me that still has my foot in recovery is able to see reality clearly.

Reality check: There are worse things in life than eating sweets for a day, or two days, or all week. And with that, as uncomfortable as I feel right now, I move on with today. Bad days don't last forever.

Hello Life!

******

Day 318: Trading Brains with an Eight-Year-Old

Today I thanked everyone who had commented and emailed with so much incredible support after the previous day's post. I knew I said that a lot, but I was always so swept away with gratitude every time so much support came in.

We truly had built a community of love, acceptance and support on my blog, and I was so grateful for everyone who was a part of it.

Thursday, December 5

I am happy to report that today was a much better day, just like you guys said it would be. Those feelings and that invisible 'kick me I have no self-discipline' sign is no longer around my neck.

I got to speak with my three little brothers on the phone tonight. As I was talking to the middle one, who is eight, he asked me what *my next step is in becoming a writer. (He really did use those words too.)*

"I don't know. I am applying for newspaper jobs. No one wants me yet," I told him.

"Shira, Hello Life is your job. Why do you need a new job? Don't worry, I will tell everyone in my class to read it. We will be the six musketeers," he said. *(In total, I am the eldest of six brothers and sisters.)*

He was so cute when he said that and it just brought the biggest smile to my face. I am not sure which part I loved more, the fact that he thinks Hello Life is my job, or the fact he referred to our siblings as the six musketeers. I think I like the six musketeers the best. Six, not seven, so no space for Ed – I like that.

When I told him he is the smartest boy I know and that I want to switch brains with him for a day, he immediately said yes. At first I was kind of surprised. He was actually into this idea.

I thought to myself, why would anyone want my brain? While it's filled with creativity and deep thoughts, it's also filled with so many internal battles, fights and self-judgement.

"If I had your brain, then tomorrow in school when my teacher asks me a hard question about long division, I know I will get it right because you are smart," he said.

That right there was a Hello Life moment. He is eight, he doesn't know the kinds of things my brain thinks about; he doesn't know the lies Ed has filled it with. And he doesn't care what I looked like today, what I ate today or any of that stuff. He cared that I was smart, and he wanted that.

He also gave me permission to use his jokes since I will be borrowing his brain for the day, and he is the absolute king of jokes. It made me think about how amazing it would be to really do that trade. I would get to have a brain where jokes matter; a brain where the only thing that matters is getting the answer right in front of your friends in your class when the teacher asks a hard question; a brain where it values it's life because it's smart or funny, not because of how much it ate that day.

The fact that he wanted my brain, regardless of the lies Ed is telling me about myself because of how I look lately, shows me the truth that Ed doesn't want me to see – that I am still valuable regardless of whether I am not the skinny person he wants me to be.

Recovery starts in the brain, in the heart and in our soul. It has nothing to do with our bodies.

Thank you to the eight-year-old little man who shone a light on that for me today. Hello Life!

******

Day 319: Being the Best Writer He Ever Saw

This day's post had to be short because I was at a concert with my cousin, and while writing meaningful blog posts was very important to me, it was also important for me to be living in the moment, and I needed to honor that on this night.

Friday, December 6

Today I had an interview with pretty much the head of my university. It was for the last cover story of the semester. At first he didn't want to talk to me, but after slightly stalking this nice man for two months, he finally did.

When I was leaving his office, he told me I was one of the best writers he had ever seen and he enjoyed my writing. He even named every article I wrote by name.

If I had weighed myself today, I wouldn't have been able to even see the major honor in that. All I would have thought about was my number and how to make it better.

But I didn't weigh myself today. I wasn't a number today. Today I was the best writer the head guy at our university had ever seen.

And on another note, I just want to say that being at this concert with my cousin has led me to the opportunity to have chicken nuggets and ice cream from McDonald's. I haven't had chicken nuggets in years and I would just like to say they are amazing. Truly amazing.

And with that I am back to living my life as that best writer at a concert with my cousin.

Hello Life!

******

Day 320: Today Was All Me

I was going out to dinner at a steakhouse for my grandma's seventy-fifth birthday on this night. Knowing this was going to take place about a week previously, I had totally planned to work out today. I mean, it was just a given. I was going to eat dinner at a steakhouse, therefore I must work out that day, right?

Well, no surprise, as this was a lesson I kept learning over and over, just like when I had woken up earlier in the week to go to the gym at 6.a.m. and then realized it wasn't worth it, the same thing had kind of happened today, and my so-called 'plans' were no longer so planned.

Saturday, December 7

I knew I only had a few hours to get things done today before I had to get ready for the dinner and there wasn't space for both working out and writing my last cover story for my university newspaper. There was only room for one.

I will be honest and say that this was probably one of the easiest decisions I have ever made in all of my recovery. Ed versus the best story I will ever write in my entire life. There was no hesitation. Ed lost immediately.

While at one time Ed would have 100% completely won, because he would have been the center of my universe, and reaching that number on a scale would be all that I would have based my self-worth on that day, today he was nothing.

I would much rather produce the best story I ever wrote than lose a few calories at the gym. So that is exactly what I did. Come Tuesday when this story runs, there will be no traces of Ed anywhere around it.

This is all me – my brain, my mind, my talent and my skills as a writer, all of which Ed gets in the way of if I restrict and value myself on a number of calories, size or weight.

There are parts of my life that Ed is still a big part of – major parts of – and I don't deny that. But when it comes to writing, it's all me. Today was all me, not Ed.

Hello Life!

******

Day 321: Just Because

There had been a whole bunch of things today that pissed Ed off, and I honestly had no valid reason to do so.

I hadn't restricted the previous day to let me think that I was allowed to eat the way I had on this day. I had actually eaten at a steakhouse the previous day. I hadn't worked out on this day to make myself think I deserved to eat what I had wanted today.

Sunday, December 8

I really didn't have some Ed-approved reason to eat these things today, but I did, just because.

I ate breakfast with my brothers and shared cookies and watched a movie in bed with them this morning, just because.

I ate M&M's in the middle of the day, just because.

I ate dinner before I was even hungry as I just wanted food, just because.

I ate the most delicious chocolate truffle, just because.

Wow, and I even ate some marshmallows with ice cream (weird combination, I know), just because.

A year ago I would have looked at this list and thought I had binged. But I look at it now, and every single one of those food decisions, healthy or not healthy, was totally mindful and thought out.

So nope, I didn't work out today and no, I didn't restrict yesterday. And I actually even know I won't be able to work out tomorrow and will also be going out to dinner tomorrow too. It still doesn't change the fact that I totally and mindfully enjoyed my sweet tooth today, just because.

Do we all always need a reason or justification to enjoy things or do things in life? In the world of a perfectionist (my old world) or in the world of an eating disorder (again, my old world that was intertwined with the perfectionist in me) you did. You ALWAYS needed a reason to do anything.

You needed a justification to eat, to go out with friends or to even smile. Usually those justifications were centered around a certain weight that day, or a size, or calorie intake. If you ate X number of calories or weighed X number, it could give you a valid excuse to possibly enjoy yourself for a moment or two.

In the recovery, learning how to accept myself world, you don't need a reason to enjoy yourself. In this world, just because is a good enough reason.

To all of us who are giving ourselves permission today to eat, live and be who we want to be, just because, I say: Hello Life!

******

Day 322: Wearing Ed's Shoes

I had been tutoring one of my girls on this day and it had been one of those days where she was just not getting anything, mixed with not wanting to do any work – all this combined with me not having patience and being extremely hard on her.

There had even been a moment where I shamefully, not proudly and so regretfully almost yelled at her and had said her answer was stupid. I couldn't believe I had used the word stupid.

Right before our lesson ended, she had put her head in my arms and she had cried. I felt so horrible – for that lesson, I had been Ed. I had been wearing his shoes, I had been wearing his clone, I had been walking in his stride. I had been thinking, talking and acting like him. I had become everything that I hated about him.

Mind you, this girl usually did very well, but today I had been asking her to be perfect, to not get anything wrong, and to get every single thing right, and I had realized that right in that second.

"Don't cry my love, everyone has bad days. I have bad days where I mess up on my homework too. I am sorry, I was too hard on you," I had told her.

I mean, was that the best I could say? That I was sorry? That everyone has bad days? It wasn't anywhere near good enough in my opinion.

Would that have been good enough if Ed had told me he was sorry and that he had just had a bad day, and that is why he had been mean to me? No way. It would never suffice. Just a simple sorry?

And more than that, I had lied to her.

Monday, December 9

I have never had a bad academic day. I am a straight-A student to this day. I hold myself to the same almost unrealistic standards that I was trying to hold the girl I tutor to, and why? She doesn't need to be me to be the best version of herself, and as a matter of fact, I hope she is far from being me.

I don't want her to be a perfectionist. I want her to know it's okay to have bad days and that it's okay to not know all the answers on her homework all the time.

But as I sit here and write this, I feel like it would be contradicting myself to not take my own advice. She had a bad day, but so did I. Just in the same way she has to know it's okay to not know all the answers all the time, I have to know that I can't always be the perfect tutor and that I too will slip up.

I didn't have a perfect day in Ed's world either. I didn't go to the gym, I went out to dinner for my grandma's birthday and I ate two desserts – yes two! I even told my cousin that I have two stomachs, one for food and one for dessert.

In the recovery world that is a great day, but it's not a perfect day. It could have been more balanced. And of course Ed is telling me that I should have avoided the whole thing anyway. But the truth of the matter is, so what? I had dessert on a Monday, and yes, it was after eating a lot of sweets yesterday.

Yes, I maybe could be more balanced in my food choices, and yes, I could have been a lot nicer to my amazing little eight-year-old girl today.

You know what the craziest part about today is? I can forgive myself for eating the dessert and the food that Ed so badly wants me to obsess over, but I can't seem to forgive myself for being an Ed to that little girl.

At one time I would never have cared if I yelled at her or made her cry, as long as I ate under a certain number of calories that day or weighed a certain number that day. Now all I can think about is how I was to her like Ed is to me – demanding of perfection.

So today was another day of imperfection. Imperfection in my tutoring, imperfection in eating what Ed didn't want me to eat and imperfection in not measuring up to be the person I know I can be.

I can't go back and apologize to that girl again right now, but I wish I could. I don't know what else to say. I hope I can forgive myself for making her cry those tears that were pleading for me to just give her approval.

After being in Ed's shoes today, and after being him for an hour, I have never wanted to be further away from him.

Today was imperfect. I was imperfect. But I am learning, and I guess that is all I can do.

Hello Life!

******

Day323: The Story that Gave Other Voices Power

Today had been a day of culmination and celebration for me.

The previous Saturday I had told everyone about how I had decided to work on my final newspaper story for my university instead of working out. Today that story had run on the front page of the last paper of the semester, as well as getting about three hundred Facebook shares and leaving multiple newsstands empty on campus.

It was a story that talked about major changes that would be taking place to the university graduation ceremonies, such as everyone only being allowed four tickets per graduate, and college ceremonies being combined. These were changes on which the students hadn't had the opportunity to air their opinions.

Tuesday, December 10

Had I been assigned this story a year ago, I would have looked at the facts, which were the changes that are being made, I would have looked at the university's reasons behind them, and I would have left it at that. It wouldn't have made me a bad reporter to do that either, as that is a reporter's job, to report the facts.

But being on this journey to recovery has done so much more than make me just physically healthy again, and it has done so much more than help me build a healthy relationship with food for the first time in my life. Recovery has changed the way I look at people and the way I look at the world. I no longer see the world in cold hard facts and reasons. I no longer just see people as people. I no longer just see myself as only a body.

Throughout finding my voice during my path to recovery and regaining it back from Ed, I have also found the importance in being able to give others a voice. That is actually my favorite thing about this blog, that it has given others a safe place to express themselves, ask for advice and expose their Eds.

When I started investigating this story, no one wanted to talk with me. They were either scared they would get in trouble or they were scared they would look bad at the university. But the majority of them didn't know what I was even talking about.

After Friday, students were starting to be notified of these changes. Yesterday I went to a student government board meeting where there was an open forum for students to voice their opinions about these changes. Some students cried when they said they couldn't choose just four people to give tickets to come watch their graduation. Some of them were the first to graduate in their entire family and they didn't know how to choose only four people to come be a part of such a huge accomplishment.

One of them cried because he wanted to walk across that stage to get his diploma and invite the stranger who once paid for his first semester of college because he didn't have the money, and now he can't.

One of them was from a foster home and said he wanted to invite all thirty of his foster brothers to come see him graduate, and now he couldn't do that.

The point is, every student had their own voice and their own story. Because I have learned to value my own voice so much throughout my recovery, I have truly learned to value the voice of others too.

The story that ran today wasn't a story that was founded only on hard facts, although that is its foundation, it's a story that gave a voice to the voiceless. It's a story that gave a megaphone to these students' voices. It's the story that gave their voice power. I know how amazing it feels to experience my own voice having power against Ed, so I can only hope these students felt that same thing today.

When I woke up this morning I felt huge – huge beyond measure. I have been eating a lot of sweets the past few days and I haven't been working out, and today was also the last day I will work with my trainer. Needless to say, I was freaking out, but I stood in front of the mirror and I told myself loud and clear that Ed won't ruin this day for me.

I worked so hard to give other people a voice and to make this final cover story of mine the best that it could be, that there is absolutely no way Ed will take that away. He has taken away so many wonderful moments for me already, and this can't be one of them.

Thank God there was no number on a scale for me to see today, because with all assurance, I know it would have ruined my ability to appreciate my story's success.

Today, more than celebrating the culmination of being a senior reporter for my university newspaper, I celebrate the power of people's voices, including my own.

On that note, Ed is still not allowed to ruin today. The rest I will have to figure out tomorrow.

Hello Life!

******

Day 324: Time to Do Some Major Soul Searching

I was no longer the top senior reporter for my university newspaper, as I was graduating, and that had been something of a hard pill for me to swallow.

Many times, I had used my front-page cover stories to define me, to justify me, and to credit me with being a good person. Instead of my scale, I had looked to other external accomplishments to tell me whether I was 'good' or 'bad'. Not having that anymore was going to be a challenge and was going to force me to look even more inwardly at accepting who I really was – not me as the writer, not me as the recovery warrior and not me as a college graduate, but just me as a whole.

So now not having a job, on top of no longer having my senior reporter status wasn't helping me feel any more valuable a person. I had never thought that not having a job could even mean anything to me. It had nothing to do with my weight so how could I even care? But, in recovery, I did care.

Wednesday, December 11

I sat here ten minutes ago and added up all my calories from today over and over and am really feeling horrible about myself for how much I have been eating lately and how I look lately.

By now I know the answer to why I am doing this. I am in the unknown again, the unknown of not having a job and not knowing what is going to happen with my life, so instead of sitting with those feelings, I let Ed show me what I indeed and most definitely do know.

I do know how to count calories and I do know how to be hard on myself. It could be very easy for me to resort back to restricting right now and go back to Ed. It would be almost like second nature.

But what good would that do for me? It would bring me solace and comfort for a moment, then it would make me feel trapped in a whole other unknown world, the world of Ed, the world of where you never know how far you can fall until you are already there.

There are no more cover stories, there is currently no job, and there is no more sick skinny body that Ed created for me to find validation through.

E, we have some major soul searching to do, and I am ready.
Hello Life!

******

Day 325: Yes, Yes and Yes

The previous Monday I had been not very proud about how I had been really mean to one of the little girls I tutored, and how I had felt as if I had acted like Ed to her in being so demanding of perfection.

Since then I had been thinking about how I would make it up to her today when I saw her. What would I say? How would I apologize?

Thursday, December 12

I know how to win this girl's heart, because after working with her for two years now, there is one thing that never ceases to make her smile and that is a vanilla Frappuccino from Starbucks. Yup, that is it, a drink, so simple and pure.

When I showed up at her door with her drink in my hand, her entire face lit up. "No way! No way! Really, Shira? Really? Wow, I am in heaven."

All of a sudden it was as if that day on Monday hadn't happened and for a moment I was feeling relieved. But about ten minutes into our session, she looked at me and said, "Shira, am I doing better than I was on Monday? Am I better now?"

Her question broke my heart. Is she better now? Was she ever bad to begin with? Did I really make her feel like she wasn't being a good person because of a few mistakes on a math problem? That is how Ed used to make me feel anytime I ate even one calorie over his approved limit.

Maybe her comment hurt me so much because lately Ed has been making me feel so unworthy as I have been giving in to my sweet tooth, and because I have been snacking more as I wasn't as busy with school, and a list of other things that I am sure I have said a hundred times this week already.

I honestly didn't know what to say, because I almost wanted to cry. How could I answer an eight-year-old girl who just asked me if she is better than she was three days ago, when the truth is it wasn't her who was ever bad to begin with, it was me who was the one demanding perfection of her? It was me who was wrong.

I just looked at her, hugged her and said, "Lola, you were never bad on Monday. I was just tired and I was too hard on you. You are amazing and I love you." I tried to show her as much love and compassion as I could.

"You are the best, Shira." That was it. One simple sentence and she forgave me just like that, and we went on to have a really good lesson together.

If she could forgive me after I was so hard on her on Monday, why can't I forgive myself? I am the one who needs to forgive myself for acting too harshly that day. I am the one who needs to forgive myself for giving in to my sweet tooth.

But, on the other hand, does giving in to my sweet tooth even need forgiveness? Does it even have to be considered a bad thing? Ed would like me to think it does, like I am doing something wrong by eating what I want, so I need to ask for forgiveness.

But really, now that I write and walk myself through this, I don't need to forgive myself for enjoying my sweet tooth, and maybe I already have permission to move on from Monday since that little girl already forgave me.

Maybe what I need to do is treat myself the way I treated my eight-year-old girl, and just how I realized I was too hard on her, maybe I am too hard on myself too. Ed is hard enough on me as it is, and I don't need to add myself to that equation on top of that.

We are our own harshest critics. When will it be okay with our standards of perfection to treat ourselves how we would treat an eight-year-old child who we love?

If we are talking about the eating disorder world of perfection, that time is never. But if we are talking about the Hello Life recovery world, the world of forty days left to reach a year without a scale, and the world of learning how to be okay with being imperfect, that time is now.

If I can treat that little girl with so much love and compassion, there must be enough of that love left for myself too.

Yes to my sweet tooth. Yes to that girl being in heaven for a simple drink. Yes to treating ourselves how we would an eight-year-old.
Yes, yes and yes.
Hello Life!

******

Day 326: Eating Cupcakes in the Sun

I had just had lunch/dessert with one of my friends, Anna, and I had a little bit of time before I needed to go tutoring, so I thought I would write about it while these positive feelings were still fresh in my heart.

Hopefully, by writing about the positive feelings I had right then, it would keep Ed from coming and trying to ruin it about twenty minutes later, when they started to slightly wear off.

Friday, December 13

Anna and I are Friday lunch and pastry partners. Whenever we see each other, it's always on a Friday and we go to lunch, then we go for dessert. Sometimes we get dessert at the restaurant we eat lunch at, sometimes, like last time, we go to a bakery. Other times, like today, we try somewhere new.
Today we went to this award-winning cupcake shop by our school. We actually went in there before eating lunch, made sure the cupcakes were up to our sweet tooth standards, and then drove back after we ate lunch to get our cupcakes. This lunch/dessert date totally took place in the recovery world, not Ed's world.

So anyway, there we were, sitting with our S'mores cupcake and our mocha chocolate cupcake, just laughing, enjoying and saying how we were happy we could eat like this together.

"Eating cupcakes in the sun, that is what life is about," Anna said.

I told her right in that moment that she just named my blog post for today. What else do I need to say? Eating cupcakes in the sun.

Sweetness, company, friendship and enjoyment, on a day that I didn't work out, on a day that I still don't have a job, on a day that Ed is telling me I am not allowed to do anything but hate myself.

Well, sorry Ed. I enjoyed my cupcakes in the sun with my friend anyway. Hello Life!

******

Day 327: Hello to My Strong and Ass-Kicking Alter Ego

Today had been the Bat Mitzvah of one of my cousins, which was a big celebration with a big party. A big fancy celebration of course meant a nice fancy dress to celebrate in.

For me, this meant potential Ed destruction. Which dress did I feel good in? Which ones still fitted me? How did I know which one to try on without getting sucked into Ed chaos?

In the past, when I had been faced with situations like that, I had been known to try on every single outfit in my closet – old clothes and new clothes. It had never ended up with me feeling good about myself or my new healthy body.

But these were the habits and behaviors that Ed had instilled in me for so many years; they were the rules that he had told me I had to abide by.

Saturday, December 14

If you are going to a nice party and you need a nice dress, of course you should try on the tightest smallest dresses you own and see how they fit you. If they fit good, you get a pat on the back, if they don't, you know you are not up to Ed's standards (this is what Ed would say).

I had the choice today of whether I wanted to continue in my old Ed habits or I wanted to try to break them.

Before I tell you how I broke those habits, let me say that while, through my writing, this victory may look like it was an easy one, it was extremely difficult. Making the choices I did today took immense inner strength, dedication and courage to stand up to Ed.

So, what did I do? I took the dress that I knew I wouldn't feel good about myself in out of my closet yesterday and gave it to my sister. She didn't even have to ask why I was giving it to her, she already knew. But I told her if she wanted she could consider it hers because I am never taking it back.

Then I took out the last dress that I remember wearing that I felt good about myself in and put it out to hang on my door. That is it. My decision was made yesterday. That was the dress and that is what I am wearing. I told myself yesterday that there will be no trying on anything else.

I am deliberately writing this post ten minutes before I need to get ready so I am left with no time to try on any new outfits, in case Ed starts to creep in.

Today took strength. Giving my sister my old dress took strength. Putting on this dress right now when I am not in the greatest place with my body and still going to the Bat Mitzvah and putting a smile on my face because I know tonight is not about me, takes strength. I think, more than anything, that is what I am priding myself on today.

I don't like my body right now, I don't like the way I look in any dress right now, and I don't particularly love the fact that I can't wear the dress Ed once thought I looked so skinny in because it no longer fits the same.

But regardless of all those things, I am able to put them aside and step into the shoes of Shira the recovery warrior, she is kind of like my alter ego. Shira the warrior doesn't let those things ruin her cousin's Bat Mitzvah and she doesn't let those negative thoughts swallow up her personality. Shira the recovery warrior is present, she is strong and she is ready for tonight.

We have already gone ahead and named my eating disorder with his own name, so why not run with the concept of tapping into my alter ego? If it works, I say I like it. And so far, it's working.

Hello to my strong and ass-kicking alter ego, and Hello Life!

******

Day 328: Go Jenna Jameson

I had been home today watching Oprah's *Where Are They Now?* show, and there was a segment that came on with Jenna Jameson, one of the world's most famous porn stars, literally one of the most bodily judged human beings of all time.

> *"I used to think I had to be X [not saying the number so it doesn't trigger anyone] pounds and look a certain way. Now I let myself eat whatever I want and be like a normal person and I forgive myself if I have a muffin top sometimes."*

That is what she had said about her life now that she wasn't a porn star anymore. I think it just went to show, once again, how we were so not alone in this battle to true self-acceptance.

Sunday, December 15

Eating disorder or no eating disorder, I am starting to think that we as human beings all fight the fight of learning how to truly love ourselves; even the sexiest of porn stars are fighting this fight. We all fight the fight of loving our muffin tops, or loving our 'this' or 'that' that our Eds won't approve of.

When I saw Jenna Jameson say how she forgives herself for having a muffin top, I wanted to shout at Ed, "You see Ed, if a porn star, who everyone once judged based on her sexy looks could love her muffin top, then I could love myself without your approval too."

Go Jenna Jameson.

Go me for not only going out two separate times today for breakfast and dinner, but for also being so present for all of it and not letting the food take over me.

Go all of us who are fighting the fight, learning how to love our muffin, cake, candy – whatever food you want – tops/body parts that our Eds tell us not to.

Hello Life!

******

Day 329: Redefining Accomplishments

Today I had really had to force myself to stick to my original good old plan.

At first I had been upset at myself because I thought I was past the point of needing to force myself and remind myself to stick to my meal plan, because I had so often just listened to my body and eaten whatever I wanted. But, like always, I learned again that I couldn't plan my recovery.

So today I found that I hadn't passed that point. Oh well, I had done what I had to do ... moved on.

Monday, December 16

Right before I was about to write this post, I was trying to find an index card for my final tomorrow to make study cards, and I came across my very first journal that E gave me.

On the very first page, it said 'Accomplishments'. In the very beginning of my recovery, E had me write down my recovery accomplishments every day. I totally forgot about them.

It started on December 28, almost a year ago from today, and it said I ate frozen yogurt and chocolate. The next day, December 29, it said I ate dinner even though I was in a fight with my boyfriend at the time.

The list goes on over the next few days to include eating dinner, one time eating cake and coffee creamer, and one time eating even though I thought I weighed too much. (Keep in mind, this was on January 2 and that I gave up my scale on January 21.)

Looking at that list made me realize that even though it's been almost a year since I wrote it, those accomplishments still need to be celebrated.

So what if I had to force myself to stick to the plan today? I still did it, and that is an accomplishment.

My favorite part about that original list of accomplishments is that every day it said I had some kind of sweets. For those who read this blog every day, you know how much I love sweets.

I am so happy that I am here a year later and able to say I am still eating sweets, and may I use today as a reminder to not forget what an accomplishment that is.

To all of our accomplishments today, whether they be big or small, or with food or with our mentality, we deserve to own them, recognize them and celebrate them.

Now that I think of it, what does the word *accomplishment* even mean? If you asked me this on a whim during the day, right now in my life, I would tell you it means that I am graduating college tomorrow and that if I only had a job, then I would feel accomplished.

But seeing this list shows me how far from the truth that is. Since when do accomplishments have to be a job, money or not having to work so hard to follow the meal plan? Since when does the word *accomplishment* even have a certain level of expectation that I need to reach in order to celebrate it?

I don't like it and I want to change that. No more rules and expectations to what I need to do to feel accomplished. My list that I made a year ago had no expectations from E when I made it. She just wanted me to find a reason to feel proud of myself every day.

So let's redefine *accomplishment* to exactly that: Finding a reason to be proud of ourselves every day, even if all we did that day was wake up and simply exist in the moment. Even if all we did, like me today, was follow our meal plan.

May I add, I found out today that this blog made it onto NEDA's 2014 Blogroll. Our journey, our stories and our support for one another made that possible, and, if anything, that is the biggest accomplishment of all.

Hello Life!

******

Day 330: Oh My God, I Am a College Graduate

I used to imagine how I would write this day's post. I remember it so clearly.

I had been in the beginning stages of writing my blog, and I remember thinking to myself how incredible it would be to write a post about how I graduated college while actually being in recovery from my eating disorder. How wonderful it would be to graduate college and not have a number on the scale to ruin my day.

Now I couldn't believe that that post had actually come and that I was actually writing it.

Tuesday, December 17

Today I officially completed my last day of college. I am officially a college graduate. I mean, I can't believe I made it to this day while being in recovery.

I had dinner tonight with my best friend and another friend, and we had to end it with Linda. Lifers, please meet Linda. She is my chocolate fudge cake at my favorite restaurant (the cake is called Linda's Fudge Cake) that everyone in my life knows I need to order and have.

Ed and Linda are not friends. There were times where Ed made Linda and I lose connection. But, through my recovery, Linda and I have rekindled our spark.

So there are a few things to celebrate today. I graduated college AND I got to celebrate with my best friend and with Linda. Perfection, pretty much.

I thought I had made it through the day without crying, which is what I usually do on any kind of occasion that has some kind of emotion, until I got to my car after dinner. I had posted a Facebook status about graduating, and one of my family friends wrote, "Great job, sunshine. Your grandpa would have been very proud."

Some readers who have been with me since the beginning and who have read my earlier posts about my grandfather, know that he was my heart, my love and my rock and now that he is no longer physically here, he is my angel. I tried to not think of him today, because I knew it would make me cry that he is not here to celebrate with me, but I also know that my family friend was right, he would have been so proud.

He would have been proud that his first two granddaughters (I have a twin sister who graduated today too) graduated university. He would have been proud that I shared it with my friends and family. He would most definitely had been proud that I shared it with Linda.

On days like today, the power that Ed once had over me is somewhere far away. Even though he is here giving me a hard time about Linda, I don't care.

I finished college while being in recovery today, which means no number on a scale or no calorie count can take away from that accomplishment. I finished college being able to say that I wrote the best cover stories I ever wrote. I finished college today and made my grandpa proud.

Actually, I finished college today and made myself proud, and it has nothing to do with what I look like, what I weigh or what I ate. I am proud ... period. No Ed excuses around it.

Oh, and I can't forget to say that I am proud that Linda and I had a date tonight.

Lastly, I am grateful that I am able to celebrate today with all of the beautiful souls who are part of this journey. Thank you for letting me share this milestone with you guys and thank you for being with me, supporting me and encouraging me along the way.

Oh my God ... I am a college graduate.

Hello Life!

******

Day 331: Stripped of Validations

I had to say thank you so much for all the incredible love that everyone had shown me after I had written about finishing college the previous day. Every comment and every email truly made me smile and brought me so much strength and joy.

On that note, my one night of feeling so proud of myself was very short lived.

I had gone in for another job interview, only to find out that it was an unpaid internship, which meant it wasn't something that would work for me right then, because I hadn't gone to college to work for free.

I think I had cried four times this day, if I counted correctly and didn't forget any. I thought I was about to face the hardest part of my journey to recovery.

Wednesday, December 18

In the beginning of my recovery and in the beginning of my journey of one year without a scale, not weighing myself for one day was a huge deal. Then, not weighing myself every day after that was a big deal and it was a huge accomplishment; enough of an accomplishment to keep me feeling proud of myself.

Then as I moved through my recovery, I was able to add more accomplishments to feel proud of myself, such as writing cover stories for my university newspaper, breaking certain food rules or getting good grades in school.

I apologize if I have been writing about this subject frequently lately, but as you know this blog is honest and real, and this is what I have been dealing with lately.

What has happened to me that now being on Day 331 of not weighing myself is no longer enough to keep me feeling proud of myself? What has happened that now following my meal plan, eating my sweets and standing up to Ed on a daily basis are not enough to keep me feeling proud of myself? What has happened that graduating college is not enough to keep me feeling proud of myself for more than one night?

I say that I think I will be facing the hardest part of recovery right now because this is actually the first time in recovery that I don't have any of those things to help me feel validated. This will be the first time in many years that I won't turn to Ed for validation when other things are not working. I am making that choice, but it's a choice that I know I am going to have to fight for every day.

It would be extremely easy to go back to the arms of Ed right now. When there is no job, no exterior accomplishments and not even a scale to validate me, there is of course always Ed and his rules of restricting to pat me on the back when I do a good job.

I don't want to go there and I refuse to go there. But just because I am choosing not to go there doesn't mean it's going to be easy.

I imagine myself as this really beautiful luxury car with all the bells and whistles – a sunroof, fancy tints, nice rims and a really good stereo system inside.

What happens when you take away the nice rims? There are only tires. What happens when you take away the tints? There are only regular windows. What happens when you take away the sound system? There is only silence. What happens when you remove the sunroof and the fancy paint job? There is just the metal frame of that car.

I am that metal frame right now. I feel like I have been stripped of so many of the fancy validations that were taking Ed's place up until now. Stripped of my fancy title as senior reporter, stripped of my grades in school (since I am no longer in school), and even my accomplishments with recovery don't feel as great as they once did.

But maybe this is all happening for a reason. Maybe this is the part of recovery where I have to look at that metal frame – no body on it, no fancy titles on it, nothing on it, but just its frame.

Ed used to be that frame for me. He was my foundation to the frame. He was the links that kept the metal frame together. This is the first time that I need to look at that frame without Ed holding it up, and it scares me that I don't know what I will find.

In one month I won't even have this blog to identify myself with. I feel like I am stripped down to the core of my being. But regardless of my fears of what I will find when I look at just my frame, plain and simple, I know this: I won't find Ed. I am not Ed, he is not me, and he doesn't make up my frame anymore.

But if he doesn't, then who does? If a job, fancy title or weight can't make me who I am, then what does?

I don't have the answers, but like everything else with this blog and this journey, I have hope that I will figure it out.

Hello Life!

******

Day 332: The End of My Pity Party for One

My pity party for one about not finding a job, not feeling accomplished and feeling sorry for myself that I had to deal with Ed all at the same time was now officially over. It had happened, it had lasted and now it was over.

Today, I hadn't even had the time to focus on my joblessness, because I had been busy fighting with Ed. I didn't know why, but Ed had just been so loud and alive today, with every single thing I had eaten and every single thing I had thought about eating.

Thursday, December 19

I had got the families I tutor all some holiday gift baskets for Christmas, and when I was at the house of one of the kids, her nanny had put out the chocolates, cheeses and snacks that I brought them for us to eat during our session.

I was just watching a Dr. Oz episode yesterday (I am not his biggest fan, but I watched it anyway) where some fitness expert said that when you really want to eat something that is not good for you, you should count to fifty. If once you count to fifty you still want it, then it's a little more justifiable to have it.

Well, imagine Ed's happiness when he saw that on the show. Not only do we criticize ourselves for eating things that he doesn't approve of, but now we actually take the time to count to fifty before doing so.

So, I am not happy to say I tried it, but I was in such a bad place with Ed in my ear that I really was trying everything I could to not give in and eat all that deliciousness in front of me, so I tried to count to fifty.

Honestly, by the time I got to fifteen I think I wanted all of that stuff more than I did before I started the whole counting process in the first place. Then I thought, what am I doing? First off, the little girl I was with was talking to me and I blocked her out because of my ridiculous count to fifteen, then I realized this was all Ed dominating me.

So, I ate what I wanted. It wasn't overload, it wasn't a binge, it was just what I wanted and craved and it pissed Ed off – a lot. He is still mad at me right now. But really, what am I going to do?

At first, I was really thinking about how unfair it is that I have to deal with my dear Ed while others during the holidays can just enjoy these holiday sweets without thinking twice. But again, it's like throwing myself a pity party. No more of that. It's even annoying me at this point.

So, I ate it. And just like my bad day yesterday, it happened and now it passed. Regardless of what Ed might want me to believe, the world didn't end because of it and I am not a valueless person because of it. Actually, I think the little girl loved me more because of it, as I got to enjoy those sweets with her.

We all are fighting, searching for validation and dealing with our own form of 'Ed', whatever it may be.

And now that I am done feeling sorry for myself, I can start to find ways to love myself again – ways that Ed doesn't control, ways that a job doesn't control, and ways that numbers, weight and counting to fifty don't control.

Goodbye to my pity party. Goodbye to counting to fifty before eating what I want, and Hello Life!

******

Day 333: Trying Every Chocolate in the Box

Today, I had written my blog early, as I had really wanted to write about an experience I had had the previous night, and I had wanted to start my Friday with it.

I hadn't written about the dating part of my life a lot over the past year because it was pretty much non-existent, but I guess for this one post I could bring it up because it was really relevant.

Friday, December 20

I started dating this guy about a month ago (super-nice guy), and I had told him that my favorite chocolates are Lindor chocolates. I said it one time and that was it.

Last night after we went for dinner, he gave me this huge gift box of Lindor chocolates. "Since they don't have a Lindor store, I ordered it online for you because you said they are your favorite," he said.

This is not about the chocolates, the gift or the dating, it's the fact that he remembered something I said; my voice was heard by him when I said that I like those chocolates.

So, what did I do? I went into my kitchen, turned the light on at 11:45 at night, sat with that huge basket of chocolates and tried every single kind of chocolate in there. There was a box of fancy chocolates within the basket, the kinds with the different fillings, and I sat and tried every single one.

At first I was scared I was about to binge, but then I realized that I loved these chocolates. They are my favorite kind. And hell yeah, I wanted to try them, so that is exactly what I did.

I don't even want to think about the number of calories in those chocolates, as the nutrition labels were on every package, but thinking of that would ruin my experience.

I loved every moment of sitting in my kitchen eating and trying my different chocolates that this person had given to me. I liked the fact that it was just me, and I liked that I let myself try each one.

When I was done, I thought about throwing all the left-over chocolates away so it wouldn't tempt me. But why? That would be Ed talking. It's scary to have them in my house, yes. But I do live with my sister and my grandma, and maybe they want some of that chocolate too? Why should Ed take that away from them? Why should Ed take it away from me? Who said I am only allowed to try every chocolate I want for just one night?

I woke up this morning with Ed making me feel not so wonderful about my late-night indulgence – actually he is trying to make me feel horrible. He is kind of getting through to me, but that is why I wrote this post right when I woke up.

For the rest of the day, whenever Ed is saying his lies about how 'bad' I am for eating what I ate, I can just look back and read about my peaceful and joyful experience of sitting in my kitchen for a late-night dessert, trying every chocolate in my chocolate box.

And on a side note, totally not relevant to my chocolate box experience, I realized that while I am able to connect with everyone via email or comments, other fighters are not able to be connected with each other.

I have been speaking with a few other fighters who said they would like to be connected to other people for support, especially with the holidays coming up. Is anyone wanting to participate in some kind of Facebook forum where everyone can speak, discuss and offer support to one another outside this blog?

I think that is the easiest way to do it. If you are interested, please let me know so I can put it together and invite everyone who wants to be part of it. Or maybe we can try a TweetChat or an online EDA group? But I think Facebook is easiest, so let me know what you guys think either with comments or emails.

So, yes, I tried every single chocolate in the box. What can I say to you Ed? Hell yeah.

Hello Life!

******

Day 334: This Is How We Celebrate One Month Left

Today had marked the official one-month countdown of our one-year journey together. So, how did I celebrate it?

Saturday, December 21

Happy one month left of our one-year journey.
I had a movie date with my eight-year-old brother, the one who said he would like to switch brains with me so he can have all the right answers in school.

Let me explain something about this little boy to you. Not only is he funny, but he is warm, loving and he loves sweets almost as much as me. So there was no one else I would rather spend this day with than him.

I would like to say that I am the one who took him out, but he had two free movie tickets, so besides the candy and cookie we ate, he actually treated me.

Before we go to a movie, I always take my brothers to this candy store by the theatre so they can pick whatever they want. Last time we were at this candy store, I remember exactly what I got – a few sugar-free chocolate-covered almonds and sugar-free jellybeans. They were horrible. Today my brother and I got our own bags each, and this time there was nothing sugar-free in mine.

We watched the movie together and laughed together, and I just kept thinking to myself how lucky I was that out of all the people in the world, he chose me to go watch it with him.

You know the craziest part? He had no idea that I was celebrating the last month countdown of my year without a scale today; no one actually knew.

On our way out to the car, we stopped to get some pastries for a friend, and of course for us too, and he said to me, "Shira, if I could make a rule for the world, it would be that everyone loved pastries." Then we both laughed and said we both wished it could be true.

The entire way home we talked about funny lines that we remembered from the movie, and we talked about how the boys' bathroom in his school is not as nice as the girls' bathroom (he says he only knows this because a girl, who he made very clear to me is not his girlfriend, told him the girls' bathroom is nicer).

This is what I am celebrating today:

I am celebrating the world of loving pastries being a rule.

I am celebrating the world of sharing movie lines in the car.

I am celebrating the world where the fact that the boys' bathroom being not as nice as the girls' bathroom is a major issue.

I am celebrating the world where the girl you talk about when you are eight years old is a girl but, make no mistake, she is not your girlfriend.

I am celebrating the world of things that really matter in life – the small, innocent, touching moments that no number on a scale, no job and no fancy title could ever give you.

I can't think of a better way to celebrate my one-month countdown.

Hello Life!

******

Day 335: We Don't Choose Our Bad Days

It's safe to say that we don't choose when we have bad or good days, right? I hadn't wanted or chosen for this day to not be the greatest day, but so far it hadn't been.

Had I wished that the day after I had celebrated one month left of my journey would be a good day? Yes. Did I wish that those bad days would stop popping up so randomly? Yes.

And when I say bad day, I don't mean not eating. At this point in my recovery, eating on my meal plan (at minimum) was just a daily thing like brushing my teeth. I was talking about the way I felt about my body. I was uncomfortable in my own skin on this day.

Sunday, December 22

This entire week has been a battle of being uncomfortable with the fact that I still don't have a job and it has caused me to really look at how I define myself and now it's returned full circle to the battle of being physically and mentally uncomfortable in my own skin.

I can't choose my bad days, but I know that I can choose my reaction. To sit here and write that I am going to just smile and move on like I am okay today would be a lie and it wouldn't be realistic right now.

While on some bad days I can do that, today is not one of them. But what I can do and will do is accept what is. I can try to fight this feeling and make myself feel guilty about having a bad day, feel guilty about all the body checks I did today and feel guilty about the complaining about my body that I have done to my sister today. But why? Things happen. Days happen. And bad days happen even after good days.

There are a lot of things about recovery that have nothing to do with our bodies, but then there are days or moments where the harsh reality that my body is changing and clothes are fitting differently are elements that I can't avoid. So, today is one of those days. I might not smile and be the happiest of people today, but I will get through it.

I think getting through is sometimes the best thing we can do for ourselves, especially on our bad days that we don't choose to have.

Here is to getting through until tomorrow.
Hello Life!

******

Day 336: Rolling with the Punches

We don't choose our bad days and we don't choose life – life chooses us. It chooses when we face certain issues, it chooses when we face certain destinies and it chooses which battles we each need to fight to make us who we are. I had learned yet again that we can't choose the way things happen to us all the time.

When I had been invited to a totally unexpected dinner the previous day and lunch today with the new guy I am dating, you can see where this lesson had been taught to me yet again. On a day when I had been really despising the way I looked, I had been invited to dinner – a big, heavy, fancy dinner. And on the day after that dinner, where Ed was ready to go crazy on me for what I had eaten, not only had I skipped my regular Monday gym session, but I had gone to lunch (lunch with desserts may I add).

There had been two choices: I could have stayed in my Ed, anti-social and isolated world, or rolled with the punches, just gone and got with life's program, and forgot Ed's program.

So I had rolled with it. I had smiled, eaten, laughed, and been present with everyone around me.

Monday, December 23

I may not be feeling good about all the food I have eaten since yesterday with these unexpected social eating experiences, but I am really proud of myself that I did it. I rolled with those punches. I went with the flow. I did recovery in real life. It wasn't what I had planned, which was staying home around my nice, comfortable and safe meal plan, but, it's what happened.

In a time in my life where everything from my job status to my body changes to what I will do when this blog is over is so unknown to me, rolling with the punches is the best advice I can seem to give myself. I guess if we can't choose our bad days, and we can't choose what life has planned for us, we can choose to just roll with it.

And on the same note of rolling with things as they come, my Facebook forum didn't work out. Either I am technologically challenged or it's just not meant to be, because it's a public forum and I want everyone to feel safe speaking with each other. So that plan didn't work.

My next idea is to have everyone who wants to be part of this fighter support group to send me your email, and I will send everyone a group email with everyone's contact info. We can do a group thread or people can email separately with whoever they want. What do you think?

And as always, sorry if I am repeating myself, but thank you again for everyone's support yesterday and today. I honestly almost cry sometimes at the beautiful messages and comments you all write – thank you so much. We are rolling on this journey together, and I am forever grateful for that.

Let's roll with the unexpected punches, the unexpected dinners, the unexpected issues that are bound to arise with the holiday family gatherings coming up, and the unexpected social eating experiences. We can do it.

Hello Life!

******

Day 337: Christmas Eve with Ed: Recovery Edition

Today and the next day would be some, if not the absolute hardest days of the entire year for people in recovery for an eating disorder, or actually in recovery for any kind of addiction.

When we spend time with relatives or close friends and family, it's easy for old memories or feelings to come up and trigger our Eds or our addictions.

I knew that for us in recovery for eating disorders, these two days (Christmas Eve and Christmas Day) would be especially difficult because they are two days that are totally surrounded by food.

Tuesday, December 24

Happy Christmas Eve everyone.

As weird as it may seem, while I am Jewish, I actually do celebrate Christmas and it's my very favorite holiday.

My uncle is not Jewish and celebrates and practices Christmas every year, so just like any other family celebrating Christmas, so do we on behalf of my uncle.

I am not sure what Christmas Eve dinner or Christmas dinner looks like for others around the world, but for us it's basically like Thanksgiving all over again. Whether you are celebrating with a dinner tonight, or a breakfast or dinner tomorrow, we are all going to be surrounded by food today.

If you have been reading my recent posts lately, you know that I haven't been in the best place with Ed. Realizing that my big Christmas Eve dinner falls today wasn't an easy thing to take in.

My first instinct was to not go, and to stay home and eat what felt safe to me. But I knew that wouldn't only be selfish and disrespectful to my family member who celebrates this holiday, but it also would be taking away my joy from a holiday that I love so much.

Here is the thing with today: I would like to say that this is my Christmas and that this is my holiday and Ed can't ruin it at all — he will be nowhere in sight. But that is just not true. It's indeed my holiday and Ed won't ruin it for me, but to say that he won't be anywhere in sight is not true and I don't think it's fair to expect it to be.

For a long time I thought that if I had Ed next to me, it meant I was failing, but I see now how wrong I was. The fact that, yes, many times I do have Ed with me, yet I am still succeeding in my recovery, speaks volumes. That is strength and bravery.

I don't expect Ed to not be with me at my Christmas Eve dinner tonight. I know he will be there. He will be sitting right next to me on my chair. And you know, I think that is okay for the moment.

Ed was with me for so many years, so to say that he would just disappear during my very first holiday season in recovery would be the perfectionist, black-and-white person in me speaking, and I have let that part of me go.

The biggest lesson I continue to learn is that none of us have to be perfect in our recovery. Today my recovery means being present and going to that Christmas Eve dinner, even when Ed is telling me not to. If he comes with me, so be it. If I need to wear my stretchy pants and loose shirt, so be it. The fact is, I am there ... period. I am there.

And to my dear friends and fighters, please know that wherever you are we are all going and fighting through these hard holiday gatherings together. At least for me, knowing that I am not alone, during a time where I feel like it's difficult for others around me to understand the anxiety around food, is a big source of support.

When you are at your dinner table tonight celebrating Christmas Eve, I will be at mine doing the same thing. When you are around the delicious holiday treats tomorrow morning, so will I be. And so will our Eds too, but that is okay.

Last year, only Ed was present during this time of year for me; Shira was not. I was physically there but my mind wasn't. Now I am here. I might be here with my Ed next to me – my little, annoying Ed who doesn't hold much power anymore – but, nonetheless, I am here.

If we have our Eds with us at our tables tonight and tomorrow, let's forgive ourselves for it. If we eat what our Eds tell us not to, oh hell yes, let's forgive ourselves for it, because it's Christmas and we deserve it. And if we feel our Eds are taking over us, let's forgive ourselves for it, because regardless of what our eating disorders want us to think, we are not perfect.

We are learning, and for me and for many reading this, it's our first Christmas in recovery. Let's love ourselves and give ourselves some slack.

Wishing everyone and their Eds (if they are present) a very happy, safe and delicious Christmas Eve.
Hello Life!

******

Day 338: It's the Holidays Ed, Watch and Learn

The previous day in my therapy session with E I had been telling her that I hoped I would get sick so I would have a valid reason for myself to not work out. I was tired, my body was tired, and I had just wanted to take some days off, but being in the place I was with Ed and being Christmas, with all the food, I couldn't find it within myself to do it.

When I was locked in my eating disorder, I would work out even when I was sick, but in recovery this wasn't something I allowed myself to do.

Well, in the true way that the law of attraction works, I had woken up on this morning sick. I had such a sore throat I could barely swallow.

At first, when this gave me permission to cancel my running plans with my friend, I was kind of relieved, then Ed woke up too and the madness began. "You are sick, so you don't have an appetite to eat today, right Shira?" he was saying. "You are sick, so you can't go to all the lunches and dinners you had planned for Christmas today, right Shira?"

Uh ... wrong Ed. Very wrong.

Wednesday, December 25

Merry Christmas everyone.

I tried to listen to Ed today. It's not something I am happy about, but I did try. But I sit here now, one lunch and one dessert session later, and two more dinners ahead of me (which doesn't mean I have to eat at all of them, but nonetheless they are there), and I can honestly say Ed was wrong. I still totally had my appetite ... and I ate ... and ate ... and ate desserts too ... delicious amazing deserts. And I will probably eat more desserts today.

Do I wish that I could take days off from working out without needing an excuse of being sick? Yes, very much so. But at the same time, I don't blame myself for not being at that point yet.

So I think this was the universe's way of giving me a day off, or possibly a few days off, and maybe I deserve that. I am sick, so I can't work out. Go me.

It doesn't mean I don't need to have my appetite, even if Ed wants that to be true. How could I not have an appetite with all this yummy Christmas food in front of me today and yesterday? How can I not have an appetite to eat the desserts that I handpicked myself to bring? Having a sore throat doesn't affect that.

Oh, and may I add that I tried ham for the very first time yesterday. Oh my God. Wow. I will never go twenty-three years again without it.

So with that said, and with sitting here now feeling sick with my sore throat because I pretty much asked for it, and yet still ate what I wanted today anyway and didn't work out, I only have one thing to say: It's the holidays, Ed.

People enjoy the holidays. People take days off from working out even if they are not sick, and they don't need to hope to get sick to do so. People eat when they are sick too, because they like the food in front of them and it's a social component.

It's the holidays. Holidays is a word you don't know, dear Ed, but that is okay because I will teach you. Now it's time for you to watch and learn how people enjoy the holidays without you calling the shots.

And if my clothes start to fit a bit tighter in the meantime of me teaching you, oh well. If I gain a few pounds that I will never be able to see since there is no more scale, then oh well. It's the holidays Ed. Watch and learn how we in the recovery world celebrate.

Hello to my first holiday season in recovery, hello to any other fighter's first holiday season in recovery, and hello to all of us teaching our Eds how we celebrate.

And last but most definitely not least: Hello Life!

******

Day 339: Holding onto the Image of Hope

We had made it. It was the day after Christmas, meaning that Christmas Eve and Christmas day had passed and we had made it. At least for me, after two days of non-stop food and holiday eating mode, I was feeling really accomplished.

I had tried ham for the first time over Christmas. I had also tried duck for the first time. I had had three dinners on Christmas Day and about three dessert sessions to go with them. I had eaten it all and loved the taste of it all, but mostly I had loved the fact that I was able to spend time with people.

If I had been locked in my eating disorder, there is no way I would have gone to my Christmas Eve dinner, or to any of the Christmas meals, and I would have spent it alone. Just Ed and me at home.

To know that I had spent it with people, with laughter, with smiles and, yes, with delicious yummy food, reminded me of the freedom that never went away in the recovery world.

Thursday, December 26

When I got home last night I decided that today was the day I was finally going to take a day off. I know I am sick and I need to rest, so why not take a mini staycation in my bed. I decided that I won't set my alarm for today and that I won't do anything but rest in my nice bed and watch movies.

I actually went through with not setting my alarm, but I didn't really relax today because I spent my time still endlessly applying for jobs, but I got fifty percent of the staycation down with not setting my alarm.

A morning where I didn't wake up to my alarm telling me it's time to go to the gym is a big win for me. I don't remember the last morning I had like that, and it was really peaceful. Even though I know I am not going because I am sick, it doesn't matter. The point is I didn't go and it felt good.

Ironically enough my twin sister is sick too with the same sore throat as me. I still ate breakfast, and was feeling really good about it, considering Ed told me not to, because since I can't swallow it means I can't eat, which is not true. So when lunchtime came around, I was honestly thankful she was here.

"Shira, I am hungry. Let's eat lunch." Um ... lunch? Ed didn't want me to eat lunch today. He told me lunch was going to be tea.

And today, I truly didn't have an appetite to eat because I am sick. But I know by now that whereas some people who are not in recovery for eating disorders may get the so-called luxury of not eating because they are sick, I can't do that – at least not right now. So my sister and I had lunch together and it was such an interesting experience for me to observe.

We both had soup, since we both have sore throats, but the way we each prepared our meals were so different. She just poured her soup into her bowl straight from the carton. No measuring or anything. Just poured whatever she wanted. I measured out specifically one cup of soup for my bowl.

She added loads of parmesan cheese to her soup, again not measuring. I measured the cheese into mine. Then I brought out a box of crackers for us to eat with our soup, and while I was counting every one I ate, she didn't seem to count hers. I don't even think she knows how many calories are in each cracker – a fact that I know very well.

I am not mad at myself for measuring my food, because right now it's what I need to stick to my meal plan. I know I need to eat and I know it's hard to eat when I am sick, so if measuring it makes me feel a little bit more in control, then why not? There is no handbook on eating when you are sick when in recovery for an eating disorder, so I am finding what works as I go.

But seeing my sister not measure her soup, her cheese or her crackers, and thinking about the idea that she probably has no idea how many calories was in this meal, nor did she seem to care, made me smile with joy. That is the world of someone who is not tainted by Ed. Sometimes, and on a lot of days, it's my world too, even if it wasn't totally my world today.

Looking at my sister gave me hope. That will be me one day. I will be the one not measuring or not counting crackers. It might not be today, or even a month or year from now, but it will be me. Holding that image of hope close to my heart is what is giving me strength today.

Hello Life!

******

Day 340: Our Bodies Have a Mind of Their Own

By now the recovery fighter support group had officially started and was active online with discussion forums already flowing, and I needed to thank the strong souls who were putting their heart, time and support out there to help one another.

Who knew that my sweet tooth would still be alive even when I was sick? Being sick had really taught me a different level of self-care. It had taught me that my body truly had a mind of its own.

Friday, December 27

Because I am sick I am not really in control of what my body needs right now. If it doesn't need exercise, it doesn't, and that is something I have to honor. If it wants food and sweets even if it's not working out, it needs that, and I need to honor that too.

This is the kind of self-care where I really need to take my own self out of the picture and just listen to my body. My body has a mind of its own, and it really doesn't care what Ed thinks.

Even on the days where we try to tell our bodies not to crave certain things, it doesn't care. It will crave them even more, right? Our bodies don't care that they didn't exercise today, they still want and need food. My body is probably enjoying its staycation from the gym in bed even if Ed is not.

My body doesn't care that Ed is telling it to not want certain foods. Praise and long live to my strong fighting body that doesn't care what Ed says.

Hello Life!

******

Day 341: A Staycation Done Right

Let me define for you what the word staycation means to me. Staycation: A vacation where you don't go anywhere and stay exactly where you are.

I had been talking about this staycation for a few days now, ever since I had been sick and hadn't been able to work out, but today was the first day that I had actually gone through with it, meaning I hadn't applied for any jobs or anything, just sat and rested. Also, I hadn't worked out for a few days.

Saturday, December 28

The beginning of the day was extremely hard for me, and I was tempted to start going through my old clothes and trying them all on to see how they now fit. Some of you may remember that this was something I used to do a lot but slowly stopped throughout this journey to recovery.

One of the girls in the fighter support group had written that when she couldn't work out because she was sick, she had made a pro and con list. So I figured if it worked for her, it has a good chance of working for me too.

It took all of sixty seconds to make my pro and con list to my staycation at home today.

Pro: Get to watch all the movies I haven't seen and watch the Law and Order *SVU marathon; get to listen to music; get to eat breakfast and lunch in bed; sing in my room to my Pandora.*

Con: Didn't get to burn a few extra calories at the gym.

That is six pros and only one, tiny, small con. In Ed's world, this one con is everything. I mean, it should be the deciding factor of my entire day. But in my world, which is the world of learning how to live in recovery, that con honestly can erase itself from this page because it really doesn't matter.

What matters is that I found time to rest today. What matters is that I listened to my body today. What matters is that I was kind to myself today.

As I was getting a little anxious from being home all day, WordPress notified me that our blog has reached five hundred followers. From my five siblings and parents to now five hundred.

It was the perfect reminder of why I am home today, of why I am learning to be kind to myself and to my body and of why I chose the path to recovery. It was a reminder that while I made the decision myself to walk this journey to recovery, I have been so blessed to not have to walk it alone. We are five hundred strong fighters and each and every one us deserves credit for being a part of each other's journey.

You know what else matters today? What matters is that I actually liked this staycation and I actually am hoping that I don't need to wait until I am sick again to give myself another one. Today was a staycation done right.

Who said you need to be sick to enjoy a day off from the gym or from all of life's responsibilities? Ed said that. What a lonely and sad person Ed is on his way to becoming without me.

Hello Life!

******

Day 342: Mom, I Need New Jeans ... Again

I had been getting ready this morning to go to a basketball game (I was still sick but this still counted as a staycation because it was fun, right?) and I had pulled out a pair of pants I had bought for myself about two months into recovery.

At the time I had bought this pair and another pair of pants, and I actually didn't think I would have to buy another pair ever again. Two months in recovery meant my body had done with changing, right? Well, apparently not.

When these jeans had fit tighter today, my first instinct was that they were tight because I hadn't worked out in almost a week, plus the holiday food fun I had been having.

But then I realized, I had bought these in the very beginning of my recovery. Who said they would always fit how they fitted at the beginning of my body getting healthy again?

Sunday, December 29

I could spend my energy bad-talking my body with Ed like I did for the first half of my day, or I could have a reality check moment and recognize that I am not in control of how my body changes.

If it has changed since my first two months of recovery, which being almost at my year mark makes sense, then I guess I need to honor that, right? Ed says no, but really, what does Ed know nowadays anyway?

So I guess my point is: Mom, I need new jeans ... again.

Thank you in advance.

Hello Life!

******

Day 343: The Best Monday of 2013

Today was the last Monday of 2013, and thinking about that had a strong impact on me.

When I was locked in Ed all of the time before I started recovery, Monday had been my most hated and dreaded day of the week. It was the day after I had let myself 'binge' on Sunday night (which looking back now from a recovery standpoint was never binging, but was simply eating), and so it was the most restrictive day of my week.

I would wake up, exercise, sweat, eat fifteen prunes throughout my entire day, then work out again at night, all in an effort to lose whatever amount of weight I had gained on Sunday. It was prison. It was robotic. It wasn't free.

I would go to sleep on Sundays feeling so full and yet so mad and angry because I knew what Ed had coming for me on Monday. I don't think there was a Monday that I ever didn't listen to Ed while I was locked in him. He had owned every single Monday. Every single Monday of 2012 was like that, and even a few in 2013.

But today, I was spending my last Monday of 2013 far away from the trapped soul I had once been when I was living, walking and breathing as Ed.

Monday, December 30

I am still getting better from being sick, so there was no working out today. Instead, there was a therapy session with E. Then when I got home it was time I organized my room, and in the process I ended up organizing my jeans.

Okay, so even for people without eating disorders, going through old clothes can be hard, but for people in recovery it's even harder. Obviously I wish I hadn't tried any of the old ones on, but I had.

I already told my mom yesterday for all the world to see on this blog that I need new jeans, and she was so happy to buy me some, so why even try on my old ones? I don't have an answer for that other than Ed.

But I tried on three pairs. Three. It wasn't all of them and it wasn't the whole drawer. They were the ones that I also got in the beginning of my recovery, which just like the ones from yesterday are now tight, so I gave them to my housekeeper. She was so happy because she said her granddaughter would fit in them. Knowing that my old jeans that at one time were my first pair of recovery jeans could now make someone else happy, made me feel happy too.

Instead of going back to yesterday's cycle of why they once fit at a time when I thought my body was no longer changing, I decided to just move on. That was yesterday's lesson, so let's just leave it in yesterday.

Anyway, right as I was about to write this blog post, I realized that I didn't do a body check this morning. This is the first time, and I mean first time, ever that I haven't done a body check in at least two years, including my time in recovery and including the entire time of this blog.

I was trying to think of what possessed me to forget about the body check this morning and I was trying to think about what could have been so important that Ed made me forget to do it.

You know what I was doing this morning? I was texting my ten-year-old brother, who has the flu and is sick at home, and I was giving him advice on what to eat and drink to feel better. My care and love for him was greater than Ed's demise for me.

From Mondays being my most hated day of the week, to this last Monday of the year being the first time I didn't do a body check, a day where I gave away old clothes, and a day that I took to rest my body because I am sick – I think it's safe to say that I have taken my Mondays back from Ed.

It was the best Monday of 2013. Save the best for last, right? Hello Life!

******

Day 344: This Was the Year of Hope

Today had started out badly ... really, really badly; the kind of bad that included almost a thirty-minute body check, which had been more like a body attack on myself. I had taken pictures of this body check (deleted right away, but still) and had felt a lot of sadness.

I was sad because I felt like I was letting Ed just swallow me up in his mean and suffocating self and I was feeling stuck in it. I had been so mean to myself and to my body in that mirror today. It was like a three-sixty from yesterday where I had my first day of no body checks.

I was upset at how my body looked, I was mad at myself for this entire month of eating all this delicious holiday food, just eating sweets for fun, and I was mad at myself for not working out this last week when I had been sick.

Somehow, I had found one moment of strength to stop myself, look at my own eyes in the mirror and give myself a pep talk.

Tuesday, December 31

At first I might have been embarrassed to say on this blog that I sometimes talk to myself in the mirror, but I am not anymore, because it's the truth.

"Shira, so what if you don't love your body right now? You are like every other American in this world who enjoyed the holiday season, so give yourself a break."

That is the only thing I could manage to say to myself, but it was true.

I don't own a scale of course, so I can't tell you how much 'holiday weight' I have gained (or think I have gained), but I figured it's no more or less than the typical average American person.

Although part of me is still in Ed's hands at the moment, the healthy recovery part of me is actually really proud of myself after that self-talk intervention.

For the first time in years that I can remember, I was like everyone else this year. For the first time in years I actually went from Thanksgiving to New Year's and ate and enjoyed yummy food, and more than that, enjoyed the social gatherings around it. If a few extra pounds comes with that, the recovery part of me says it's so worth it.

Not only was this the year that I was like every other American and indulged during the holidays but it was also the year that I started living in recovery.

This was the year I rang in with my now ex-boyfriend, who is no longer in my life. This is the same year that I left our three-year relationship to go find my own voice and my own strength, and it's the year I left him, knowing I am deserving of someone to respect my voice. This was the year that I left his family, who had become my family, back in my past. His family was Ed's family too. We loved them. I loved them. It was one of the greatest heartaches I have felt this entire year.

This was the year that loneliness and self-doubt often kept me company, but it was also the year that I have grown closer in my friendships than at any other time in my life.

This was the year that twenty days after 2013 started, I decided to give up my scale. This was the year that I stopped using my weight, my calories and my clothing sizes to define me.

This was the year I was forced to unlearn every truth I ever thought was true about myself, many of which Ed taught me, and the year I was forced to create new truths for myself.

This was the year that my truth now begins with my story. This was the year that my truth begins with my soul, my inner being and my spirit, not with my physical looks.

This was the year that not only was I the top senior reporter for my university newspaper, but the year I graduated college.

This was the year that someone sent me an email saying this blog saved their life.

This was the year that strangers from all around the world have now become friends and support systems for one another through this journey. This was the year that an online support group was created out of this blog, a support group that will live on so far longer than this blog ever will.

This was the year that my black-and-white way of thinking turned into gray.

This was the year that I have learned how to finally start showing myself the kind of unconditional love that I have always shown to others.

This was the year that I decided to change my life for no one else other than myself.

This was the year Hello Life was born.

This was the year of hope.

Hello *Life!*

January 2014

Day 345: I Will Love Myself More

I HAD spent pretty much all of this day responding to the beautiful and kind email messages and comments from everyone, and I had spent a lot of time being part of our online fighter support group chats. There was no other way that I would have liked to have spent the first day of 2014.

I had spent all day being inspired, uplifted, touched and moved by not only reading such kind words, but by being surrounded (well, virtually surrounded via internet) by such strong people. We truly had a special community on my blog, and I wanted to thank everyone who was part of it.

Wednesday, January 1

Happy first day of 2014 everyone. Happy New Year fighters, supporters and beautiful souls.

My plan today was to wake up, go to the gym (now that I am feeling better), and that was pretty much it. Instead, I woke up, ate breakfast, took a nap, answered my emails, took another nap, ate lunch, and now am about to go watch a movie with my grandma and my sister.

So much for plans, right? And so much for Ed's plan at that. I guess the gym just didn't have a place on the first day of my new year today, and I am actually really feeling okay with that.

I was all excited that the 'holiday food season' was over after New Year's and I could get back into my routine today, but like always I have learned yet again to not plan every part of my life. The holiday food season might be over, but the days of lazy days in bed and movies with my family are thankfully not over.

Another fighter asked me what my New Year's resolution was and, up until she asked me, I really hadn't thought about it. I have never been one to make New Year's resolutions, and if I did they were Ed's resolutions, not mine.

Right after I read that, my aunt sent me a picture with the following caption:

> What if the only resolution you made was to love yourself more?

It couldn't have been better timing. Essentially, I have been working on this resolution since I started recovery, so instead of setting a new goal for myself, I have decided to keep working towards my goal from 2013.

I think I will work on this resolution far past 2014, 2015 and 2020, and as long as I can say I am working to still love myself more, Ed is not winning.

I will love myself more through my hard days, through my body checks, and through my sometimes-negative self-talk.

I will love myself through my body changing, through my good and bad moods, and through my hard days of recovery.

I will love myself more on my easier days, my peaceful days and my quiet days, and try harder to not be upset with myself and think that because I had an easy day, I must not be trying hard enough.

I will continue to work on loving myself through the last twenty days of this one-year journey that we have left together. I don't know where I will be in twenty days from now when we reach the end of this one-year mark together, but I do know this:

I will have loved myself more in these past three hundred and sixty-five days of this blog than I ever have before.

Hello Life!

******

Day 346: Food Comas

Today had been my first day back at the gym. I had been sick for a week and half and couldn't work out during that time. I would like to say that I had walked in there feeling good and strong, but I hadn't. I had walked in there feeling like I was bulging out of all my clothes in every area and pretty much just uncomfortable in my own skin, and for moments of time I had really thought that I was one of the biggest people there.

This was so not true, and would probably never be true, but this was the kind of stuff Ed tried to feed me with, and I use the word feed because when I listened to his lies, I literally felt like I was swallowing them into who I was as a person, and for that quick moment I would let it define me.

I had looked in the mirrors at the gym while I was walking on the treadmill, after I was done walking, and even as I was walking out to my car. Ed, Ed and more Ed.

He had been holding my hand the whole time I was there. He had hugged me, held me and pinched any extra skin he didn't like on my body.

This was when I had thought, "It's okay Ed, it's okay. I will just eat totally on the meal plan today, nothing extra, and you can just be quiet."

That didn't quite happen because I went out to dinner with my grandma and my sister at this restaurant where they would fill your table with all these yummy foods that were never ending.

Deliciousness, yes. Ed-approved, no.

Thursday, January 2

Let's start off with the fact that I am currently in a food coma, and a major food coma at that, while I am writing this post.

I am also writing this post knowing I am taking my cousin to lunch tomorrow for her eighteenth birthday, and I also know I have a big family dinner tomorrow night too.

Ed wants me to not go to either because of this dinner tonight. He wants me to sit here and cry because of how full I am. And to be honest, it wouldn't be so hard to do that. Actually, it would be easy to do that considering how I am feeling at the moment.

I looked in the mirror way more times than I would like to today. I am not happy about my current food coma. But yes, I am still going to go to that lunch and dinner tomorrow anyway. And you know why? Because I would rather sit here in my food coma and even cry over it if I have to, than cry another night because I am scared that my heartbeat is too slow because I didn't eat, or cry another night because I ate one extra piece of gum that I should not have.

If I cry over this food coma, let it be a victory to me that the reason for my tears is not one that my eating disorder caused. They will be tears caused by my recovery. I can live with that.

And with that, I just finished reading an email that another fighter sent me in which she told me she just tried pasta for the first time in a long time, and she ate this amazing dessert called Hershey Symphony.

If she can do that, I can get through my food coma. I even told her that I need to try Hershey Symphony now too. And I will, so it might be another food coma night.

That is okay with me, because what is life without Hershey Symphony and dinners to enjoy with friends and family? It's a life filled with food comas; some uncomfortable ones, yes, but it's also a life filled with freedom, family and deliciousness. Don't we all deserve that?

I guess I can handle a few more food comas in that case. Bring it on. As she wrote to me today, "Hello Hershey Symphony, hello shrimp pasta, hello snow, hello 2014, hello life."
One more time: Hello Life!

******

Day 347: The Other Side

I had written the previous day about taking my cousin out to lunch today for her eighteenth birthday. This was a lunch that Ed had been begging me not to go to.

After the previous day's food coma that uncomfortably lasted all night long and even into my breakfast on this morning, this lunch was the last thing he wanted me to go through with.

But I had a very special and personal reason for taking this eighteen-year-old woman out to lunch – her and I had a very special relationship. Other than being family, we were also friends, and I was also her tutor.

I had been her tutor for a few years by this time, including during my worst times of my eating disorder. And while I had been battling with my own eating disorder, so was her mom, but her mom had been battling for years.

I had seen first-hand with my own eyes how her mom's own Ed crept had into her life from an early age. She had told me how she wanted to lose weight, which diet she was trying, and I would see the papers on her door that were taped up there that listed all the ways she could lose that weight.

I had seen all of this when I went to her house to tutor, and what had I done when I saw this? I stood in front of her mirror, lifted my shirt up and told her how fat I had got and how I was the one who needed to lose weight, not her.

I had also let her mom, who because she didn't eat, found solace in feeding others, give me food to take home that we both knew would be thrown away.

But this girl, my cousin, she was the other side of Ed. She was the side that we didn't talk about. She was one of the loved ones affected by our Eds, who when we are so locked inside our own disorders, fail to see the impact it has on them.

Along my road to recovery, she had stood by my side, she had lifted me up when I was down, and she had tried to get her mom to read my blog in order to help her, although she never had read it.

Friday, January 3

It was crucial for my recovery that I went to this lunch today. Going to this lunch meant showing my cousin that it's possible to live a life free from an eating disorder, even if her own mom is still stuck in it. Going to this lunch meant showing her the beauty in the fact that we can now eat together and have a good time together.

I was proud to walk into that restaurant with her next to me, and right as we sat down, the most unexpected and most inconvenient thing that could happen, happened. Out of all the places to eat and out of all the people in the world, in that exact moment I happened to see my ex-boyfriend's sister, husband and their baby.

This was the same family I wrote about only a few days ago who I said leaving had caused me the greatest heartache this year that I have ever known. This was the same family for whom I was the maid of honor at their wedding. This was the same family for whom I cried tears of joy when I found out she was pregnant with the baby they were now with.

As we made eye contact and I got up to say hi, they walked away. Just like that. They got in their car and drove away. I was shaking and I was heartbroken all at the same time.

This lunch was my cousin's lunch, it wasn't about me. But in that moment, there was nothing I could do but just say, "Oh my God," a hundred times over.

I didn't want to eat anymore. I didn't want to be there anymore. I wanted to cry. But just like my cousin was the other side of Ed who we don't want to talk about, so was this family. Except they were the other side of my heartache and my past that I don't like to talk about. It's the other side that I need to let go of.

I had two other sides standing right in front of me. One, my cousin, whose side of the 'Ed world' she lives on, deserved to be free of today with me. And two, the other side of leaving my past behind me had just walked away.

I had to choose which side I wanted to save. I chose my cousin. It took me a few minutes to gather myself together, but I decided I was going to stay present during this lunch.

We ended up talking about her friends, her surprise birthday party that she just had and her plans for going away to college.

When we finished eating lunch, she even thanked me for sharing our meal together because she enjoyed eating it with me so much. And of course, not only because I love dessert, but because it was her birthday, and what kind of birthday is complete without a dessert, we had to get dessert.

She asked me if I would have some. At first I was thinking to myself, "Girlfriend, are you serious? Of course I am having some!" But then I remembered that this is the same girl who I once ate cake with on her mom's birthday, only to leave early because I had to go to the gym to work it off. This is the same girl who I told I ate a bag of carrots a day as my meal.

I was no longer shocked why she asked me if I would share this dessert, and when I said, "Hell yeah," we ordered and it was the best dessert ever, not because of how it tasted, but because of what it meant.

She was once part of my Ed. As if being part of her mom's Ed wasn't enough, I let mine into her life too. She represented the other side of my eating disorder, the side where I didn't care who was affected by it, as long as I was 'skinny' that day.

Today, she became part of my side in recovery. That dessert became part of my side in recovery. And with one part of my past leaving me today forever, I let a new part into my life, the part where I showed my cousin the recovery side of me and celebrated her eighteenth birthday with her eating lunch and dessert.

And as far as I get in my recovery, I hope to never forget those on the other side who were affected by my Ed. It's because of that reminder that I find strength today to continue in my recovery and let my past be my past.

On with recovery we go. Hello Life!

******

Day 348: My Extended Holiday

My alarm had gone off this morning, waking me up to go to the gym, and the first thing I felt was that my body was sore from the food I had eaten the day before.

Feeling that soreness was Ed's way of making me feel guilty about whatever amazing food I had eaten, and it was his way of telling me to go work it off today. But I knew I was meeting my friend Anna for lunch (and I was meeting her for dessert too, as Anna and I always needed dessert) and I had really wanted to dress up and feel really good when I went. I don't know why, but I did.

I only had time for one or the other: Go work out then see Anna while feeling sweaty and in yoga pants, or take my time to get ready, do my hair and feel good.

Despite Ed telling me to go to the gym because of the food I knew I would eat with Anna, I had decided to stay home and get ready.

Saturday, January 4

Sometimes I think that getting ready and feeling good about ourselves, whether it be the way our hair looks, the outfit we choose to wear or the makeup we wear, can make us feel even better than some workout at the gym.

Indeed, that was the case for me today. It was a different kind of self-care. And when the jeans I decided to wear were a little tighter than usual, (which I already knew, as these pants are kind of tight, and it was a totally Ed-based choice to wear them, probably in the hopes I would feel guilty and eat less today because of it) I decided to throw on a loose shirt over them and carry on.

The problem wasn't solved forever, but the problem was temporarily solved. I looked good. I felt good. I felt comfortable. I didn't feel like I just had some great workout, but I felt pretty, and I think that actually felt better than sweating at the gym today.

So Anna and I went to have our lunch and two desserts. Two ... yes two ... two amazing desserts.

At first I left that restaurant thinking, "Oh my God, Shira, you have been eating so badly for a whole month straight now. Holiday season is over. Stop with these lunches and mid-day desserts." But then when I really sat and thought about it, and walked myself through my own thoughts, I realized that while it's true that holiday season is over, the birthdays I celebrated this week were not over, the birthday I am celebrating tomorrow with another cousin is not over, and my lunch dates with friends are not over either. So maybe my holiday food vacation is a little bit extended?

Even though I do feel guilty and anxious right now about this entire month of sweets and big lunches and dinners, part of me is feeling proud and part of me is laughing at Ed that he can't stop me from enjoying them.

I am in the time of my life right now, where I am transitioning from college into the working world, trying to find a career and trying to establish my life. If in the meantime I happen to have time for birthday lunches in the middle of my day with my cousin, dinners with my family during the week and lunches and dessert for no reason at 2p.m. on weekends with my friends, then why not?

Although I might not feel so great right now, I know that there will come a time in my hopefully soon-to-be career and job-oriented busy life, where I am sure that I will miss the days of mid-day lunches and desserts, and miss the days of birthday celebrations and dinners in the middle of my week.

So for now, even if Ed is trying to ruin it for me, I am going to try to enjoy my extended vacation, delicious food and all. And it's really not the food that makes these lunches, birthdays and dinners so special, it's the freedom that comes with being connected with others that makes it special.

However, if I had to choose between a special meal with loved ones that included Ed-approved food, or choose between a meal with loved ones that is downright delicious and yummy, even though it's not on the safe calorie list, I would take that one.

It's not that long ago that I let Ed keep me in my house every day and every night away from the world – isolated, deprived and unhealthy. Now that I am able to go to lunch, dinner and dessert, I think it's okay that I let these extravagant meals and social gatherings last a little over the one month allocated to holiday eating, like other people do. After all, I have many years that were taken by Ed to make up for.

Hello to my extended holiday, and Hello Life!

******

Day 349: Hello Bad Day

I had written my post on this morning in hopes that by writing I would bring myself into a better place of mind.

I had written my blog while sitting in my car after dropping my sister off at the airport, and I was parked right outside my gym. I just couldn't seem to go inside, with so many emotions weighing heavy on my heart.

So I had decided to spend half of the time I had allocated to working out today sitting there in the quiet and writing my blog post in hopes of giving myself my own kind of therapy.

Sunday, January 5

My body is so sore today that I can barely move. The skin on my stomach hurts, my chest hurts and my back is sore – sore to the point where I feel I am bruised everywhere and my skin is so tender I can feel it every time I move.

It's one thing to indulge in yummy foods like I have been allowing myself to do for this past month, but it's another thing to wake up the next morning after one of those indulgences, something that was supposed to be enjoyable, and feel physical pain everywhere.

How will I move today and deal with feeling this pain? How will I sit and be present through my other cousin's eighteenth birthday at my favorite steakhouse today, and not even get to fully enjoy it because I have to be so careful to not make my soreness worse?

I remember when I used to weigh myself, that number I saw every morning would be with me all day. Just like a person has a cell phone number to be reached at 24/7, I had my number that Ed could reach me at 24/7.

Today, instead of that number, I have the physical discomfort of my body soreness. It's a constant reminder of the 'punishment' I get for eating everything Ed said not to. And despite the dozens upon dozens of times I have gone through this soreness, this one is just really hard. It's making me cry as I write this.

I am sixteen days away from my one-year mark without a scale and of being in recovery, and my body has still not found its way of naturally healing itself from all of Ed's torture.

It's draining. I don't have any answers today and I don't have the inspiration to give myself that I am in need of at the moment. All I have is my truth today, and sometimes holding onto our truths during times of self-doubt and self-judgement is the best thing we can do.

My truth for the moment is that I am having a hard day. That is it. Letting myself acknowledge that and letting myself have that is actually the most free I have felt since I woke up this morning.

I just posted a picture on the Facebook online fighter support group that said, "One hello could lead to a million things," and I asked what the other fighters would say hello to.

I said hello to self-love, but now I want to say hello to my bad day, because by saying hello to it, it means accepting it and then saying 'see you later' to it tomorrow.

Maybe I can even say 'see you later' to it later today. I won't say goodbye to it because it's impossible to say goodbye to bad days forever. But for now I need to stick to my truth.

So, hello bad day; I hope we can get through this and soon you will be able to leave me. In the meantime, I am going to accept that you are here and just take it moment by moment.

Hello Life!

*****

Day 350: The Selfless Love Ed Can Never Take Away

Before I wrote this day's post, I had to say that I honestly didn't have the right words that could even begin to suffice to thank everyone for their love and support of the previous day.

Every single comment and personal email had truly given me the strength and hope to continue through my day yesterday and today. From the bottom of my heart I thanked everyone for their love yesterday and gave a special thank you to my girls in the online fighter support group, who were literally there second by second if I needed them to be.

Monday, January 6

I wish I could say that today was a lot better than yesterday, but it just wasn't. I woke up with my body still sore and with that bruised feeling that I had yesterday, but I was able to distract myself for half of the day with job searching and a writing test I had to do for a reporting job I applied to.

When that was over and ended, I just was in a place of defeat. Even the girl who used to train me at the gym saw me today and said that my eyes looked like I was in a faraway place. She was right.

I couldn't even look at myself in the mirror today. Why I am having such a difficult few days is something I am not sure of, but I know that it has to do with far more than just my physical body.

I know that not eating, restricting or exercising all day won't fix how I am feeling, although those facts are something that I need to remind myself of constantly today because they are easy to lose sight of when I am feeling so bad about the way I look and when I let Ed's voice drown out mine.

There was a time early in my recovery when I spent a majority of my days feeling this kind of defeat, and while I am thankful that is no longer the case, it doesn't make the days that I do still spend like that any easier.

So instead of spinning inside Ed's world, I reached out to the three people I know who, no matter what place I am in, can make me step out of Ed's world of self-judgement and step back into the present world – my three little brothers. Well, four actually, if I include my twenty-year-old brother who towers over me as little, which I guess he technically is – so my four little brothers.

Getting dressed to get ready and go see them was honestly such an internal battle with Ed, I almost don't even want to write about it. Nothing looked good. Nothing. I switched shirts at least five times, and when tears started coming to me, I found a way to swallow them back.

Normally I am a big believer in that crying things out can make you feel a lot better, but after yesterday and my day on Friday, I need a break from my own tears.

But there is something about being with my three younger brothers that makes me almost untouchable to Ed. Maybe it's that when they are here, I would never let Ed touch them, so I make sure I stay present. Maybe it's because I know when they hug me and tell me they love me, it has nothing to do with how I look.

I am not sure of the reason, all I know is that they are the three sole people in this entire world who can make me drown out Ed. When they were hugging me and kissing me tonight, I kept thinking to myself about how I could explain to them that I just wanted to hold them, because in their presence I feel beautiful all over again, and because I feel so loved for just being me.

When my five-year-old brother got showered and dressed in five minutes all so I could take him to get his favorite black-and-white cookie (also my favorite cookie), how was I supposed to explain that the few bites I will share with him will mentally erupt Ed? I couldn't explain it and I never will.

Why can't I find it in me to love myself the past few days the way they always unconditionally love me? I could ask that question to myself a hundred times and come up with a thousand different answers.

If I can't seem to completely find my own love for myself today, I will find, embrace and live through the love of others who do love me – from this blog, from the support group and from my family and friends.

Of course Ed is telling me that if I can't even let him love me or myself love me, then I am weak for letting other people love me instead. But maybe letting other people's love for us be our own source for loving ourselves in days of self-judgement is not such a weak thing to do. Maybe it's just another way of fighting and hoping for a better day tomorrow.

Regardless of what Ed is telling me, I will let the love that those three angels have for me be the love I live off tonight and hope that it carries me into a better day tomorrow.

I did share that black-and-white cookie with my brothers, and I even made them and myself dinner. It's my love for them that allowed me to do that tonight. While it's not as good as saying it was my love for myself that let me do that, it's good enough for today because it shows that even though my own self-love can't beat Ed today, my love for my brothers can.

It's a kind of selfless love that I will never let Ed take away from them or me.

Hello Life!

******

Day 351: We Are Worth Fighting for Ourselves

While today hadn't been as good as my many of my good days in recovery had been, at least it was better. I had still done way more body checks than I would like to admit, I had tried on two pairs of pants just to see how they still fitted, and I had let Ed talk to me for a little longer than I would have liked. But it had been a better day than yesterday.

Tuesday, January 7

There were definitely hard moments in my day today, like when I went to go get frozen yogurt with one of my brothers and I let myself put on some extra toppings. Ed wasn't happy. There were hard moments when I was eating dinner with my brothers, because I didn't know how the food was made. But above it all, never once did I space out into Ed's world and never once was I not in the moment.

Every single second spent with those three beautiful souls today was spent with them in real life, not in Ed's faraway life. I made sure to smile, laugh and love each of them as best I could, even when Ed was trying to hug me as I was sitting there hugging them.

Today wasn't better because Ed was any quieter than the past two days, because he wasn't. It was better because I am actually taking a moment right now, as I write this, to be proud of myself, which is something I don't do too often.

Despite Ed's voice today, I surpassed it. When he tried to wrap me with his presence, I wrapped myself with my brothers instead. When he told me to not eat with them, I smiled through my own self-doubt instead.

It was hard, but it was also showing me that I still have the same fight within myself that I had when I first started this journey almost one year ago. And as many good days as I might have, and as many bad days as I might have, I am beginning to see more and more that nothing can take that fight away from me.

A year ago, Ed would have won me over today and I wouldn't be sitting here in front of this TV sipping hot chocolate with whipped cream and watching a movie with my little brothers.

It doesn't matter what kind of Ed battles I had to fight today – the jeans, the food, the mirror checks. The fact that I am here on this couch in this very moment reminds me this fight is worth it.

I don't know if fighting for a life of freedom from Ed and a life of living in recovery truly ever stops, but I do know that we are worth fighting for ourselves.

Hello Life!

******

Day 352: Chef Shira Is in the House

I had started this day by saying hello to the good days that we have after the bad days, because it's after such bad days that we can truly appreciate the good ones, and that was where I was at right then.

I was appreciating this good day that I had had, and I was really excited to tell everyone about it.

Wednesday, January 8

I don't know what inspired me today, but I decided I wanted to cook myself dinner. I was home alone and it wasn't even dinner time, it was mid-afternoon, but the feeling just came over me. Knowing that it's sometimes difficult to eat when I am by myself, I decided to seize the opportunity before Ed could talk me out of it.

So I made dinner. Well, I made it and then saved it for when I would later eat it, but I made it. It was fun. I had my TV on, I could hear my pan sizzling and I felt like a real chef.

I used to cook all the time when I was locked in Ed. I would cook for everyone in my family and for my ex-boyfriend who I lived with at the time, but I would never enjoy my own cooking. I would cook them something really yummy, then make myself my 'Ed' food, which was usually a plate of veggies.

Even throughout my recovery, cooking is not something I have done too often just because I am usually really busy. But I decided that if I still don't have a job and am graduated out of school, I guess I could take advantage of the time I had today to cook myself dinner.

It was a dinner that I have made in my head many times before, but I had just never done it. It wasn't anything insane, difficult or gourmet, but it was what I wanted. It had all the components a balanced meal has – proteins, fats, carbs, and just deliciousness.

When I went to go eat it about an hour ago, I decided that for the first time in a while I was going to eat just at the table with no distractions. I usually watch TV when I eat alone so I have something to do, but when I do that, I often can't focus on my food, which sometimes works for me if Ed is there. But today I really wanted to focus on this food; I cooked it and it's something I really wanted and have been wanting since I made it earlier in the day.

At first, sitting and eating in silence felt really lonely, but then I began to really enjoy the act of what I was doing. I was enjoying my own cooking. It was a beautiful moment. And even though I had portioned out my meal according to my meal plan, I went back for seconds. No meal plan in recovery is ever against seconds, right?

I took my plate to the sink, thinking, "Wow, I am a good cook. Chef Shira is in the house."

It was just yesterday that my little brother, who is now five, asked me if I still eat prunes. Prunes used to be my Ed diet, and there were many occasions when I took my little brothers out to eat at a restaurant and instead of eating with them, I would just bring my little plastic bag of prunes to eat for myself. They always asked what it was and I didn't really know how to explain it, so I told them they were my special healthy food that is good for you.

Last night, out of nowhere, he asked me, "Shira, do you still eat those things in a bag that are healthy for you?" At first I couldn't even believe he remembered that, but at the same time, I guess it's kind of a hard image to forget when you see your sister eating from this little plastic bag whenever you ate together.
I looked at him, smiled and said, "Nope, not anymore."
If only he would see the dinner I made tonight, he would give me a big high five. No more prunes baby, and no more plastic bags at the table.
Hello Life!

******

Day 353: Winning Is a Journey

I had been to the park today to go for a short run instead of going to the gym because I had felt like being outside, only when I had started running, my body was just not having it.

I ran cross country in high school and I usually actually enjoyed the feeling I got from running (as long as Ed wasn't there with me), but today I had thought to myself, "Wow, this is really just not fun." It wasn't what I had expected and it wasn't what Ed expected. I had expected to run. I mean, other than wanting to be outside, that was why I was there.

Every time I walked, I felt like I was moving one mile per hour, but the more I had tried to push my body to run, the more miserable the experience had become.

As I started walking, a song came on my Pandora and it had a line in it that said: "We have a choice to make, whether we choose to win or lose, and I choose to win."

I wasn't sure if it was because of the state of mind I was in, but that line had hit me really hard. In that moment I had honestly felt like I was able to step outside of my own body for a moment. There was me as my soul and then there was my body. We were two different entities.

Thursday, January 9

Since the beginning of my recovery, I have felt that me as a person and my body are two separate things. While that may not be true, that is how I feel. We are like a married couple that is bound together for life, that went through a period of distrust, and through this past year we have been relearning how to trust each other and getting to know each other again.

So, my body didn't want to run today. After all it's done for me and after all Ed has put it through, I am learning to listen to it and to respect it. So if it doesn't want to run, it doesn't run.

In that moment, I truly felt like I was winning. I was winning because I was making the conscious choice to listen to my body instead of listening to Ed. I was making the choice to grow in this relationship with my body. We are a couple, and we are growing and learning together.

Since the day I chose recovery, I knew I chose to win, but today, after hearing that song, it just made me think about it more. What is winning? I don't even think there is one direct answer for that.

Every day my definition of winning changes, especially when it comes to winning back my life from Ed. Yesterday, winning meant making myself dinner. The day before that winning meant eating frozen yogurt with my brother. The day before that winning meant simply getting through my hard day.

Today, winning meant walking instead of running. Today, winning meant eating the soup the lady I tutor for made for me. It wasn't winning because it was me eating, it was winning because it was me showing compassion to someone else the way I would want them to show me. Today, winning was eating dinner with my sister, even AFTER I ate that soup because I knew she was waiting for me. Again, the win wasn't the food, it was me *honoring our time we had set aside for each other and not letting Ed take that away.*

Winning is connecting with the fighters in the online support group.

I don't know what shape or form winning will take tomorrow, and I am not even sure if I will win tomorrow. Maybe tomorrow I won't win and it's a tie. Maybe some days I will feel like I am losing.

By choosing to win, it doesn't mean I choose to always be undefeated. It means I choose to persevere. It means I choose the hard path – the path of walking instead of sometimes running, the path of listening instead of acting, and the path of learning how to love myself for who I am just the way I am.

Winning is a journey, it's not a one-time race with a one-time winner's title. The closer this blog gets to the end of its one-year mark, the more I am beginning to see that.

Hello Life!

******

Day 354: Being Accepting of Just Okay

Today's post sounded a lot like my other posts from this week, so I apologized in advance for me writing about my brothers again. But like I had always said, I really did write my blog honestly and this past week they had been major parts of my days, so it was unavoidable to write about it. However, there had been something different that happened today when I was with them.

Friday, January 10

Throughout this past week, I have written many times about how eating with my brothers and sharing treats with them have been huge steps in my recovery. I even wrote about how my five-year-old brother asked me the other day if I still eat "those things in a bag," which were the prunes I used to take with me as my meal when I took them out to eat. I wrote about how proud I was to tell him that those things are no longer in my life.

So today when I made them macaroni and cheese for lunch and ate cereal with milk and fruit instead (totally on the plan but not what they were having), you can see why at first I felt like I was failing today.

"Again, they are seeing me eat something different from what they are eating," I thought to myself.

But honestly, I was craving that cereal and milk since yesterday, and I really wasn't comfortable eating that mac and cheese. Some days I can be comfortable eating outside of the meal plan and other days, like at lunch today, I am just not.

It took me few times of walking myself through my own negative thoughts to bring myself to the final conclusion that I am writing about now. Recovery doesn't mean always eating exactly what everyone else is eating. Recovery doesn't mean always eating things we are not comfortable with. Recovery means being present.

So, yes, maybe I ate a meal that I was more comfortable with than the mac and cheese they were eating, but I was still present with them at that table. I had a bowl, a spoon and a plate with food. It was definitely a different image than the old Ed-controlled me with my plastic bag of prunes at the table. And later, when I made cupcakes with them and I even let myself have one, I was again back in the moment, eating with everyone else.

Recovery ebbs and flows, and today is one the days that I see that. My point in writing this is really to remind myself of what I was saying yesterday – that winning is not one definition and neither is recovery.

One part of today, recovery meant eating a cupcake with my brothers, and on another part of my day, it meant sitting with them at lunch all together but eating something I was comfortable with. And that is okay too.

The only one who expects me to live life as this perfect 'recovered' person who always eats what everyone else is eating and doesn't even think twice about it, is me. I don't even think my brothers cared about what we ate or what I ate. They cared that I was there. They cared about sitting outside in the sun together, cuddling together and watching movies together.

Despite what the perfectionist in me is saying, I know that I did a pretty okay job today, cereal and milk, and cupcake in all.

I like being accepting of the word okay. It's not perfect and it's not terrible, it's just okay. And I like it.

Hello Life!

******

Day 355: Ten Days Left Video

This day had marked ten days left of our one-year journey together. It was a big milestone for me, so I had decided to make a short video/slide show of the year's biggest moments up until this day.

Saturday, January 11

I apologize for the not so great music, which also ends about thirty seconds before the presentation does. I had to choose from the songs YouTube gave me (not many options), but it really is worth watching the five minutes of it.

Here is to the last ten days of the beginning of this lifelong journey of finding true self-love and self-acceptance – something that no number on a scale could ever give me.

Hello Life!

******

Day 356: Don't Eat Dessert Without Me

I had to apologize in advance for today's blog post being a little shorter than usual, but I had come to write it just as I had finished dinner with my brother, sister and some of our friends, and they were still there, so I didn't want to keep them waiting for too long.

The reason that I had cooked dinner tonight was because my brother, who was twenty, was leaving the following day for two weeks, so I wanted to give him a nice goodbye dinner, along with my sister.

I had invited him the previous night, before I knew that I would wake up with my body sore this morning (yet again). Right away, Ed had wanted me to cancel this dinner. I had actually thought about it, and I thought about ways I could get around it.

I thought that maybe we could go to a restaurant where I could order something different to everyone else. Even if I had decided to do that, it wouldn't have been bad, but the point was that I had said I would make dinner, and I was really looking forward to it.

Sunday, January 12

I used to cook for my brother all the time when I was locked in Ed, and I never got to enjoy the food with him, so tonight was going to be a special occasion.
I didn't have to think about it too much. It was one of those days where I just knew what I had to do, and so I did it. Stuffed salmon, roasted butternut squash, roasted Brussels sprouts, champagne, and bread rolls later.

I can say that, although Ed is not happy with me, and he is very much with me right now, I am happy. I am happy because when I hear my brother laughing right now from up in my room, I know it's this dinner that made that happen. I am happy because he, my sister and I just sat around a dinner table and enjoyed good conversation. Regardless of how many times I have to shut Ed up tonight, this dinner was worth that; it was worth the connectedness, the selflessness and worth the company.

My brother even came wearing his Hello Life bracelet, which I forgot he even had.

And right as I left the table to come write this post, I told them very seriously and matter of factly, "Guys, don't eat dessert without me."

On that note, I am off to enjoy my dessert, even with Ed next to me. We will be fine Ed. It's time for dessert.

Hello Life!

******

Day 357: Closer than I Was Yesterday

I had been sitting in E's office today, telling her how I felt so chubby and not good in my body. I was expecting her to say something like, "Let's find out why you are feeling this way," or something like that, but that wasn't what she had said.

She had just asked two simple questions: "Why do you have to be chubby? Why do you have to look a certain way in your body?"

I hadn't got it at first. "Um … what do you mean? If I am not chubby then what am I?" It was a serious question.

"You are Shira. Why can't you just be Shira?"

I didn't know how to answer. I think it was one of the first moments in therapy all year that I actually had nothing to say for a split second.

Monday, January 13

Why did I have to define myself as chubby today? Why do I have to define myself by my body checks every single morning? They are good questions that I don't totally have the answers to yet.

Why do I think that being Shira means having to tag on a label about my body, like chubby, skinny or whatever other word that can be used to describe someone's physical being? I have spent pretty much my entire life since I was eight years old calling myself these labels.

In some parts of my life I labeled myself fat, in other parts I labeled myself chubby, and other times I labeled myself skinny. Regardless of what time period I was going through, I always used one of those words as my label.

And of course, I used my weight as a label too. I still remember how much I weighed the day my grandfather passed away, because it wasn't a good number, but I 'allowed' myself the extra room because I was so sad. I told myself I could give myself a break.

These numbers and labels have been such a huge part of how I have defined myself for so much of my life. It was honestly mind altering when E asked me why I even had to be any of those things.

Almost one year into being scale free, and I never thought about that. Who would Shira be without her being attached to a chubby, or to a skinny, or to an 'I am sore today'? It's one of the hardest things I have ever had to think about.

I know who I am without my number on my scale for almost a year now; that I know because I have been learning that through this year. And I love who I am becoming without that number to define me.

I love the writer in me. I love the reporter in me. I love the sister in me. I love the friend in me. I love the fighter in me. But numbers and labels are two different things. A number is fact, a label is a feeling. But just Shira. Plain and simple, no extra labels – that is totally different.

I guess what I walked away with today, because it was a day of much self-doubt also in other areas of my life, is that when this blog is over eight days from now, I am not going to have all of the answers I thought I would have. I may still label myself with those names or those words. Or I may not. I am learning.

I used to think that after this one-year journey it would mean that I was cured from Ed and cured from all the negative ways I used to view myself. That is far from the truth, and I am glad I can be accepting of that.

The closer I get to this blog ending, and the more I start to wrap things up, the more I am learning that this one year wasn't meant to be a solution or an answer; it was meant to be the beginning of something.

I have a long way to go, far past this one-year journey, until I think I can figure out who Shira is, with no labels attached. But I am okay with that.

I am not where I thought I would be at the eight-day countdown to this one-year journey being completed but, then again, how could I ever know where this journey would lead me?

But I do know I am a lot closer to being where I want to be than I was yesterday, I am a lot closer than I was the day before, and I am a lot closer than I was three hundred and fifty-seven days ago. Hello Life!

******

Day 358: Exactly Where I Need to Be

I had woken up this morning scrolling through Pinterest when I had seen this quote.

"We are what we repeatedly do."

After writing my post the previous day about me thinking that I wasn't where I wanted to be by that time in my journey to recovery, this quote really had stuck out to me. It had made me think about what kinds of actions I did on a daily basis that made me who I was.

After going through those daily actions in my head, I had changed my mind about what I had written about not being where I wanted to be right at that time.

Tuesday, January 14

I actually am exactly where I want to be at this point in my journey. Let me tell you why.

If I had to list the things that I repeatedly do every single day and so make up who I am, or at least the things that I have been doing every single day for this past year since I started recovery, here they are:

I am kind to people, to strangers and to those around me.

I am a sister – a caring, compassionate, selfless and loving sister.

I am a daughter, a granddaughter, cousin, and niece.

I am a best friend.

I help others from the deepest place within my heart because I want to feel their joy with mine.

I am a writer.

I am a reporter.

I read poems off the clock to the little girl I tutor.

I am open about my journey to recovery.

I take care of my body and its needs.

I nourish myself.

I proudly wear leggings on most of the days that Ed tells me to wear my now too-tight jeans.

I share desserts with my friends and with my loved ones.

I take my brothers to the bakery to get their favorite black-and-white cookie on a random Monday night.

I cook dinner for myself and for others.

I order chocolate chip pancakes at breakfast sometimes.

I might look in the mirror every morning at how my body looks, but I know my worth is based on what is within.

I practice being mindful.

I practice telling myself I am worthy.

I am kind to myself when Ed is not, and on the days that I can't be kind, I am understanding and accepting of what is.

But most of all, every single day for the past year, if I have done one thing repeatedly, it's that I speak my truth. My truths may not have all the answers, but they are more than enough to show me that I am indeed where I want to be right now.

I do truth. Every single day, I do truth. Therefore, I am truth. I am my own truth; a truth that Ed or anyone or anything else can never take away from me.

This one-year journey of giving up my scale meant giving up my old truth. My old truth was only one thing – that number. My new truth doesn't have a definition, a number, or a size, and it doesn't have answers. All it has is me, and for today that is exactly where I need to be. Hello Life!

✶✶✶✶✶✶

Day 359: My Recovery Heroes

I had let someone else pour milk into my coffee today without me measuring it. I had eaten a piece of the special black-and-white cookie today that my grandma had bought me the day before. I had even had a job interview today that I thought had gone really well.

But that wasn't why today had been a good day. Today had been a good day because I had been inspired, lifted and filled with complete joy. This joy hadn't come from Ed and it hadn't come from my own personal recovery. It had come from the recovery paths of others who had been walking this journey with me.

Wednesday, January 15

As you know, there is a Hello Life fighter support group online. Over the past few weeks these fighters and I have grown to become friends, supporters and safe people to lean on for one another. Over the past few days, they have blown me away.

Today it was just the icing on the cake – totally no pun intended, but I do love cake, I do love icing and I do love these strong women, so I think it's okay to say that.

We have one fighter who is eating a lunch tomorrow with her co-workers. It's a prepared lunch that she didn't make – a social lunch. She is a recovery hero.

We have one fighter whose New Year's resolution included being more kind to herself. She is a recovery hero.

We have one fighter who is the spiritual guide for this entire online support group. She is a recovery hero.

We have a fighter who just joined our group and sat at a table with her children while they ate food. She is a recovery hero.

We have one fighter who is letting her mom move in with her in order to help her stay on track with her recovery. She is a recovery hero.

We have a fighter who, despite not feeling well and being in physical pain, stays full of light, hope and optimism, and continues to not let Ed be her escape. She is a recovery hero.

We have one fighter who ate a Hershey Supreme with her family this past month. She is a recovery hero.

We have a fighter who cooked her husband's favorite meal for his birthday this year. She is a recovery hero.

We have a fighter in France who continues to push through her hardest days. She is a recovery hero.

We have a fighter who reached out when she was having a hard day. She is a recovery hero.

And lastly, we have one fighter who right now has friends over at her house, where she put out a chocolate cake, cheeses, crackers and pepperoni and veggies with dip. She even posted a picture of this on our support group wall. She is being present tonight. She is not letting Ed have her disinvite her friends over tonight because food will be there. She is a recovery hero.

Seeing those pictures almost made me cry. They symbolized freedom. They symbolized her taking her life back from Ed. So this post is in honor of her, in honor of the recovery heroes, both in the support group and outside of it, who email, comment or read this blog every day, and who are all around the world. I wish I could list everyone but it would be hundreds of people.

If this year has taught me one thing about others, it's that nothing in the world, even our relationships with our own eating disorders, is stronger than the support and understanding that we can have for each other as people.

Today, these heroes are my inspiration. They will be my inspiration when I go out to dinner right now. They will carry on being my inspiration way past when this blog is over in six days.

In honor of my recovery heroes: Hello Life!

******

Day 360: A Journey Coming Full Circle

It felt a little bit crazy and bittersweet to think that this was our last official Friday eve post together. With that being said, today's post was probably one of the most meaningful ones I had ever written.

Thursday, January 16

When I was locked in my eating disorder, every Thursday night I would go to dinner with my grandma. (This was before I lived with her like I now do.) Thursday nights were our night to be together. Every Thursday we would go to the very same restaurant where I would get the very same salad of lettuce, carrots and cucumber, with no dressing. It was crucial that Thursdays were Ed's days because Fridays were a major judgement day for my weigh-ins.

On Day 18 of this blog, I wrote about how on the night before, the second Thursday of this one-year journey, I had decided to take my Thursday nights back from Ed. That day I told my grandma that we could go to a new restaurant for our Thursday night dinner. We went to a fish house that she liked, that I liked and that my cousin, who was going with us that night, also liked.

I remember writing that post like I wrote it yesterday, because I remember sitting on my bed crying tears of victory and joy as I wrote it. I felt like I could fly. It's similar to how I am feeling right now too.

Tonight, the very last Thursday of this one-year journey, my grandma had planned to go to dinner with my aunt, uncle, cousins and us to that very same fish restaurant. When she asked me if I wanted to go, I almost couldn't believe it. I didn't even realize the irony in the entire thing until a few hours later.

I could have not gone tonight. I was tutoring late and I could have said no and everyone would have understood. But for some reason, eating at home tonight alone with Ed, even though it would be a more comfortable meal for me, especially on a day that I only worked out for about fifteen minutes, just didn't seem as appealing to me as it once was.

What once would seem like a perfect night for me at home alone with me and my Ed food, no longer seemed like a fun night tonight. I cut my tutoring ten minutes short so I could make it to this dinner on time.

I was starving when I got there. I don't know why, but it was just one of those days where you just have to listen to your body, even if it's hungry all the time. Luckily for me, the waiter brought out a fresh loaf of bread and butter right as I sat down, and he even messed up my order. The two side orders I got were wrong, instead I got the two wrong side orders and the two right ones a few minutes later, and I enjoyed all four of them, including my main meal and my bread and butter.

I even got a ketchup stain on my jacket. A ketchup stain, guys. Ketchup was something I didn't eat for years when I was locked in Ed, and now it has stained my jacket. If it doesn't come out, I will proudly wear that jacket anyway because of what it symbolizes.

I remember sitting at the table tonight, feeling nice and full, and thinking to myself how this journey has truly come full circle. Three hundred and forty-three days ago I sat at that restaurant with the same people, and I remember the one bite of bread that I had. I even remember the butter I put on it. It was unlike anything I ever remember tasting.

And now, I sat there tonight, choosing to be present and choosing to honor my family, but this time around, three hundred and forty-three days later, I was so much more free than I was the last time.

In that post on Day 18, which I titled 'A Victorious Thursday', I wrote: "Eating at a new restaurant may sound silly to some people, but for me, it was symbolic of telling Ed that he will no longer get in the way of my relationships with those who I love and care about in my life."

Here I am on Day 360 and I wholeheartedly can say that I have proved that line to be true. From my second Thursday of this one-year journey starting at this restaurant with me trying a bite of bread, to my very last Thursday of this journey ending at this restaurant with a ketchup stain on my jacket, and a few pieces of bread and my four sides later, I can truly say that this journey has come full circle.

I called it from Day 18 Ed. You won't get in the way of my life anymore. I was right.

Hello Life!

******

Day 361: The Small Victories that Still Count

I had eaten a hamburger for lunch today … with fries and with ketchup. I was full all day after it.

I hadn't worked out today because I had wanted to get my hair done instead before I left to go visit my mom in San Diego.

I hadn't measured the dressing on my salad tonight at dinner.

I hadn't blotted the oil off my pizza that I had at dinner either. I hadn't even taken off the pepperoni.

I had eaten pizza even after I had a hamburger for lunch – a hamburger that I had eaten because my family members I was with had wanted to go to this restaurant, and I didn't want Ed to get in the way of that.

Until Ed had set in later, I will say that the hamburger was pretty good. My pizza was good. My dressing was good. However, Ed wasn't good and he wasn't letting me off the hook easily. But I could tolerate Ed because I was proud of my small victories today.

Friday, January 17

It's not about the food, it's about not letting Ed dominate and control my life and I didn't let him tell me to choose food that only he approved of. I chose food that everyone around me wanted.

Making that choice might be small but it counts. Eating ketchup still counts. Not dabbing the oil off my pizza still counts. Not changing restaurants from what my family wants to something Ed wants still counts.

Even though I only have four days left of this one-year journey, these small challenges are not that much easier. But by the same token, they are also not less accounted for just because it's almost been a year that I have been in recovery.

These small victories still count, even though part of me feels like I should be at the place where these challenges should be normalcies – where ketchup should be normal, where a hamburger and unmeasured dressing should be normal. But they are not normal yet and that is okay, because as long as I can still celebrate them I am still winning.

Today I celebrate my challenges that turned into victories. I celebrate the small victories that still count. We don't get to pick when our challenges become things that are no longer hard for us, but we can pick to celebrate being a victor of those challenges while they continue to choose to present themselves.

As long as my challenges are still here, I will celebrate my victories from them. And as long as I can do that, I know I will be okay ... maybe even better than okay.
Hello Life!

******

Day 362: My First One Year Hello Life Celebration and Getting the Hammer that Will Smash My Scale

This night had been my first celebration of my one-year mark of my blog, which would officially be on the coming Tuesday. It had been at the same steakhouse in San Diego that I celebrated my six-month milestone.

All I have to say about this dinner is that I loved the bread and butter, wine and steak, and mostly I loved the icing, frosting and whipped cream that came on the chocolate cake.

I also loved the family who I was able to celebrate this first celebratory dinner with, and my menu that said, 'Congratulations Shira on 1 year, "Hello Life"!!'

I had also gone earlier this day to get the hammer that I would be smashing my scale with at the end of this journey.

Saturday, January 18

I set up a poll for everyone to vote on what to do with my scale, and the results overwhelmingly say to smash it, so that is what I am going to do.

My stepmom and my brothers had actually taken the time to make me a special hammer for this day about a week or so ago, and even painted it yellow, Hello Life's colors, and wrote Hello Life on it. It was a beautiful gesture and it's a big indicator of the kind of role they played in this journey.

But as they were making it, I wasn't able to help them. I didn't even want to pick up the paintbrush. I wasn't ready yet to come to terms with the fact that this one-year journey is almost over. I realized that in order for me to truly prepare myself for the moment of me smashing my scale, I had to go through the preparation process myself.

At first I ordered a hammer online, but it wasn't sufficient enough. I decided that if I am going to mentally prepare myself for this moment, then I need to start with going to the store and picking out my hammer myself – feeling it, imagining me using it to smash my scale – and sit with that idea for a while.

This scale was my everything for so many years. It was my definition of who I was. It was my good days. It was my bad days. It was my birthday. It was every day. While smashing it will be one of the greatest acts of self-love I can ever do for myself, it's also going to be smashing away a part of who I used to be.

So today I went to pick my hammer. I even got yellow spray paint to color it with Hello Life colors. I picked up every single hammer in the aisle – the light ones, the big ones, and even the ones I couldn't easily pick up. It took a while until I found the right one. After practicing picking it up and pretending to smash something with it, I had chosen the right one.

My hammer that my family made for me is going to stay with me and in my room forever as a reminder of what it symbolizes – love and unconditional support. For whatever reason, that hammer was meant to serve that purpose for me as a reminder of that love. But this hammer, the one I got today, will be the destroyer of my scale.

So today I took one step toward accepting the ending of this journey and also one step toward celebrating the end of this one-year journey. I celebrated with my mom, aunt, sister and grandma, and had the most incredible dinner ever.

My sister even asked me how I felt, and I told her that I can't believe it's real. And when I looked at her when she asked me that, I couldn't help but remember the very first day I got my meal plan, and she came and ate lunch with me because I couldn't do it alone.

Tonight was a celebration of not just this one year of recovery and one year without a scale, but a celebration of the relationships and love that come from being in other relationships than just with Ed. And I got the hammer that will be used to smash my scale.

I am still not sure I am ready to accept that Tuesday is quickly approaching, as this blog has become a huge part of my life, but I am doing all the right steps to mentally prepare for it.

Hello to my first celebration for this one-year journey, hello to the hammer that will smash my scale, and Hello Life!

******

Day 363: How Blessed I Would Be to Spend the Rest of My Life in this Gray World

Today hadn't been the easiest day.

It hadn't been the easiest when it came to eating, since my body was sore and Ed was loud after my incredible dinner and dessert the previous night that I had let myself fully enjoy without him in my way.

It hadn't been the easiest when my dinner plans that I had made got cancelled, which other than feeling kind of lonely had also left me to eat with just Ed. This had been an experience that, while it was hard, I can say I had done pretty well and was proud of myself for.

But I had learned throughout this past year that not every day, every hour, or even every meal for that matter, was going to go the way we planned it. And sometimes it's okay for things to be canceled, or to feel a little lonely, or for meals to be a little hard.

Sunday, January 19

Maybe a year ago, before I began walking this path to recovery, I would have thought that today was a terrible day. I would have thought that whoever canceled on me is a terrible person. I would have thought that because Ed is loud today it means I really messed up yesterday. I would have thought that feeling lonely meant that I am alone in this world. But I sit here tonight, and I truly don't think any of those things are true today.

The person who canceled on me had another plan come up, and while it's not the same thing I would have done, they are just a human being who, like me, deserves some slack.

Just because Ed is loud today doesn't mean I messed up yesterday, it means I stood up to him yesterday and enjoyed myself with my family. Good for me.

And just because I am feeling lonely at the moment, I know that I am so far from being lonely in life. If anything, this journey has brought me the closest that I have ever been to my loved ones and friends.

I guess what I am trying to say is that where at the beginning of this one-year journey I was scared to leave my world of black and white, I can now officially say that I have learned and embraced how to live in the gray. I haven't mastered it by any means, but I think I have done a pretty good job of learning how to live in it – of learning how to live in a world where canceled plans don't ruin my day, where Ed being loud doesn't mean I am a failure, and where feeling lonely is not a finite definition of my life.

I don't think perfectionism can exist in a gray world. I don't even know if a perfectionist can live in a gray world. With that being said, I don't know if I can say that I am 100 percent free of my old perfectionist self, but I can say, that I have let go of a lot of her throughout this year.

The more I let my perfectionist self go, the more I learn how to master living in the gray. The gray used to mean unknown weights, unknown calories and unknown foods, but now it means understanding canceled plans, it means knowing that feelings don't define us, and it means knowing the difference between Ed's voice and my own voice.

If I am seeing this beautiful part of the gray world after just one year of recovery, I can only imagine what other beautiful parts of this world are still waiting for me to come discover them. That is definitely a journey that will take more than a year, and maybe it might even take a lifetime.

How blessed I would be to spend the rest of my life living and uncovering this gray world, and not another day living in the perfectionist, Ed-dominated world of the black and white.

Hello Life!

******

Day 364: A Goodbye Letter to My Scale

With the following day being the very last day of my one-year journey, I had decided that it would also be the day that I smashed my scale. The poll that I had up on the website had almost 50 percent of votes saying to smash it, so that was what was going to happen.

Throughout my recovery, I had written many letters on my blog. I had written letters to Ed and I had written letters to myself. Now I was going to write a goodbye letter to my scale. I apologized to my readers in advance for it being so long, but I just had a lot to say.

My letter to Ed hadn't been a goodbye letter, as I didn't think that Ed would ever leave my life forever. However, I could, would and had learned to live above him and to live free of him. But this letter to my scale was indeed a goodbye letter, because after tomorrow, when I smashed it, then threw it away, it would forever be gone.

Monday, January 20

Dear scale,

My precious, only, trusted, heavy and white scale. Where do I begin to start to say goodbye to something that over many years, and pretty much my entire life (except this one-year journey) was such a huge part of my life?

Every day, and often every hour, particularly for the past three years, you specifically were my life. There were other scales over the years but you were the one that Ed and I picked for the worst few years of our time together.

I remember standing on you on my eighteenth birthday, on my nineteenth birthday and on my twentieth birthday. I remember standing on you the day I had surgery. I remember standing on you the day my grandpa passed away. I remember standing on you on my twenty-first birthday and my twenty-second birthday too. This year, for my twenty-third birthday, you were not around.

Do you remember the many times that I tried to give you up, and yet I always came back? One time I gave you up for a week. One time it was for a month. And one time I was even sure I could do without you because I placed you at someone else's house, only to find myself speeding over to that house once everyone left for work to go stand on you once again.

Do you remember when your batteries ran out and I was late to my family dinner, because I had to go to the drug store to buy new batteries for you?

Do you remember the times at 3a.m. when I would pull you out from under my bed and stand on you when everyone around me was asleep? It was like our own little secret. Just you and me.

Do you remember when I came rushing home from my vacation in Big Bear last year just to run and stand on you to see what bad news you would give me?

I am sure you remember everywhere I put you – under the bathroom sink, under the bed, and even in the kitchen one time. I am sure you remember the way my feet felt when they stood on you, because I sure remember the cold metal parts of you on my feet too. I remember the clicking sound you made when I had to turn you on. That sound will haunt me forever. It was the sound I woke up to every single day, and sometimes in the middle of the night, for years.

And no matter how many other scales I stood on at a doctor's office or someone else's house, you, my dear scale, were the only one I trusted.

You didn't even start out as my scale. You started out as the scale of someone else, someone who I lived with. At first, I only took you out of her closet when everyone was asleep. Then you moved with me into my new apartment. Then you moved with me into a new home. Somehow, along the way, Ed and I made you ours. We didn't even care that you once belonged to someone else.

But last January 21, 2013 I gave you up for good. For the past year you have resided somewhere with E. I don't know where, and I really don't care to be honest. I know that E doesn't care about you either. I gave you to her because her strength is far beyond yours and I knew your presence wouldn't bother her like it would bother me.

I wonder how you feel now that you haven't been turned on for an entire year? Do you feel lifeless? Do you feel dead? Because that is how I felt every time I stood on you. Maybe now you can understand my life with you for those years.

And I might add, dear scale, that tomorrow I will be smashing you. But before I smash you, I will make sure to remove your batteries. You will never be alive again.

I am not sure if you will break completely but I will be using the heaviest hammer that I can hold and I am going to read you this letter. I am going to smash you as hard as I possibly can, then I am going to throw you away.

Do you know what I have accomplished this year without you, scale?

Do you know that I was the top senior reporter for my university newspaper, even without you telling me what number I weighed during it?

Do you know that my brother called me his hero all because I decided to value myself on who I am, not on you or Ed?

Do you know that, without you, I graduated college? I graduated college on a day on which I have no idea what I weighed, and it was the best day ever. My Facebook status for it got over one hundred and forty likes. Your weight for me could never get that kind of popularity.

Do you know that my family still loved me this year, even though I wasn't the number I always wished you would show me? Yup, they loved me, supported me and carried me through even without your number.

You used to be my only truth; my only definition of who I was. But I have learned over this past year that I am not a number. I am not a size. I am not even a definition of anything. I am me. And me is no longer a part of you, and you are no longer a part of me.

Therefore, tomorrow we will officially part ways. I am not only smashing you for me, I am smashing you for every single person who is part of this journey. I am smashing you for the other birthdays and days and lives of others you have ruined. I am smashing you for every single fighter in the support group, and I am smashing you for the many people who said this blog saved their lives.

Do you remember when I gave you to E? My only words when she asked me if I had anything to say were Hello Life! I remember that.

I have found that my soul is my new truth and your number no longer defines me, dear scale. And because of that, I officially say goodbye to you.

Sincerely,

Shira

Hello Life!

******

Day 365: Let's Smash this Thing

The day had arrived. One whole year without a scale. I had done it. I didn't write a blog on this final day. I simply posted a video of me smashing my scale to bits and this picture of the smashed scale.

About the Author

SHIRA Lile began her advocacy work for those with eating disorders when she began to write her blog, 'Hello Life: A Year Without a Scale'.

Through her blog, Shira met hundreds of people around the world who were inspired by her journey.

Over the years, Shira has mentored people all around the world who are striving to recover from their eating disorders.

She founded a non-profit organization to help others battling eating disorders to extend hope to anyone who wants or needs it.

It's Shira's life passion to walk alongside others in their journey to eating disorder recovery.

More information about 'Hello Life: A Year Without a Scale', the blog, can be found at www.hellolifeblog.com

Author's Thanks

Thank you with all my heart to Ivan, who without his incredible talent and endless hours of work, this book wouldn't have been possible.

This book was developed and edited in the UK by:
Ivan Butler MBA
Coachhouse Business Services
Copy-editing & Proofreading Professional
Email: ivanbutler897@btinternet.com
www.coachhousebusinessservices.co.uk

Made in the USA
Middletown, DE
11 November 2020